The X Press

Presents

Michael Maynard's GAMES MEN PLAY

Published by
THE X PRESS, 55 BROADWAY MARKET, LONDON E8 4PH.
TEL: 0171 729 1199   FAX: 0171 729 1771

© Michael Maynard 1996.

Distributed by Turnaround, 27 Horsell Road, London N5 1XL
Tel: 0171 609 7836

Printed by BPC Paperbacks Ltd, Aylesbury, Bucks.
ISBN 1-874509-22-0

1
Life's A Bitch

Homie had a phat night. As I rolled around under my sheets I had that feel good factor. The feeling you get the morning after you've been with a fly chick; it makes you wanna shoop all day long.

Thought a brotha would be used to this shit by now, but when a hoochie knows her shit under the covers it always leaves me mellow. See, you don't have to play 'General', 'cause she reads your game plan to the letter, and her lips and fingertips are so sensitive to your E-zones that all you do is lay back, catch the scores and perform your endzone shuffle.

Good sex always gives me an appetite. As I lay daydreamin' about the juice Amanda had sucked, pummelled and pricked from my body I felt a Mega Mac hunger. Damn...must be a conspiracy between white boys and the sistas to say white women can't do the nasty—just to keep live wire niggaz like me away from finger testin' the home-made cream of wheat.

Don't give me all that shit about history and unity. The black *thang*. That shit don't work with me.

I'm a reality man dealin' in the here and now and in my book there ain't no difference between the fruits on the tree, except one's a paler shade. I sparked my first Dutch and checked the Hitachi clock-radio. Shit, it had let me down again. It was five past four. Amanda must have left ages ago. Bitch didn't even say goodbye. I turned over onto my back. The last thing I expected to find in the bed was last night's protection against the nightmare of a baby, but there it was sticky and rubbery. *Damn!* When did it come off, before or after we did the nasty? Mama would trip if I came home with a half-white kid. See, she had a beef with white people ever since the early sixties when she touched down in Birmingham from Jamaica— a wide-eyed twenty year old expecting life to be rosy, streets paved with gold and every shit to be peaches and cream. Instead she was greeted with 'No Niggers' signs outside boarding houses. Worse still, Pops did a Houdini with a white woman when my twin sister Janet and me were still in diapers. Word has it I have half-caste blood relatives living in the capital. Mama has never forgiven the white race for striking those blows against her soul.

1

But according to Uncle Sylvester, white people didn't have shit to do with it. He once let on that Mama drove Pops away. Said she had a mouth like she ate Brillo pads for breakfast, lunch and dinner, and that her bitchin', moanin' and accusin' him of not standing firm against the white man gave Pops no alternative but to seek quieter pastures.

Mama still feels the same way about white people, despite the fact that every other nigga she's dated since Pops has dissed her. She didn't actually say it in so many words but her actions made it crystal that she wouldn't tolerate me or Janet bringing home a white partner. Man, she almost caught her goddamn death when I brought home my main squeeze, Cheryl, for the first time. Chick is so red-skinned she could pass for white. I practically had to go on my knees to convince Mama that Cheryl was a sista. That's why this white girl thang's gotta stay confidential. Homiez like to have a helping of cream on their apple pie. In my case, a double or triple helping with no strings attached. But the sistas don't like to hear that. They want the X-rated loverman, a phat wallet and the whole CV thang. Then they'll start talking about settling down and getting married, when all a brotha wanted was a one night stand. Stuff like that freaks me to shit out, y'knowha'msayin'?

With white girls—once you get past the 'is it true what they say about black men?'—they're usually cool and will settle for the X-rated performance in bed without the emotional G-clamps.

And one more thing: they're ready and willing to keep your bank balance in credit. You won't find too many sisters willing to bankroll a homie in return for a little tenderness.

I decided to make the move to get my black ass out of bed. The crib was a mess. I picked up a ring off the floor, my only memento from three years at Delaware Union College. I picked the remote off the floor and activated the video for some NBA action. Isiah Thomas and his Detroit Pistons 'Bad Boys' were running the wood against Cleveland. I stood in front of the television admiring Thomas' dope moves on the opposition.

Started bouncin' an imaginary ball...man I was there at the Auburn Hills, Michigan, alongside Isiah and the boys in front of twenty thousand fans. Shit didn't mind that I was dreaming, as far as this homie was concerned, I was running with Isiah, naked butt an' all.

"Yeah, Zee, check da rock," I shouted, caught the dream pass, jumped two foot off the ground and sent the invisible ball swishing

2

through the hoop. I lost concentration when Isiah lost possession.

I placed the ring on the bookcase which housed the trophies and certificates I earned over five years at the local comprehensive in Handsworth. I picked up one of the certificates: it read *Winston McKenzie, Most Valuable Player, 1985.*

I heard the sound of my mobile above the roar of the Auburn Hill fans—took me a good few seconds to locate it under all the mess. Eventually I found it under the settee cushion.

"Whad up!" I shouted.

"Winston McKenzie," a strange male voice came back.

"Who dis?"

"Is this Winston 'Macca' McKenzie?"

"Damn punk, y' got da mobile digits, who y' think it is?"

"Winston, this is Brian Murphy—sports reporter from the Birmingham Evening Echo."

"Okay," I replied—kinda happy that after five months these local jerks had finally caught on I was back in the hood.

"We're going to run an article on you in Saturday's edition. I just wanted to make sure I've got the facts straight and get a few quotes."

"I'm wit'cha, fire away dude."

"First a general one. What made you take up basketball?"

Shit—this reporter really wanted to start at a basic level.

"Man, I was a shit hot athlete durin' school. You name da sport and I could play it. But b-ball was my vocation, my Route 66 outta da ghetto, y'knowha'msayin'? Once I got da rock in my mitts man, dat was it. Never wanted to do shit else."

"Sorry?"

"Man, I didn't wanna do anythin' else, 'cause being a good sports-man at school brought you props. Y'know, teachers would treat you wit more respect. Homie would always get off with a warnin' while other kids got da bamboo, y'knowha'msayin'?

"Then da teacher would always encourage you in sports, push you harder and have one-on-one conversations wit'cha. Dat shit never happened in normal lessons."

"Did you mind being only recognised for your sporting ability?"

"Man, I had no prob wit it whatsoever, 'cause I was no bookworm and I also got time off lessons to go to matches. Other homiez who tried to bunk off school got done for truancy, but I was an athlete and somehow missin' lessons to play sport for da school was a virtue. Y'knowha'msayin'?"

"Didn't you think it was wrong that you should miss lessons to

3

play sport?"

"Like I said, man. I was no intellectual and if sport didn't get my butt outta there somethin' else would—y'knowha'msayin'?"

"You sound so American..."

"Man, I was there three long years. Homie picked it up."

"So you have. Ah...tell me how did you get there, to America?"

"By plane, fool, whaddya think, I stowed away on da QE2?" Homie was beginning to think they'd put some two-bit reporter on my exclusive. Cheapskate punks, this is a big time diss.

"No, no," the jerk interrupted, as I was about to call time on his sorry ass. "I mean how were you spotted to go to Delaware Union College?"

"Okay, I gotcha, man. Let me see. At sixteen I left my callin' card scrimmagin' at da National Schoolboys final—"

"Right," he interrupted. "By all accounts you had a good game."

I paused for a moment to watch Isiah on the television score another basket.

"Right, man. Posted up a triple double."

"That 's scoring double figures in three categories, right?"

"You're on line. I kicked back thirty-five points, eleven assists and ten rebounds. A scout spotted me and wanted me to go to high school and then university in da States—but my Mama refused to play ball. As far as she was concerned America was bad news, had a worse rep than hell."

"How did you feel about that?"

"Shit, man, I was knocked back, y'knowha'msayin'? But it didn't come as no surprise though."

"Why was that?"

"Look, me and Mama ain't exactly parallel in our thinking. When she said A, I did Z. When she did B, homie wanted C, y'knowha'm-sayin'?"

"So you don't get on with your mum?"

"Yo, don't go print dis shit. Dis is off da record, man."

"Okay."

"Look, da bottom line is: muthas bring up sistas. Pops bring up homiez. Mama tried to raise me like a Pops 'cause I didn't have none, but da shit wasn't goin' down, y'knowha'msayin'? Shit worked against my street vibe. We collided head on every time."

"So how did you eventually get to America?"

"When I turned eighteen I was my own man. Delaware put da b-ball scholarship up again and I was off."

4

"What about your mum?"

"Shit, she didn't see it da way I saw it, but it wasn't a prob, 'cause at da end of da day, a man gotta do what a man gotta do. And I was da man, pure and simple. She moaned 'bout it, but couldn't do shit to stop it. It was my call and I didn't shirk from makin' it."

"So how is your relationship with your mum now you've returned home?"

"Man, we talk, and dat's all I'm sayin' on da subject."

"Okay. You were supposed to be at Delaware four years but you only stayed for three. Why was that?"

"Man, I don't wanna discuss that."

"Why not, Winston?"

"Look dude, don't go questionin' me 'bout my personal. It's not on da agenda," I shouted.

"I've got reliable reports saying you were kicked out because of some criminal activity."

"Wha' you talkin' bout man? I left under my own steam. Nothin' 'bout no criminal activity."

"Isn't it illegal in the States for an undergraduate on a sports programme to sell season tickets to fans and keep the profits?"

"Don't know shit 'bout da rules and regulations."

"I think you do, Winston. You know it's illegal 'cause you have been caught. Isn't that true?"

Dude sounded like Roger Cook.

"You gonna print dis?" I asked.

"We're going with it."

"Damn you punk ass, muthafucka. Y'know what you wanted from da off. Just playin'."

"Give us your side of it."

"Ain't got nothin' more to say."

"Well we'll just have to go with what we've got. It would look fairer if we had your side of the story."

"Okay, punk, you got me by da nuts," I said, rubbing my hands through my high-top fade.

"See, in America college players don't git paid up front. Niggaz sweat their jock straps off packin' da joint out and don't see a cent as a thank-you. Niggaz have to go undercover to make a buck, y'knowha'msayin'?"

"So you did it?"

"Man, I had to, didn't have no snaps to buy shit wit. Man, I don't wanna talk no more. Print wha' da shit you like, I'm outta here." I pressed the off button and I was gone.

I didn't know they took this ticket scalping that seriously in America. College kicked me off the team and it then was impossible for me to stay just as an academic. Anyway, it was probably for the best, since I wasn't getting much burn in the team. I know I was good enough but the coach had a thing against foreign players. If he had given me some court clock—or this scalping shit hadn't come up—then I reckoned that by the end of the next year I would've had a shot at the professional ranks of the NBA. A one-way ticket to the black millionaires' club. Brothas have a monopoly, making more money in a fortnight than Coca Cola. Make Fort Knox look poor. I'm not sayin' I could do all that Your Highness Jordan shit. Fly through the air like an Exocet, yes. Dunk like a madass slam jammer at five foot ten inches, no. Not in my wildest dreams.

But I can handle the rock, fake and dip and play mad house D.

Anyhow, my American agent said it would be best to go back to my home town, chill out and let things blow over for the season, then he would try and interest some top clubs in Spain or Italy in a homie's potential for next year, 'cause I know they pay big bucks.

So now I'm back here playing in front of two hundred people for Handsworth Warriors, a third-rate team with fourth-rate management. Still, it's nice to rest off back in Birmingham and spend some quality time with my sis and I suppose my mama, though she still holds a grudge.

The pungent stink of last night's love session was still lingering and combining with the smell of my soiled basketball training gear to form a violent odour. Five empty cans of Red Stripe littered the floor, the drainings of a bottle of wine sat beside two fallen glasses and the remains of a ten pound blunt completed the mosaic of vice.

Shit. Did we smoke and drink that much? Maybe gettin' busy wasn't that busy after all, and it's the blunts and alcohol that's messin' with my system...

I pulled back the curtains. The sun shone aggressively but because of the draught seeping through the cracks in the wooden window frame I could tell it was bitch cold. Handsworth on a cold day was as unwelcoming as a hoochie with no bootie on a 2 Live Crew video set. Even when the sun shone over the niggahood the place just looked like shit warmed up.

I watched a young black woman—no older than nineteen—drag her son through the street. She was yelling "If you don't come on, you can stand here and cry!" She walked on a few yards. The little man, who looked around four, stood his ground. She walked back towards him, slapped him across the head, told him he ain't no man yet and dragged him on his way.

Got a homie thinkin', *what a life*. To be caught up in that dead end shit at such a young age. Don't they know about contraception?

I moved to press playback on my answer machine, but a piece of paper lying on top of it caught my attention. It was a note from Amanda; so she wasn't a total bitch. She gave me high fives for the night's performance and wanted me to pop her again.

For a moment a homie's ego hit the roof—then it slithered down the walls and rested on the varnished wooden floor of my living room when I remembered who Amanda was. She was the white-ass ho of a homie called Zorro, who had a rep larger than his six-foot-three-inch, two-hundred-and-fifty-pound frame.

No man in the hood could wield a blade like the man from Balsam Heath—known in Birmingham as Sodom 'cause of the thug mentality of its homiez. Sodom was a place where everyone was lookin' to be a ghetto star; the Jack City payback mentality.

My weed supplier, Hector, has one of Zorro's motifs burnt in on his cheek like the swoosh on Nike trainers. A slash the shape of the letter Z was his reward for tryin' to pass off some weed mixed with Handsworth Park's finest grass shoots as legit.

Zorro was also a big-time pimp, but Amanda was his special chick. I met her at a wine bar just outside downtown yesterday; I gave her the eye; she responded. Had a few drinks. She wasn't lookin' for anythin' long term and I wanted a piece of her so I popped it; simple as eating an Oreo.

If only.

She was so fly that I didn't check the consequences. If Zorro ever found out I serviced his bitch, I'd be next in line to wear one of his trademarks. But who would spread the word? If Amanda did, she wouldn't just be putting my life in the danger zone—she'd need a plastic surgeon herself. Homie's heard psycho stories about how Zorro beat on his bitches who failed to deliver his cut of their earnings on time.

To tell the truth I don't know why I took this shit on. I suppose it's another case of my dick rulin' my head. It's done a lot of that recently. Damn, why can't I leave these white chicks alone?

I only got used to white flesh at lilywhite Delaware. The only other blacks on campus were my team-mates. There were very few sistas in the entire state, and when you did see one looking fine she was always stuck like a postage stamp to some white dude. It was a mixed-up place in more ways than one, but the Yankee gyal loved my English accent and were queuing up for a piece of my black ass.

What else could a homie do? Shit, I had three options: celibacy, homosexuality or waxin' some white honey. And the first two weren't no real option for a homie.

Despite this, Cheryl is my main tenderoni. She is the blueberry on top of the muffin. She put up with seein' me only at Christmas and during the summer vacations for the past three years and I know she remained true to a homie. I don't know if she believed all the bullshit I wrote her from America about not being down wit da bitches, but she didn't say shit to me about it when I landed back at Gatwick.

Hunger pangs hit me again. The lactic levels in my body were still in the red zone from the weekend game. My eleven stone felt like twenty-two as I stretched my aching limbs, while Detroit continued to slap up Cleveland.

I turned the volume on the answer machine back up, pressed playback and went to the kitchen; it was in a state. Last week's plates, cups and pans were still in the sink. When the tape finish rewinding, the message tone sounded like an air raid siren.

"Winston, it's Cheryl. I'll call you later."

Cheryl was the only woman who had my home digits. The rest of the bitches get my mobile number. Take it or leave it. I can't have them phoning here freelance, especially if Cheryl happens to stay the night—particularly since she has this nasty habit of listening to my personals.

The machine made that excruciating sound again. Man, I felt like throwing it in the sink with the rest of the shit. "Macca, dis is coach Bailey. I only goin' tell you dis once. It important you be at trainin' on time tomorrow. Six-t'irty please. We have some new moves to go t'rough for de game on Sat'day."

"Yeah coach!" I yelled. "Man, you don't pay me enough to git my shit there on time. Eight hundred green backs a month? That's just two hundred a week, forty a day, a piss poor George Stevenson an hour! Shit ain't worth gettin' outta da sack for, so stop timekeepin' on me. Pay me what I'm worth, then you can chime like Big Ben."

I opened the cupboard under the sink to find nothing but a box of corn flakes. I poured myself a bowl and took an almost empty carton of milk out the fridge. I looked at the best-before date: the 3rd of October, 92. Today was the 5th, but it smelt okay so I poured it on and moved to the settee. The beep went again.

"Winston, why are you not at home? Phone me as soon as you get in. It's urgent."

Urgent my foot. It was Cheryl again checking up on me. I could tell by the way she slammed the phone down that she was in one of her moods; if you're not there to answer their every moan they catch an attitude.

"Black sistas, damn you!" I blurted through a mouth full of corn flakes.

The machine paused for a few seconds before the next call.

"Wha'ppen star? Hector de Inspecta comin' live and direct. Macca, me 'ave de finest weed straight outta Jamdown. Y'ave first refusal, den it's first come first served, y'know wha' I mean? Hey and turn y' fuckin mobile on, man, me nah like discuss business 'pon machine 'cause dem drug squad beas'bwoy all round, y'know. Later."

Hector got slapped with the moniker Inspector 'cause come rain or shine he would always wear this knee-length Mackintosh coat like Lieutenant Columbo's. He was also a better storyteller than Maya Angelou. Like Five-O, he never let the facts get in the way of a good story.

Hector was a small time dealer who had aspirations to be big time—and not big time Handsworth or Moss Side, but big time South Bronx. Brotha was down constantly on the American tip; mouthin' off shit about maximising profits with expansion overseas. The man may talk like he got some paper qualifications in economics, but the only education he's likely to get in the South Bronx is a bullet up his narrow black ass to go with Zorro's souvenir on the side of his face.

The machine beeped again. Damn, it was Cheryl again.

"This is the third time I'm phoning your sorry ass. It's one in the morning, where are you?"

"I'm in da sack havin' da time of my life," I shouted at the machine. "Anyway, what da hell you doin' phoning me at one in the mornin'? Man needs some peace."

Cheryl's voice overran mine. "You were supposed to pick up the curling tongs from your sister. I've been waiting seven hours for them. I told you I was perming my hair and I need them to style it for work in the morning. Winston, you're just a shaper." She slammed the phone down.

Damn! I forgot the tongs. I knew she'd wanna give me some tonight so I decided to phone and keep her sweet. The phone rang

9

twice before she picked it up.

"Whassup, Chez?" I said, in my sexy LL Cool J drool, expectin' her to kick off with some Millie Jackson shit.

"What do you mean what's up? Winston, I left three messages for you to call me last night. Where were you? I had to go to work with my hair like a white woman because you didn't get the tongs from Janet!"

Damn, she was really trippin'. Homie just sat back and nodded like I had already read the script.

"Cheryl, why you sweatin' me? Let me give y' da live SP," I crooned—but she cut me off. "I've had enough of your bloody excuses. Since you got back from America you've been acting like some kinda prima donna. Just 'cause you have that phoney accent and think you look like Wesley Snipes, don't believe you're indispensable, 'cause you're not; you hear me?"

"Ba-a-a-by, don't."

"Don't baby me, you jerk," she shouted. "If I knew this was what I could expect after three years I would have told you to keep your show-off ass out there with all those white girls."

It was the first time she had mentioned the white girls in America. Got a homie thinkin', did she really believe the shit I wrote her from Delaware? I took a spoonful of corn flakes before I continued.

"Don't take it like that Cheryl, ple-e-e-ease honey, sweet thang. Someone must have turned the volume on the machine down."

"Someone like who, Winston? You're the only one who lives in that stinking dive. Who in their right mind would step foot in that filth?" Man, she really wanted to get personal, homie felt like givin' her a rundown of some of the finest bitches this side of the Atlantic who had wined, dined and done the nasty at my crib; filth don't matter when you your manhood does the talkin'.

"Babes, take it easy. I'm sorry, okay? Look, I'll go to Janet's, get the tongs and bring them right over," I said, hoping it would cool her out.

"Please yourself. That's what you do anyway." She slammed the phone down with such ferocity that any harder would have registered on the Richter Scale. Put me right off my corn flakes. I went back to the kitchen, dropped the bowl and spoon in the sink and checked the time. Damn, it was five-thirty already. Shit, ball begins in an hour and I still had to get the tongs from my sister on the other side of the city and take them to Cheryl. In more ways than one life is a bitch.

After a quick shower I took a good look at my lean, well-defined body in the full-length mirror. Man, if I ever went to drama school Snipes and Denzel would be out of a job. I had both their shit rolled into one bundle of promise. I was patting my high-top fade when I was disturbed by a knock on the door. I didn't hear the bell ring so it must be Mrs O'Farrell, my Irish landlady. She must have been tossing and turning like a spinning top listening to us bump and grind last night. Old-timer always bangs down the door the morning after, like the DEA on a narcotics bust, to kick up a stink about my love sessions keeping her awake. It's not my fault she rented me a crib with a sack that creaks every time a homie breathes. Seems she ain't got nothin' better to do than listen to me anyway, 'cause in the five months I've been here, no man—nor woman, if she's that way inclined—has been to her room to service her. I quickly dragged on my grey sweats, opened the door and found myself staring into her big face, red from the after-effects of alcohol. "Whassup, Mrs O'Farrell?"

"Winston, I thought I would bring these up to you." She handed me two letters, eyeing my bare torso. "They came this morning but I noticed you hadn't been down to pick them up."

"Word, Mrs O'Farrell."

"And don't forget the rent is due today."

"I'm down wit dat."

As I went to close the door, she gently placed her hand on it. "By the way, Winston, you were at it again last night—I didn't get a wink of sleep, you know..."

"Sorry, Mrs O'Farrell."

"I know you coloured chaps like your thing, but you must have some consideration for me and my other tenants."

"Yeah, I'll chill things out next time, Mrs O'Farrell," I said—knowing she must have used a stepladder to get her ear closer to the ceiling to listen in. As I pushed the door closed, she headed back downstairs muttering.

I could see one of the letters was a rent slip from Mrs O'Farrell—God knows why she posts them when she could push them under the door. The other was from Tiffany Goldberg, a white jewish girl from the States, who hit on me like Bo Jackson's baseball bat on a home run. She wrote that her father was buying a b-ball franchise in New York in the semi-professional CBA league. Damn—always knew she was a rich bitch; come to think of it I always wanted to spend more time with her, but I had to spread myself thin to keep all

11

my admirers happy.

I threw the letters on the table and pulled on my Nike tee-shirt and Delaware Union College Starter jacket; slipped into my Air Jordan trainers, packed my training bag, grabbed my mobile phone, dark shades, Atlanta Braves baseball cap and keys and left the room with speed.

The route from Newtown to Nechells took me past the HP Sauce factory. Though my windows were sealed tight I could almost taste the shit as the spicy smell stunk out my car. How could people in the area stand it? Frank Bruno and his damn commercials had a lot to answer for.

I turned the radio on to the local pirate station. They were playin' Arrested Development, but I was in no mood for that new age, rap-bumpkin, southern shit. I sorted through my tapes, pulled out the Wu Tang Clan and wired it up live and direct.

The city council had tried to give Nechells a facelift—and changed its name to the more upmarket Waterlinks—but it was still the dumpin' ground for all Birmingham's social outcasts. My sis is part of this tier of society, but Janet's different. She used to have a regular dude, Joseph, and they lived up in the 'burbs of Great Barr. Things were going well for them. He had made a bank selling insurance policies to brothas and sistas in the hood.

When other homie sharks caught on and saturated the market the bottom fell out of that; so he moved over to selling computers to businesses.

Then Joseph found out, after twenty-eight years, that his mother was really his step-mother. He couldn't cope with the bull his parents were layin' on him. After a couple of years his mental health hit rock bottom and he was diagnosed a nutter. They committed him to the loony house, where they injected him with all kinds of medication. Janet says now he's like Karloff in one of those horror flicks; doesn't even recognise her.

She would write me in the States saying she didn't think he needed the heavy dosages prescribed by the shrinks. She told them so, but they kept right on increasing the amount and Joseph kept on becoming more of a zombie.

When she visits him now Janet doesn't take their four-year-old son, Uriah, with her for fear of frightening him.

She lost the crib in the 'burbs when she couldn't keep up the mortgage repayments and had to kick it at a loss. Then the council moved her into Nechells, the worst cesspit in the universe.

Night was setting in, but a group of young black kids played on mountain bikes. Their eyes widened when my E-reg metallic blue Ford Cabriolet pulled up, music rockin' the white leather interior. You've got to have a good ride to have the rep. And paramount is the thumpin' decibels, rattling both machine and bones. My shit was bulletproof, and the look in their eyes said the kids knew it too.

"Whassup, li'l homiez?" I said, stepping out of my ride. Today you had to treat kids with the respect of an adult.

"Hey, where d'you get the jacket?"

The one who asked was no older than seven.

"States, man."

"You play basketball, don't ya?" asked another.

"Word."

I pressed on the remote alarm. The lights flashed to indicate it was set. "Look after my wheels, li'l men," I called as I headed for Janet's block.

"What's it worth?" came the reply.

Shit; I remembered when I was a pee wee homie, wasn't even allowed to play out at this time, let alone try to work money out of strangers. Damn, times have changed.

"Man, I'll give the five of you a quid each when I come back down."

"A fuckin' quid," one replied. "That can't buy squat. Make it a tenner between us."

Shit. This was more expensive than the city NCP but I agreed anyway. The lift was out of order yet again so I started to climb the stairs, through the stench of stale piss. I started wishing I could have stayed in the States instead of coming back to this hell hole. But once the league authorities found out about the ticket scalping the college forced me out—despite the fact that their athletic department gave everyone on the team a quota to sell as a back-hander for signing with them.

It probably would have been different if a homeboy had been caught, but I was the English scapegoat. It made it seem they were dealin' with the problem by gettin' rid of me. It made big news on the east coast of the States—and soon will here after this bum of a reporter prints his story. But since I didn't finish my final year I walked through customs with $9,000 in my back pocket from selling the tickets. The exchange rate was wack on my return. The dollar was down, so I only pocketed £6,500. I splashed out a third on my cabri-

13

olet from the motor salvage, spent roughly the same fixing it up, and gave my sis the rest to pay off some of her debts. I didn't tell Mama 'cause she'd only start trippin' bout how I left before obtaining my degree. What the hell, I wasn't going to get it anyway. Well not in a up-front sense. I was supposed to major in Humanities but I was on the blacktop seven and eight hours a day.

Afterwards, I'd be too tired to eat, let alone study. All the hoopers were given high grades just for turning up to exams and scribbling their names. Anyway—like most of the brothas out there—my eyes were firmly on the prize of an NBA contract, not a worthless qualification.

When I reached the top floor my thighs were as heavy as lead. How did sis manage these stairs with a small child and heavy shopping? Must have biceps like Lee Haney by now. I walked across the open air corridor and knocked on Janet's door. She opened it, holding Uriah by his hand.

"Whassup, Jan? And how's da big man?"

I pinched Uriah on the nose.

"We're both fine."

She sounded fed-up. Despite her troubles Janet still kept herself lookin fine—a bit on the skinny side, but she could still turn the homiez' heads.

We don't look like twins. She's slightly lighter in skin tone and—many said—much prettier. Her hair was straight permed and tied back in one. She had a cute face, but it always looked troubled. Janet was always the quieter of the two of us and had a calming influence on me.

She always understood my brief better than Mama. Saved my ass from a belt whuppin' many a time. There ain't shit I wouldn't do for Janet.

She went into the kitchen with Uriah while I waited in the dining room. It was sparsely decorated; a settee, an old Amstrad stereo, some plants and a TV. Shit, hated to see my sis livin' like this. A one year NBA contract on minimum salary would be more than enough to take her out of this dump.

Janet and Cheryl had been best friends since Cheryl joined BBC Pebble Mill from BBC Bristol. In fact it was Janet who introduced us five years ago; she left work when she became pregnant, but Cheryl still works there in the press office. They're so close that I have to cool my shit out on the Cheryl front in case Jan starts frontin' on my ass. Sometimes homie feels like a trapeze artist on a thin wire between the two of them. One wrong move and you're fucked.

"Tell Cheryl thanks for lending them to me, and I'll see her at the weekend."

Janet handed me the tongs wrapped in a shopping bag.

"Word, sis. I can't stop, I'm late for ball..."

I raced for the front door; she came up behind me.

"Winston, when are you seeing Mum again?"

"Dunno. Why?"

"You know she's not happy with you."

"I know, Jan, but she gotta loosen da shackles man. I'll git round ta seein' her. Look after yourself and Uriah. See you soon."

I gave her a kiss on her cheek.

"When will you see her?" she asked quickly.

"Whenever," I shouted back as I ran down the corridor.

I raced down the stairs, switched off my car alarm and jumped in. Just as I was about to pull away a scrawny little black hand tapped on my window. It was the little homie and his gang who I'd promised a Charles Dickens. I searched my pockets and found two Dickens and a Stephenson. I pulled out the fiver and wound down the window.

"Look, homiez, man gotta settle for a blue."

"That's not da deal."

"Shit, well nigga, I ain't got nothin' else, so take it or leave it."

He grabbed the five.

"You owe us, fool."

"Niggaz, you been watchin' too many Jack City movies. You're too young to play this mercenary shit!"

I raced through the streets, burning rubber in an effort to get over to Cheryl's in ten minutes. Luckily there was little traffic and, more importantly, Five-O was nowhere to be seen.

Cheryl lived in a nice little one-bedroom ground floor apartment in a smart section of Moseley. She opened the door within seconds. Either she smelt me coming or she was waitin' there all evening fully strapped with an AK-47 ready to blast as the bell rang.

As I looked at her, my heart hit a faster beat. Baby looked well fly. Average height and superbly trim thanks to her three visits a week to Curves gym in the city centre. Her face had a homie dreaming of Vanessa Williams, but Cheryl had larger breasts and the kind of booty you could slap every time you saw it. She had on a pair of blue leggings and a the grey Malcolm X tee-shirt I bought her in the States. What the hell did I see in other chicks when I could have somethin' like this every night?

15

She stood on the top step and stared at me with contempt.

"Look, Chez. I know you got my number but shit, I'm cumin' correct now. Damn, I've brought the curlin' tongs with me. Please don't trip on me."

She stood in complete silence. She wanted me to suffer. I made up my face as a kid about to cry. She smiled. I cracked it. Her smile was the flyest on this earth.

"Gimme a hug, babee," I said, walking up the steps with my arms opened wide. As she moved in snugly, I could feel her warm breasts against my chest.

"You've got a hard on, you dirty devil," she chuckled, pulling me closer.

I kissed her on her lips twice.

"Yeah, but I have to go and shoot some ball now."

I handed her the tongs.

"Pity. I thought you were planning on scorin' with me this evening."

Damn, I almost came in my sweats.

"I'll be back after I deal with some perpetrators on da blacktop."

"Winston all this American talk is losing me. You were only there three years."

"Chill, man. I'll be back for some sweet stuff after training. Is that better?"

"Hmm..." she replied.

I skipped down the steps and ran to my wheels.

"Janet said she'll see you at the weekend."

Minutes later I was heading for scrimmage at Aston University in the city centre.

2
Quotas

"The social philosophy of black nationalism only means that we have to get together and remove the evils, the vices, alcoholism, drug addiction and other evils that are destroying the moral fibre of our community."

His Sony Walkman filled Calvin's ears with the words of Malcolm X as he sat alone in the university changing rooms tying the laces of his size sixteen basketball boots. "We ourselves have to lift the level of our community, the standard of our community to a higher level, make our own society beautiful so that we will be satisfied in our own social circles and won't be running around here trying to knock our way into a social circle where we are not wanted."

"Yeah, brotha, tell it like it is!" Calvin shouted in agreement. He was in his element listening to Malcolm. He was no Muslim, Nation Brotha or Five Percenter, but believed a lot of what they said about African self-help and economic empowerment. It made sense. He was tired of seeing the young brothas walking the streets without hope or direction. Tired of hearing about the black on black violence and disappointed by the general disrespect for elders within the community. His mission was to try and change things, to make a difference—and listening to Malcolm gave him a sense of power, gave him hope.

It was like Malcolm was standing in front of him in the cold, hollow shell of the changing room, those words reverberating off the walls and hitting him full between the eyes. Calvin could see the whole African diaspora sitting with him on the wooden benches nodding their heads and clapping their hands along with him.

He felt a tap on his shoulder and turned to see who was disturbing him at such an important time.

"Coach. What's up, brotha!" he shouted, watching Coach Bailey's lips move without hearing a word the man spoke. He finally pressed stop and peeled the headphones off.

"What did you say, Coach?"

"Me seh, wha' dat yah a listen to?"

Coach's ageing eyes glistened with interest behind his silver-rimmed glasses.

"Malcolm at his best, brotha. The X-Man's Ballot or the Bullet speech."

"Aah, me remember when 'im did come down ah Smethwick inna de sixties. Me shake 'im hand, y'nah."

"You shook hands with the man, Coach?" Calvin's eyes gleamed.

"Yeah man, top a Dudley Road by Rolfe Street."

"Go on, touch me brotha. Your fifteen minutes of fame."

Calvin held out his hand and Coach slid his rough-skinned palm across it.

"You must pass the word on how it felt. Give a talk for some of the younger brothas down the Centre."

"Y' still do dat voluntary work down deh?"

"Yeah man, still tryin' to get the young brothas and sistas to wise up to the realities."

Calvin stood to his full gangling six-foot-six height.

"Dat's good, dat's good. Y' must keep dem t'ings up. So Courtney Johnson still a run t'ings down deh?"

"Yeah, but the brotha's a Nation man now. Changed his name to Abdullah Rashid. He's keepin' a tight ship."

Coach looked surprised.

"Me never know 'im turn Muslim."

"Yeah, for two or three years now, brotha. Hey Coach, we've got a march planned around Handsworth against drugs in the community in about two months time. You should show your face, maybe make a speech there. The brothas still don't realise the reality of the situation for your generation when you first came here."

"Well, me haffe t'ink 'bout it. But me nah t'ink me could walk all dat way. Done all my marchin' in de fifties and sixties. Anyway, is up to unnu young people to tek up where we older ones left off."

"You're not old, Coach. You must be—what...fifty-five, fifty-six?"

"Me older dan dat, but never mind."

Calvin smiled. Despite his age, Coach could still carry the swing when it came to dress sense, with his brown suede jacket, Levi jeans and Timberland boots.

"So how you feelin' these days, brotha?"

"Alright. Doctor say I must tek it easy after de heart attack, so dat ah wha' me goin' do."

"So you're definitely out of here at the end of the season?"

"Yeah, me nah wan' to but me have to," Coach replied with a half-hearted smile. "Too much stress. Doctor say, it nah good fe me. Anyway, we 'ave more important t'ings to deal wid. Calvin, wha' we goin' do 'bout Winston? 'Im late again, y'nah!"

"You're the Coach, brotha."

"And you is me newly appointed assistant coach-stroke-team captain, soon to be coach when I retire," he announced. "So y'ave fe tek part inna decision mekkin'."

Calvin knew something had to be done about Winston. Since he joined the club he'd been late for almost every practice and every game. The brotha needed to understand that it took years to build a winning philosophy and discipline, and one man couldn't be allowed to destroy it. But as both a player and part of the management, Calvin had to tread carefully. He wanted the other players to respect him as an equal, while conceding him the authority of a coach.

And he knew Winston didn't like authority...didn't like anyone telling him about his shortcomings as a player or as a man. As far as Calvin was concerned, Winston represented the side of the brothas he could do without; the selfishness, the motormouth attitude outta control, the disrespect for all things and people other than themselves and—of course—the white women. Calvin had a particular beef about that. He let it be known the sistas were woman enough for him, but for the most part, kept his rantings to himself, since most of the team were indifferent, to say the least, on that particular subject.

But Winston was a good ball handler who brought a variation to the Warriors' attack and a determined attitude towards defence, something they had always lacked.

But he was beginning to divide the team—just when they were at last united behind the goal of winning the First Division championship and moving up to the Premier League. Gone was the internecine warfare of the past; it was all for one and one for all. But Winston was causing a lot of resentment because he got higher expenses than the other players. That made him the Man. No-one on thirty-five quid could possibly tell a twenty-four-year-old homeboy on two hundred—plus a thousand pound signing bonus—how to shoot the J...not even the assistant coach.

"You should fine him," Calvin told Coach, shrugging his narrow shoulders as if he really didn't want to make the decision.

"Me did ah t'ink dat y'nah. You right, me a go talk to Mista Lindsey and see wha' 'im say."

Coach shuffled slowly out of the changing room; Calvin watched, feeling nothing but respect for him. He admired the militant fighter even though he had mellowed with age. He sympathised with the problems Coach must have faced as one of the first to arrive from the Caribbean in the '50s...forced to live in one-room digs with three or four other people, doing the jobs the white man refused to do, fighting off racist teddy boys, and still managing to keep his family together and links with home intact.

He also respected Coach's knowledge of the sport. He found it remarkable that someone could know so much about the game without actually playing it.

Coach was introduced to the game in the early '70s when he visited his brother in Brooklyn. He had come back and set up a youth club and a basketball team, and they'd been going ever since. For Calvin that summed up Coach Bailey; he was the man.

He grabbed his bag and the suitholder containing his work clothes, and headed for the gym. His progress was halted when a body crashed into him.

"Brotha, you're late again," Calvin said, blocking Winston's entry to the changing rooms.

"Nigga, please," Winston replied, as if he wanted to run Calvin over.

"Have some respect for yourself. Stop using that word. Y'know it don't look good. Like Malcolm says..."

"Damn y'punk," Winston interrupted. "Man, I ain't here for none of dis black nationalist shit. Got it by the tankful from yer clean-shaven, sweet-talkin' Islamic bros in da States. I'm here to play ball and git paid, and talkin' black shit ain't gon' git me some. So quit frontin' on my ass and tek care of yer own homie."

"Brotha man, the club's payin' you big money considering the state of its finances, so at least you could do the right thing and get here on time."

"Club ain't payin' me shit. Can mek triple da snaps a homie's rollin' here in Europe."

"Then brotha, go to France, Italy or wherever you can pick it up."

"Man, my agent workin' on it dis very second."

"Well until then, you got to abide by the club rules and that means at training on time, every time."

Calvin moved aside and let Winston pass before heading for the gym door.

"Calvin, Calvin, y-y-y-you see dis? Y-y-y see it?"

Calvin turned and saw the short, podgy figure of Mr Lindsey rushing towards him—a copy of the *Birmingham Evening Echo* in one hand and a lighted cigar in the other—sweating like he had just finished a sprint. He handed Calvin the paper with the back page uppermost. "L-l-look 'ere," he said, excitedly.

Calvin read the headline: *Owner dodges mortars to sign Bosnian.*

"At las' dem get it in deh," Lindsey smiled, then squinted as he took a puff of his cigar. "Y'know how long me gi' dem dat story?"

Calvin scanned the opening lines then handed the paper back to Lindsey. He had respect for him as one of the leading black business-men in the city but felt the success of his night club, The Star, was despite his business acumen. Lindsey also had a reputation for being tighter than Scrooge.

"S-s-s-so, wha yuh t'ink, eh?" Lindsey asked, his milk-chocolate coloured face almost melting with satisfaction.

Before Calvin could reply, Lindsey started again, this time push-ing the paper under his nose.

"L-l-l-look wha' dem say: *'Warriors owner Maurice Lindsey went far-ther than any UN troops when he evaded gunfire and shelling to sign ace Bosnian player Joni Krantovic'.* Y'hear dat? Me famous!" Lindsey chuckled. "Further than any UN troops..." he repeated, running his chubby finger under every word.

"Famous huh?"

Lindsey didn't like his tone.

"Dat's wha' me say innit?" he retorted.

But Calvin knew the story was one of Lindsey's promotional skanks. He knew the closest Lindsey had ever got to a mortar explod-ing at his feet was when he accidentally dropped his cigar on his loafers.

"W-w-wha yuh t'ink, eh, Calvin?" Lindsey asked, drawing deeply on his cigar.

"Brotha, I'm disappointed."

"D-d-d-disa-wha?"

"Mister Lindsey, the deal from the end of last season was to get two top-notch African-American players to help the promotion push this year. But what we've got is a British-born player with a phoney accent who's going to cost us big time one day and a six-foot-eleven Bosnian who can't even play."

Lindsey looked perturbed.

"But wha' 'bout de publicity me get, uh? Look, gettin' a refugee from Bosina, or wh'ever it call, goin' bring de club 'nuff media atten-tion and public sympathy money.

"B-b-but a black Brummie back from de States, dat is back page news. No black American goin' bring us dat unless 'im a bigga crim-

21

inal dan Robin Maxwell—"

"Robert Maxwell, "

"Dat's wha' me seh innit?"

It made sense to Calvin. Maybe Lindsey was shrewder than he'd given him credit for. Anything that would bring in sponsorship money was to be welcomed. As it stood, the Warriors had a minimal deal with Black People Radio Line, BPRL. But because BPRL was a pirate station they couldn't shout it from the rooftops or the league would surely put a stop to it. For an all-black team in Handsworth, sponsorship was near enough impossible.

Nearby areas had higher crime rates, but as far as non-residents were concerned Handsworth was synonymous with black and therefore with badness; and in the eyes of the media every shooting, stabbing or riot that occurred in Birmingham had its origin in Handsworth. People that lived there said they lived in Lozells or Newtown or even West Bromwich; but if your postcode read B19 or B20 you were in Handsworth as far as outsiders were concerned—and a fully paid-up member of all that went with it.

Lindsey tried to appease Calvin:

"L-L-L-ook, t'ings a go work out. W-we don't lose dis season yet inna six game."

"Brotha, we haven't played anyone of note yet."

"Look, wid de side we 'ave we can deal wid anyt'ing dis league can fling at we. S-s-ee, next year, we goin' be in de Premier, 'nuff publicity, sponsorship and me can even afford to pay unnu some more corn. And y'see all me? M-m-me gonna be bigga dan dat Doug Ellis. Y'watch and see!"

"How much you payin' the Bosnian?" Calvin asked, changing the subject.

"D-d-dat's management business."

"Brotha man, I am management. You forget you made me assistant coach at the beginning of the season?"

"But you still one ah dem and y'nah need to know. Anyway, me have to get back to de club. Me 'ave a business to run. Me a go leave dis wid you to show de rest ah dem."

He folded the paper and handed it to Calvin.

"You know the brothas are not going to be too happy when they find out some white refugee is picking up more than them. Things not fair and you know it, brotha man," Calvin shouted as Lindsey headed for the door.

"But who gwine tell dem? You suppose to be management!"

22

Calvin walked on, and dropped his suitholder opening the gym door. Andre Beckford, who played shooting guard and was also his closest spar, picked it up and handed it to him.

"Working tonight, Calvin?"

"Yeah, bouncing at McGriff's again."

Calvin and Andre grew up on the same street and had been friends since primary school. At eleven Andre headed for grammar school while Calvin went to the local comprehensive, but they remained close, and Calvin occasionally had to protect Andre from the bashings the comprehensive tearaways used to give the grammar school boys.

Andre realised the value of hitting the books at school. He passed a string of O and A levels.

Calvin was happy to just drift through, then, but it was something he had lived to regret. He now saw it as the main reason he had to work nightclub doors to make ends meet, while Andre was a legal executive at a top firm in the city centre.

Andre had married Heather, a good friend of Calvin's from the comprehensive. Calvin was seeing Heather back in the fourth year at school, but they were still friends now. The three of them would joke about how Heather could have ended up married to Calvin. But Calvin knew she'd made the right choice; Andre was a safe brotha with prospects.

He looked around the gym. Eleven players on the Warriors' roster were now present. The twelfth—Winston—still hadn't emerged from the changing rooms.

Calvin placed his bag and suitholder behind the fence that separated the court from the seats; he saw the Uh Huh Girls, the three eighteen-year-old sistas that the team had named after the Ray Charles Pepsi advertisement.

The Uh Huh Girls followed the team everywhere and turned up to most of the training sessions. He wouldn't call them groupies, exactly, but he thought it was strange that they couldn't find anything better to do with their time than watching the Warriors train three times a week.

Maybe they got a kick out of seeing these athletic black bodies flexing in their vests and shorts. Maybe they were even hoping to be invited out one day—only no-one had bothered to find out their real names, let alone ask them out. Lets just say there are eighteen-year-old women and eighteen-year-old girls, and the Uh Huh tribe were definitely of the latter variety.

They waved. Calvin nodded. One got up and came running down the steps.

"Calvin, can I have your autograph?"

She handed him a piece of paper and a biro. "It's for my cousin from London—she came to the game last Saturday. She fancies you."

Calvin didn't feel much like a celebrity but felt good that he was known and signed it all the same.

"What's her name?"

"Dawn," she replied, smiling through a mouthful of braces.

"Okay, sista."

He handed the pen and paper back to her.

"She says she's coming up for the game this weekend and she'd like to meet you!"

"Does she, sista? Tell her the brotha's already spoken for."

He picked up a ball that had fallen loose from the backboard after a shot by six-foot-seven inch Lemuel Wright. He bounced it twice on the hard wooden surface before passing in the direction of Lemuel's massive frame—which was spoilt by a stomach that looked like he'd emptied the contents of a fridge into it. Lemuel caught it with hands like shovels, then threw to the small dark figure of Benji Daniel, who bounced it behind his back before making a one-bounce pass back to Calvin, who caught it and gingerly took two long steps before laying the ball up off the backboard and through the hoop.

"Calvin, when me gonna get me place back from dis white bwoy?" asked Lemuel, as Calvin retrieved the ball and flung it towards him.

"Lemi brotha, if you stop eatin' and get yourself on a serious training programme, you might reclaim your spot."

"Wha' yuh sayin', me fat?"

"Exactly, brotha."

"Me nah fat, me jus' big bone. Me mutha always tell me dat."

Lemi tried to pull his skin-tight shorts up his backside but they wouldn't budge above half way. Benji started to laugh. Lemi shot him a look.

"Wha' you laughin' at, Blackie?"

"Alroight, fat boy, don't start on me please," Benji replied in his thick Brummie accent.

Calvin smiled and started to stretch his limbs. He looked down the far end of the court and saw the muscular figure of Marcus Codrington taking on light-skinned, well-toned Levi Lewis. The two

24

were rivals for the power forward position and never wasted an opportunity to go at each other. They both had what the Warriors needed at the spot—aggression and speed; they were strong under the rim and good scorers. Calvin watched as the sweat dripped off their faces and soaked their tops. They were both six-foot-four, but Marcus was almost twice as wide as Levi. He grunted as they barged against each other like it was the final of the NBA championship.

Calvin's view was obstructed when Selwyn Harper put his thieving Samuel L. Jackson lookalike face in front of him.

"Elastic man!" Selwyn shouted, and placed his hands on Calvin's shoulders as he was bent over, holding his ankles and stretching his calf muscles.

"Look, geezer's sellin' top range, brand new size fifteen Air Jordan's, half price. Coming to you first 'cause I know you're a man that likes to look the biz on court. These kicks will make you a star."

Every session Selwyn had something to sell. "Brotha, I've still got the basketball you sold me last month and the thing hasn't bounced yet."

"C'mon, geezer, give me a break. That was legit' merchandise, that were." Selwyn said, placing his hand on top of his jheri curls.

"Brotha, I'm not interested. Anyway, I'm size sixteen."

"What's in a size? Okay, geezer, you know how difficult it is to get kicks to fit those canoes you got there. Don't say you didn't have first refusal."

Selwyn went across to Patrick 'Roots' Cartwright. Calvin saw Patrick flashing his long dreadlocks from side to side as if he too had been burnt by Selwyn before.

"Time out, time out, come round," Coach Bailey shouted.

The players formed a huddle. "Well, y'all know we 'ave Wolver'ampton on Sat'day and y'all know my feelin's 'bout dem..."

"Yeah, Coach!" everyone said, clapping loudly. Someone shouted: "We ah go stuff dem like the twenty-pound turkey Lemi just eat." Loud laughter echoed round the hall.

"Ssshh!"

Coach moved to reassert his authority.

"Stuff dem, yes. But we must do it by out-t'inkin' and out-playin' dem. Dem 'ave we assistant coach for five years now as dem head coach, so 'im know our game inside out. We 'ave to come up wid somet'ing new. But remember: widout discipline, we lose de game.

"Wolver'ampton is our closest rival and we can't afford to slip up against dem. Last season did one a piece but dis year we a go teach dem to poach our coach fe dem side."

As he was running through the tactics the gym door swung open and Winston sauntered in. Everyone turned and looked at him.

"Sorry, homiez," Winston said, a half-hearted smile on his face.

"Winston, I even lef' a message 'pon y' machine. Look, dis not good enough," said Coach. "I'll 'ave to speak to Mr Lindsey 'bout finin' you for lateness."

As Winston put down his bag his mobile rang. Everyone either kissed their teeth or sighed in disbelief. He answered the phone.

"I can't speak to you now, Amanda," he said in hushed tones, then he switched off the phone before finally joining the training session.

After a half-hour of calisthenics the squad did basic ball drills and then went through some plays with the starting five—Winston at guard, Andre at shooting guard, Marcus Codrington at power forward, Calvin at the other forward position and Joni at centre—against Adam Young and Benji Daniel at the guard positions, Patrick Cartwright and Levi Lewis as forwards and Lemuel Wright at centre.

John Nettlesford and Selwyn Harper sat on the sidelines. Neither got on court and why they religiously turned up to practice was a mystery. On the rare occasions when John actually started training he never finished—he was always complaining about some new injury, which earned him the nickname 'Sicknote'.

Calvin thought scrimmaging against the bench players was fun. They all wanted a starter's place and Calvin and the other starters knew it. Sometimes it would get rougher than actual games and on occasion Coach had to intervene.

Today wasn't too bad, although Winston was letting his mouth run ahead of him again. He cursed out Adam, the player he had replaced in the team, who in turn taunted Andre about taking his place in the side, since he couldn't do anything but shoot.

Adam's words were beginning to have an effect on Andre, who was way off with his shot. Winston got him open several times but Andre couldn't sink a bucket if you paid him.

"Sch-itt, homie, if ya can't deliver da result mek way for someone who can," Winston shouted at him.

They were nearing the end of the session when the gym door flew open with a bang and in marched a burly figure in a leather baseball cap, an ankle-length black leather coat and a pair of dark shades that were too small for his round face. It was the man from Sodom, Zorro.

What the hell is he doing up here? Calvin wondered. He hadn't come to hire a badminton court.

26

Calvin used to work the doors with Zorro until he sliced up two men after a minor disturbance. Now his face was screwed beyond belief. Some man screw up their face just to look hard but Zorro's menacing look had a permanence that made you wonder if he had a bad experience in the womb. He stared around menacingly for a few moments, and then stormed back out.

Once the training session was over, on their way to the changing room, Calvin walked up behind Andre and Adam and listened in on their conversation.

"Look I'm working on my game twenty-four, seven, and I'm hot, bro. Got some new moves to reveal." Adam boasted.

"Yeah—you've got all the time in the world but some of us have to work for a living." Andre countered.

"Okay, Birdman, you gotta big job, so what? You ain't got a game. Watch out bro, I'm burning your heels."

"You haven't got a chance in hell of taking my spot."

"Listen to yah, like some English bwoy. Coach knows I have a game, he's just biding time."

Calvin was under pressure to keep Andre in the starting five. For most of the season he had been off. A shooting guard has to be relied upon to score, has to be the main threat, but Andre was failing big time this season. His game was getting worse, and if Calvin hadn't used his influence with Coach Bailey Andre would have been warming the bench several weeks ago.

Calvin caught up with him when Adam had gone to the changing room. He put his hand around Andre's shoulder.

"What's up, brotha? You were off today."

Andre ran a hand over the red shaving pimples on his almond-coloured face.

"Yeah, don't I know it. I just couldn't concentrate."

"What, you got exams, brotha?"

Andre shook his head.

"Next round doesn't start until spring...just as well, I've got a lot on my mind."

Heather had already told Calvin that they were going through a rough patch; Andre's boss had been giving him hell at work and he spent little time at home because of it. Calvin wanted to help, but he couldn't get involved if Andre wouldn't speak to him about it. Andre had been that way since they were boys; he was a very private person. Andre changed the subject suddenly.

"How are your mum and dad doing?"

"Fine," said Calvin, "considering what's happened. I think it's affecting mum more than Pops, but it's hard on them both, y'know."

"When are they heading back to Barbados?"

"Brotha, I wish I could tell you. Supposed to have gone two months ago...shipped all their belongings over, even had their airline tickets, but their lawyer on the island said it's best they cancel and stay here until the problem is sorted."

"How long have the squatters been in there now?"

"They're not squatters, brotha. They were legal tenants, but when Pops wanted the house vacated ready to settle back they refused to move. Said they have to find another place to rent before they move out. It's been two months now."

"Can't you get a court order to force them out?"

Calvin sighed.

"Brotha, the law works differently over there."

"Thirty-five years they've been in this place. Now when it's time to call it a day, they can't. They just sit in an empty house waiti..g for a phone call. Brotha, if I had the money I'd go over and turf them out personally."

As they entered the changing rooms big Marcus, Lemi and some other players were on their way out.

"Oh, Lemi," Andre shouted "My car needs looking at. Thing needs a kick in the mornings."

"Bring it by tomorrow afternoon," Lemi managed to say through a mouthful of chocolate.

Calvin sat on the bench next to Andre. He didn't have to be at McGriff's until nine-thirty and the drive to Redditch only took twenty minutes. He could hear Levi and Adam discussing some women they had met at a club the night before. Levi described in graphic detail how he'd made love to one on top of a pool table, while Adam creased up with laughter. Then Adam told how her sister squeezed his manhood so tight that he thought she had ruptured him, and the two of them dissolved into hysterical laughter. Then Levi boasted that his twelfth kid—he had children by eight different women—had been born last night.

"Way to go, bro," said Adam—then raised his hand and they went high fives.

Calvin wondered how on earth he could get through to young brothas who saw their fathers and older brothers behaving like horses at a stud farm—revelling in providing a sperm donor service.

Across the room, Selwyn the Spiv was still trying to off-load his

28

gear, this time to Sicknote, John Nettlesford. John was five-foot-nine, so size fifteen boots weren't likely to be much use to him.

Roots was building a spliff. Calvin shouted across to him:

"Brotha, there's no smoking in here and specially not what you've got there."

"Cha mon," Roots kissed his teeth, rolled up the spliff and put it in his coat pocket.

Winston had already showered, but was unusually quiet as he got dressed. Thank Allah for small mercies, Calvin thought. Coach went over to talk to him about his timekeeping and they were still talking when Calvin came out of the shower.

Andre was sitting with his head in his hands. He pulled them down the length of his face to reveal worried features.

"Who's Villa playing tomorrow?" he asked.

Calvin knew that was not what was on his mind.

"I don't know."

"It's some second or third division side in the Coca-Cola Cup," Andre mumbled.

"Sorry, can't help brotha." Calvin put the Malcolm X tape in the Walkman and passed it to Andre.

"Listen to this, bro," he said, then finished dressing and checked himself in the mirror. His black suit had seen better days but he only wore it for work.

Joni came up beside him and smiled.

"Look good," he said, standing behind Calvin to pat his hair. Calvin nodded unenthusiastically. Mr Lindsey breaking up the all-African thing at the club was one thing, but to insist on giving Joni quality time on the floor was too much. Coach Bailey and Calvin argued constantly about replacing him in the starting line-up, but every Friday Lindsey would check the team sheet. If the Bosnian's name wasn't there he would replace whoever was at centre with Joni. Lindsey didn't know a thing about basketball but argued that he knew about business. He couldn't have the potential sponsorship puller on the bench.

Coach always sided with Lindsey, saying Joni needed time to settle in, but Calvin had already seen enough of him and in his view they should have shipped his long ass back to Bosnia.

The centre is the crucial position. He's the pivot of the side—he must be able to score, rebound, block shots and above all intimidate; the man has to instill fear in the opposition. Joni was a loser on all four counts, especially the last. But who would replace him? Lemi

29

was the only one with the height and size to clog up the paint and to snatch the boards.

But with Lemi eating enough chocolate to keep Cadbury's in business, Calvin just didn't have a replacement to argue his case. He finished combing his hair and went to pack his stuff away.

"Who is this?" Andre asked, handing back the Walkman.

"Malcolm, brotha," Calvin answered.

"He's that Moslem dude, ain't he?"

"Yeah man, serious brotha."

"He certainly is. Where did you get it?"

"We have copies down at the centre." For months Calvin had been trying to get Andre to come down to the X Centre and tune into the African cultural rap, but he always gave some excuse about being busy with exams, his kids or work.

Calvin grabbed his bag and made to leave. Andre walked towards the showers. "Got to hurry," he said.

"Why, brotha? Heather can't be that worried."

"Man, I've got to get back to work. I've got an important case. Can't afford to mess up."

Calvin felt almost disappointed in Andre. At a time when he should be home to kiss his kids goodnight and be with his wife, he was heading back to the office. Heather wouldn't be pleased.

"Make sure you give Heather a ring," Calvin shouted.

"She won't understand, so why bother?" Andre shouted back from under the shower.

Coach and Winston had finished their one-on-one and Winston left looking nervous. Andre looked round from the showers, his whole body layered in soap suds. "Hey, tape's fine, but give me Wynton Marsalis any day!"

They both laughed.

"Go in peace, brothas," Calvin said to Coach, Adam and Levi. As he was leaving, he caught a glimpse of Zorro hurrying out of the building. *What the hell was he up to?*

He saw Zorro pull something shiny out of his coat pocket; seconds later, Zorro had Winston pinned to the wall, threatening him with a ten-inch blade.

"I'm gonna cut yah, y' li'l bloodclaat," Zorro spat.

Calvin rushed him from behind, throwing his left arm around Zorro's throat and gripping his right wrist to keep him from slashing Winston. Big though Zorro was, Calvin's extra height made a lot of difference. They wrestled for a moment but Calvin quickly estab-

30

lished enough control to push Zorro away.

Winston collapsed in a heap behind them, coughing.

Zorro looked angrily at Calvin.

"Dis 'ave nut'n to do wid you, so fuck off!" The knife in his hand glistened under the street lights.

"Cool down, Zorro," Calvin said. He was trembling and his heart beat at a crazy pace, but he knew that Zorro would steam in for the kill if he sensed fear.

"Wha' y'mean cool down? Dis li'l bloodclaat a tek steps wid me and y'ah tell me fuckin' cool down?" the big man shouted in a crazed voice, pointing the knife at Calvin's face.

Calvin hoped that because he knew him he would just cool off. But Zorro wanted Winston.

"Don't do it, brotha man!"

"I gonna kill de li'l fucka. Get out me way!"

"If you want him, you have to come through me," Calvin said, thinking: *All this for Winston? It might be better if someone did teach him a lesson.*

Zorro's features screwed even more as he eyeballed Calvin; sweat poured down his jet black face. Then the doors to the centre swung open as Andre, Coach and some other team members came out.

"Shit!" someone shouted, and they all rushed over.

As he left Zorro pushed the blade back inside his leather coat. "Tell dat li'l fucka I goin' fuck 'im up next time."

Winston leapt to his feet, still a little shaken.

"Fuck you nigga, I'm hangin' wit' da lynch mob," he shout as Zorro's black BMW zoomed off. "Y' come back here again, y' punk ass muthafucka, and I'll put a cap in yer big black ass!"

"What's happening?" Andre asked.

Calvin shrugged.

"Just came out, and saw Zorro roughin' up Winston."

Winston broke in.

"He ain't rough me shit! Da nigga jumped me from da rear. See, everyone wants to play the Gangsta. Fuckin' phoney G try to mess wit' me, trippin' for no damn reason."

Calvin smirked.

"Well brotha, if it wasn't for me you'd a been sliced like a turkey."

"Fuck you man, I was just catchin' my breath to turn on his punk ass. I can handle my own shit. Don't need y'ass to fight my corner."

"Looked like you were having some trouble, Winston," Andre said, hiding a smile.

"Fuck you, li'l buggie bwoy. Go tek da phat suit and play wit' da white punks and git outta my face, homie. Shit! Da man messed up my fuckin jacket."

Calvin couldn't believe that after such a close shave, all Winston could think about was the mud on his jacket. But he knew the brotha had better watch out. Zorro was not a man to give up easily.

Public Enemy's *'Fear of a Black Planet'*, blazed out of the car stereo as Calvin drove from Birmingham to Redditch. He drummed on the steering wheel and rapped along to every phrase he understood. He was late, so he had to put his foot down.

He thought about the incident with Zorro and for a moment felt quite chuffed at the way he'd handled it. But his satisfaction was short-lived. He'd had to stop one brotha from stabbing another to death—where was the joy in that? It shouldn't have happened in the first place. He knew the notion of brothas and sisters living peacefully with each other was too idealistic for some—but not for him. He had to keep believing, otherwise he'd end up shrugging his shoulders like Winston and saying *'dat's how Niggaz is, Bro!'*

He had read somewhere that by the year 2000 one in four black brothas in America will be either in prison, on drugs, in a mental institution or dead. He could see the same thing happening here. Only last weekend a mad-ass went into a house party and started firing bullets into the ceiling. The next day another young brotha was stabbed to death. Things were getting serious. The young brothas were getting outta control. Why couldn't these fools put their efforts to more constructive things?

That was his motivation for organising the youth conference, so young people could come and talk about what was going wrong and how things could change for the future. It might not be the whole solution, but he had to do his part.

It was twenty to ten when Calvin arrived at McGriff's, Redditch's number one nightspot, and it was busy for a Tuesday; there was a long queue outside. He walked straight in, acknowledging the two white bouncers on the door. In the three years he'd worked there, there had only ever been three black bouncers and they were always behind the bar, never on the door. Calvin knew the reason, but the man was paying his bills, so he kept quiet. He felt a tap on his shoulder as he entered the cloakroom.

"Cal, Cal."

It was Mr Vance, the owner, a short, bald, nervous man. Calvin hated when he called him that.

"Gerry's just phoned in sick and I've got a lot of new guys on tonight. I want you to supervise."

Gerry, the head bouncer, was as racist as the KKK. Although he was ex-CID, he was as yellow as they come. Whenever trouble erupted, he would be right there—at the end—and order the others to throw the culprits out.

Calvin looked down at Vance.

"What's the rate?"

"Rate? What d'you mean, Cal?"

"I mean, if I'm doing Gerry's job I'm entitled to his rate of pay."

Vance rubbed his hands over his mouth.

"I thought you would've have been glad of the experience, Cal. You know Gerry won't always be around."

What a little creep! Calvin could have picked him up and thrown him over the bar. Vance was offering him work experience for a job he could do with his eyes shut.

"I'd prefer the extra money."

Vance sighed, then gave him a sickly smile. "Okay, okay Cal. Tell you what...I'll give you a ten pound increase on your nightly rate. How does that tickle you?"

Vance really thought he'd offered him something special. Calvin knew Gerry must be on at least seventy a night. How else could he afford the payments on his brand new Volvo? But to save arguing he agreed and Vance scuttled away to the safety of his office.

Now he was in charge, Calvin could make decisions. His first was to put the two white boys on the inside while he and Nigel—another brotha—worked the outside.

It was cold enough to make him feel lucky that he'd been working inside for the last three years. But he stuck it out anyway, if only to vex Mr Vance—and he made sure that, during their stint, plenty of black men came in. Some seemed surprised that they'd gotten past the door, let alone the frisk table.

After two hours he changed the rota and was about to enter the main hall when Mr Vance came running out, his face a furious shade of red.

"Cal, Cal, who's on those bloody doors?"

"Me and Nigel just came off. Why?"

"Why? You asking me why? Look!" He held the door open so Calvin could see into the dancehall. There were more black men in there than he'd ever seen in the whole of Redditch.

33

"So what's the problem?" Calvin asked.

"Problem? Jesus Christ man! You asking me what the problem is? My regulars can't get a bleedin' dance, that's the problem! All the girls are flocking round those darkies, ain't they?"

Calvin was ready to deck him when Vance caught himself.

"Look, this ain't on, Cal? You know the score."

Calvin's expression was stony.

"No, I don't. Enlighten me."

Vance sighed.

"Look, I run a respectable club. My regulars are going spare; I mean, they feel insulted. Whoever's on the door now, you tell 'em not to let any more blacks in, okay?"

Much as he wanted to, Calvin didn't hit Vance. He just slowly untied his dickie bow, slid it from around his neck, then rammed it in Vance's face, knocking him backwards with the force. Then he headed straight for the door, ignoring Vance's shouting and shrieking.

Calvin lay naked across his bed, absorbing the warmth of the centrally heated room. His head still hurt from the vodka he'd drunk at the Star Club after leaving McGriff's. He was teetotal, so the alcohol had sent his head into orbit. He remembered Vance's stupid face and his even stupider threats, and grinned broadly. He'd been waiting a long time for a chance to put the little runt in his place, but it had been well worth it. The phone rang. He got up and tried to keep his head steady as he walked to the living room.

"Hello," he croaked.

"Calvin, did I wake you?"

It was Heather.

"No, no. What is it, sista?"

"Nothin' really..."

"You got me out of my bed at...what time is it, anyway?"

"Two-thirty."

"Two-thirty a.m? What's happened? Where's Andre?"

"Nothing's happened. And Andre's still at work, probably."

"Damn, he's putting in some serious hours."

"Tell me about it!"

"Well, I suppose he's gotta do what's he gotta to do."

"Calvin, what he's gotta to do is spend some time with his family. Y'know, I've hardly seen him over the last month."

"Heather, the brotha's just trying to do the right thing for all of you."

"How can you say that? He comes in, grunts hello, eats his dinner, lies around listening to jazz all night. Four times this week I've had to wake him from that position."

"Maybe he has problems, sista."

"Then why doesn't he discuss them with me? Am I some kind of ogre?"

"Course not. He probably just can't talk about them. Maybe he misses his parents or something."

"We can't use that excuse for all his behaviour."

"You never know. It's a difficult thing to get over."

"Calvin..."

"Yes, sista."

"Will you answer me something honestly?"

"I'll try."

She fell quiet for a moment.

"Is Andre having an affair?"

"With who? Sista, you're gettin' paranoid. Phone him at work. The brotha's probably buried under a mountain of law books."

"If he was, would you tell me?"

"Sista, you don't want me to answer that. The brotha's my best spar."

"So what am I?" she asked abruptly.

"You're a good sista friend."

"I see. But you still wouldn't tell me?"

"Heather, don't corner me."

"God! You men are all the same. Always overing for each other."

"Sista, you need to talk your differences through with your man."

"But that's the problem! Andre won't talk to me..."

He was at a loss for what to say next.

"Calvin, have you ever cheated on Lorna?"

"Sista, this isn't about Lorna and me."

"Have you, though?"

"I'm not answering that question."

"You have, haven't you?"

"I didn't say that."

"You don't need to. I can hear it in your voice."

"Heather, I think you need to get some rest."

"You've got someone there now, haven't you?"

Calvin sighed.

"Go in peace, sista."

He signed off before she could reply.

35

3

A Different Reality

Today cold nah raas; the street favour the North Pole. And slippy? Almost bruck me neck coming off the 91 bus. I stepped carefully up Hunter's Road, carrying my Adidas bag and balancing like some tightrope walker. When I reached the corner of Hockley Hill I bumped into someone I never wanted to see. One short-ass teefin' bwoy I grew up next door to, called Shorty.

"Wha'ppen Marcus?"

I detected a nervousness in his voice. I nodded.

"Shorty."

"Long time no see. Is where yuh been man?"

"Me deh 'bout. Y'know 'ow t'ings run."

I pulled my leather duffel coat closer to shield me from the cold wind.

"Bwoy is where yuh get a body like dat?" Shorty asked, placing his two meagre arms around my shoulders. "Yuh look well solid."

"Hard work. Yuh know say me always a train."

"Me know, me know. Mus' be fifty-inch chest."

"Fifty-two." I expanded it to make it seem even bigger.

"Bloodclaat! Yuh wan' enter one ah dem body-building contest and mek some coinage."

"Nah man, me nah inna dat."

I began shuffling my feet on the icy pavement.

"So...yuh see Bigga recent?" he asked hesitantly.

"Yeah, last week. Me goin' check 'im dis mornin' too."

"Yeah?" Shorty began to look uncomfortable. "Well tell 'im wha'ppen and me a go check 'im soon. Eh, me sight yuh old man de other day y'know."

"Cha, 'im still a jester," I said. I didn't really want to hear anything about him.

Shorty always had plenty to talk about, like a blasted woman. Man couldn't stop chat about how me get so physical. Like just about every man I know, Shorty say he want to look like me. People t'ink it easy, but your mind have to set right. I told him to do what I do, pump iron three days a week, one hundred sit-ups and two hundred press-ups a day, a three-mile run every other day, plus I play ball. He looked disappointed to hear about the hard work, but yuh know what dem say—no pain, no gain. Anyway he could never look like me 'cause he's only about five-foot-six and look like him never train a day in him life. After five minutes standing talking to him, I had to go. The cold was ripping through my body. I had finally made up my mind to go and sign on. I left work two weeks ago and, being in the catering industry, I thought my next job would come easy.

In the three years since I last sign on I must ah had five different jobs, one after the other. But it look like t'ings change now. Maggie gone, but hard times still deh ya. Although me's a man who don't need—or even want—plenty money, when I found myself down to my last few buff, I decided is time to mek moves to put some shekels in my pocket.

That's why I checked Mr Lindsey last night. I've been carryin' his rahtid team for five years. Been top scorer in all that time, leading rebounder twice and voted the club's Most Valuable Player four times. They only gave the last award to Calvin, season gone, 'cause I got suspended for the final ten games.

I didn't want Calvin to know that I was looking for more shekels when him came in the Star last night, cause it don't look right y'know, team spirit and all that. But I needed to raise some cash, so if I could get it through Handsworth Warriors then all the better. I wasn't looking for no big increase on my forty notes a week expenses, 'cause I know the club don't have the cash upfront with the lack of sponsorship—but if I can reason with Lindsey to set me up with twenty buff a week extra I'll be satisfied. I had to see him later today 'cause he wanted to sleep or hibernate on it, or some foolishness.

Rahtid day was well miserable and standing at the bus stop by the Hockley Flyover jus' mek it worse. Damn bus drivers dem ah ramp this morning, 'cause I was there over twenty minutes and I didn't see one of the three buses to take me up Soho Road. Had a good mind to go to the depot and bamboozle a double decker and drive meself. Cha! If dem stupid people never move the blasted dole office I coulda walked the half mile up the hill. Now me hear them move it up by the West Bromwich Albion football ground, three rahtid miles away.

I see man in their brand new cars just whiz past me standing in line like some idiot bwoy. I know most ah dem. Come from the same stock. But them have money to splash 'pon car. Me? My foot bottom is my Michelin tyre. Me nah teef or go sell drugs and kill off people pickney, just to drive pretty car and impress nobody.

The cold started to hurt my ears, so I pulled up the hood of my duffel coat. My Hush Puppies were white like the frost on the ground, and to tell the truth I didn't even know if my toes did still in deh. Couldn't feel a t'ing. The queue at the bus stop stretched way back. Most ah dem was black and from their faces they must have been going to sign on too. You can always tell. They just look miserable, like there's no future. Is living in Handsworth mek people feel so; 'nuff times I think about steppin' from the area, but you have to have money in your pocket. Talk about life sentence. No parole from this place 'til you bloodclaat dead.

"Bout blasted time, too!" a woman in front of me muttered.

I looked up to see a bus slowly creeping over the frosty road towards us. Everybody started to pick up their bags and surge forward. Look like it was going to be a fight to get on, but me big and me hand middle thick so no matter wha' me haffe do, I know I was getting on first.

But the bus driver just hold his head straight and drive, never even think about stopping. I could see the bus was jam-packed, people did up front practically sitting 'pon top of him, but I was vex same way. I wanted to sort out my business at the dole office quickly so I could get to Winson Green Prison for ten-thirty. I was going to visit my brother, Bigga, on remand for armed robbery. The old lady nearly had a stroke when she saw the photofit of him on *Crimewatch*, as one of three men Babylon wanted to interview about a security van hold-up. They only manage to pull up Bigga 'cause some fool bwoy worker, playing the hero, dragged off his mask before one of the others shot him in the leg. When they gave the description of the man who pulled the trigger Bigga didn't have to say a word, I knew it was Shorty.

The old lady's Christian faith meant she couldn't harbour criminals, so she begged Bigga to turn himself in—believing that if he was innocent like he said, there would be no problem. She lives in a different world.

Bigga has spent a good portion of his adult life behind bars and it's surprising that the local beastbwoy didn't put two and two together and haul him in before the old lady convinced him to give himself up. Now she has it on her conscience. And if him go down, well, it's gonna break her heart.

Four packed buses came down the hill in a row before I was able to get on one. It was nine-forty. As I sat down on the back seat I stared at the photo on my bus pass. T'ing was taken over two years ago when I had a beard like a Sikh and a afro like when Michael Jackson was a bwoy. Now me chin smooth like a baby butty and me head skiffle like Kojak.

Soho Road looked like the set of one of those Indian movies on Channel Four. Everywhere you look is Indians; they owned ninety percent of the shops. Apachi Indian fly posters were pasted on walls that were once reserved for the likes of Dennis Brown and Gregory Isaacs. Despite what he says about his ragga style bringing the Asian and black cultures together, I ain't seen no black man working in one of them Indian man's shop.

I didn't know exactly where the dole office was, so I had to keep a close watch. But fifteen minutes later, when half the long-face passengers stood up to get off, I realised it must be the stop for the unemployed. I jumped up and hurried down the steps, then followed them. We had to pass the Albion football ground. As a yout' I was a regular down the Baggies, 'cause they had three black players—Laurie Cunningham, Cyrille Regis and Brendan Batson. Use to call them the Three Degrees. They played wicked football; skillful, none of that kick-and-run stupidness. Whenever one of them scored I used to feel so sweet, y'know, could big up my chest in front of the white bwoys at school.

But I used to catch up with them nazi bwoys 'nuff times. On matchday the whole of Soho Road was sell out of bananas, 'cause them bwoy buy them up to pelt at at the black players, like them was monkeys in a zoo. Even the Baggie fans used to throw at their own players when things went bad. It used to vex me, y'see. One time, me hear one white man a call Regis a black bastard. Then 'im look at me and say, "Sars mate, I don't mean you loike."

I shot him a box 'cross him face y'see, man went out like a light. Cha. Me one nearly mash up the whole place, 'til seven Babylon fly down 'pon me, and fling me out. Since then I never went back, black players or not.

Finally, we reach the dole office. I couldn't believe the new building. Last time I was in one of these places the staff were behind thick glass screens. Now them bold as brass, sitting there like 'boasty Pete' behind desks in an air-conditioned office. Bloodclaat, there were even comfy chairs around for the claimants to sit. This was some improvement. No glass, no barrier, nothing between you and them. Mek yuh feel almost human. But they were taking a chance, 'cause me know when some of dem raggamuffin yout' let off, dem workers would have to hurdle like Ed Moses to get outta deh. I hear 'nuff of them get them head open like a can of beans when dem refuse people dem

39

corn.

I looked around the office. 'Nuff black gyal did ah rush round the place like dem important 'cause dem have job. Just one black man was in the place. When my turn came I went to the front desk where a sweet-looking black woman was sitting. She looked well professional in her nice grey suit and white silk blouse.

"Take a seat, sir," she said—without even looking up at me. But at least she show some respect and call me sir.

"Me wan mek a fresh claim."

"Sorry?" she said, like is the first she hear the lingo. "You want to make a claim?"

"Yeah."

"Okay. You fill out this booklet and I'll make you an appointment for an interview."

She handed me a green booklet.

"Interview, fe wha'?"

"It's just standard procedure, sir," she replied. "When would you like to come in?"

I kissed my teeth.

"Whenever."

"Will tomorrow at three suit you?"

I gathered myself. " 'Ow long it a go tek?"

"About forty-five minutes maximum, sir."

"T'ree is alright."

"Your name, sir?"

"Marcus Codrington."

"Address?"

This t'ing was already getting on my rahtid nerves. I hate people questioning me about my private business. These bloodclaat dole people asked too many bloody question.

"17 Hatfield Road, Lozells."

She could sense the hostility in my voice. "Do you have your National Insurance number, sir?" she enquired nervously.

"Cyan' remember it."

"Okay, Mr Codrington. I'll see you at three tomorrow," she said, smiling.

I snatched up the booklet and cooled my temper before walking out.

I was thirty minutes late for visiting time at Greens. The outside of the building always frightened me as a yout' when we used to go past it on our way to Sunday school. It favour the Addams Family yard. I was sure it was what make me try hard to stay on the straight and narrow. Inside the wardens were giving me the normal eye-balling. I cleared security and went to the registration area. I wrote Bigga's real name, Carlton Codrington, as the person I came to see, then sat on one of the benches that stretched the length of the waiting hall. The place was full of gyal waiting to visit dem man. I found myself nodding at practically every one ah dem. Seemed like the whole of Handsworth was inside Greens.

A burly-looking warden came into the waiting room and shouted: "Marcus Codrington!"

To me, he looked like the true image of a prison guard, y'know, a big bruiser type who loved to cuss, swear and knock the convicts around just because he had on a uniform. As I reached the door he held it open for me, saying:

"You've got fifteen minutes."

In the visiting room, there were about fifty desks, arranged in rows, with an inmate behind each one. Bigga stood up when he saw me come in. I put my clenched fist up to acknowledge him and manoeuvred past baby prams, hysterical crying women and mean-looking wardens to get to him.

"I taught unnu forget 'bout me," Bigga said as we touched fists.

"Nah, mon, is jus' me had fe sign today."

I pulled out the chair and sat opposite him.

"Sign on, wha' fe? Yuh lose yuh job?"

"Nah, not exactly," I said rubbing my chin.

"Wha' y' mean 'not exactly'? You a sign on and a work too?"

He was sounding like the blasted dole people.

"Easy nah Bigga."

"So wha'ppen, man?"

"Me lef' de place," I said, leaning back in my chair. "De owner did ah tek steps wid me. Wan' me sweep floor and clean out toilet when me suppose to be a cook. Me have few words wid 'im and ruff 'im lickle. Nothin' serious, y'know."

"White guy?" he enquired.

"Wha' y'expect?"

"Bwoy, to tell truth, it nah mek no difference what colour dem is. When people get a little position it go straight to dem head. Tek in here for example. De black screws jus' the same as de white ones. No bloodclaat difference. But Marcus, yuh haffe watch yuh temper."

"Me know, Bigga man. Me 'ave t'ings under control," I told him,

41

with more certainty than I really felt.

Bigga was thirty-three—four years older than me. He had the longest dreadlocks in Handsworth—almost touching his broad backside. He got his pet name because of his size. He was built like me, but his body was soft and untrained. His gut hung over his trousers like a balloon and his breasts were sagging like a woman who born ten yout'.

The old lady brought the two of us up more or less on her own. The old man left when I was twelve, after Bigga sized up to him for licking mom. Man was no rahtid use, anyway. He'd go out and whatever money he didn't give the bookie, he used to get stupid on rum. The gas, electricity and mortgage went unpaid. 'Nuff times bailiffs turned up to cart off the furniture 'cause of him. Then he had the cheek to tek out his grievances on us, especially the old lady. The man was a bully. He was six foot and about seventeen stone of solid muscle and the old lady was half his size—but big enough for him to use as his personal punch bag.

One time he cuff her so bad she had to stay in hospital for two nights. I remember it clear as day 'cause him made some lumpy mash potato and cold gravy for me and Bigga to eat, tellin' us the old lady gone to see auntie in London even though we saw her run out the house screaming after he hit her.

We couldn't understand why the old lady always forgave him and never reported him. Anyway, as soon as Bigga was an equal size to the old man he started to give him a taste of his own medicine. He was too big for the old man to lash with his buckle belt, and he couldn't take it. Him feel he was no longer the man, he who must be obeyed, and him just dig up. He still lives in the area and me sight him regular but I just say wha'ppen and leave it at that.

After the old man left, Bigga began to look after me and the old lady. He started mixing with Shorty and his posse and got dragged into selling weed, and it wasn't too long before the Babylon joined the bailiffs in banging down the old lady yard in the early hours of the morning.

"So 'ow's Mom?" Bigga asked.

"Holding up."

I could see Bigga didn't want to dwell too long on the old lady 'cause he knew he'd let her down; but he had to ask about her 'cause Mom refused to visit him inside.

"Wha' bout y' gyal, she still givin' you problems?"

"Bwoy, Marcia still a mess 'bout, man."

"She still nah let yuh see de yout'?"

" 'Ow yuh mean? De gyal tek out court injunction. Ban me from goin' widdin a mile of she yard. Cyan' even send Charmaine a li'l chocolate, never mind see she."

"Cha, yuh see 'ow women evil man? Dem evil, let me bloodclaat tell yuh."

Bigga shook his head in dismay.

"Me stay away fe de last two week, but de t'ing a burn me inside. Y'know wha' it like when yuh cyan even sight yuh two-year-old yout'? Me feel fe just trod up to Wolverhampton same way."

"Me know 'ow yuh feel, but watch yuhself. Don't go messin' wid dem injunction t'ing, 'cause yuh may find y'self in here wid me. And we cyan do de old lady so."

The fifteen minutes went like five. When the screws called time, we both stood up and touched fists.

"Later," I said.

"True," he replied, as I turned to leave.

"Yaow!" Bigga called.

I turned back.

"Yuh see Shorty?"

I nodded. "Me see 'im earlier."

"Tell dat short-ass raas to get 'im backside up 'ere quick, seen?"

It was rahtid seven o' clock when I finally headed home after working out at the gym. Today should ah been my day off but I was so bored I had to do somet'ing. I worked my legs and back, but I was so shattered, I felt like I was squatting five hundred kilos instead of two.

On my way home I passed Calvin's parents' yard. For months now there's been a big 'for sale' sign outside with SOLD SUBJECT TO CONTRACT tacked on underneath. Looks like people don't want to put pen to paper. Anyhow, it's nice to see Calvin's people still together and planning the rest of their future. I don't know wha' me old lady goin' do when she get older.

When I got home I picked up my mail. The first letter was the electric bill. I didn't even bother look at the rest, just flung them on the dining room table. I went to the kitchen, cut two thick slices of hard dough bread and added turkey slices and coleslaw to make a crucial sandwich. Then I opened a tin of banana Nurishment and turned on the TV in the living room.

I get as bored as hell when there isn't any basketball training. I flicked through the *TV Times* to see what was on the box. Four channels, but not a rahtid took me. *Sportsnight* was on later but that only had snooker, tennis and an interview with Martin Offiah.

And since Sky took it away from Central, football has been dry, 'cause if you can't pay you can't play. And right now I can't pay.

As I crabmashed my way through the sandwich, the phone rang. I put my plate down and answered on the second ring.

"Yaow."

"Marcus? Is so you answer de phone, bwoy?"

"Mom, how yuh goin'. Y'alright?"

"Mmm, me alright. You?"

"Surviving, y'know 'ow it go."

"Well that's all we can do 'til de good Lord come to save us."

I smiled. The old lady always worked the Lord or some Bible passage into the conversation. Since the old man took off and me and Bigga left home, that's the only thing she lives for.

"You see Carlton today?" she asked.

"Yeah."

"How is he?"

She sounded sad and concerned.

"Him look good. Y'know Bigga, never mek anythin' bother 'im. Him ask fe yuh, y'nah."

I hoped she'd realise what I was hinting at.

"But 'im nah must, 'im nah forget 'im mother."

I tried the more direct route.

"Why yuh nah go visit 'im? 'Im a look out fe you, y'nah."

"Marcus, I prayed to de Lord to give me de strength to go and visit Carlton, but I can't tek seeing my boy in dat place wid all dem murderers, rapists and evil people. And knowing is me help put him there—" her voiced dropped. "—I just can't go. It's too much."

"But Bigga's no rapist or murderer."

"I know son, I know. But I can't go."

I could tell she was feeling bad.

"Okay Mum, me overstand."

"Thank you, son. Anyway, what about you? You eatin' properly?"

I looked at my half-eaten sandwich.

"Yeah, me well full." I hated lying to her, but if I told the truth, she'd be round in half an hour with a double helping of rice and peas and chicken; and I didn't want her to worry.

"Good, good."

I was surprised she stopped there. Normally she'd ask what I had for breakfast, lunch and dinner.

"Yuh father was 'ere earlier," she said, trying too hard to sound casual.

"Wha 'im want?"

"Marcus, why yuh sound so? 'Im jus' come to say hello."

" 'Im only come round when 'im want somet'ing. Yuh too easy wid 'im."

"But I must be able to forgive."

"All me a say is watch 'im."

"Don't go worryin' y'self, de Lord will look after me."

Like he looked after you before, I thought. But I didn't want to vex her by saying anything against the Almighty.

"Yuh see Marcia or Charmaine lately?"

"Nah. She still a play stupid game," I said, not really wanting to discuss Marcia with her.

"Marcus, what I keep tellin' you 'bout lookin' after me grandchile? You is de man and must tek de lead. If she won't come to you, then you go to her and stop messing about. Yuh nah get any younger, y'know. An' I couldn't stan' fe lose another grandchile."

She kept dropping that on me, even though the story was fourteen years old.

"Mom, why yuh don't jus' forget 'bout Samantha? Her mother tek her away long time."

"And you let her go."

"Yuh know Nadine jus' up and run gone a Canada without even tellin' me."

"Only the Lord knows wha' do 'er. I don't know wha' fe seh," she relented. *Praise Jah!* "So when I goin' see yuh, Marcus?"

"Me 'ave basketball training tomorrow evening, so I goin' pass round Friday afternoon."

"Okay, I'll have some cow foot soup ready when you come, y'hear, son?"

"Yes Mum."

"Okay, see you Friday then."

I smiled.

"Yeah Mum. Later."

"The train now arriving at platform eight is the 21:48 Inter-City to Manchester Piccadilly, calling at Sandwell and Dudley, Wolverhampton, Stafford, Stoke-On-Trent, Crewe, Stockport and Manchester Piccadilly."

What the blasted hell I was doing at New Street Station ticket office I never know. I was taking a chance with life going up to Wolverhampton to see Marcia, but I had to try and smooth t'ings over with her. She can't keep up that militant stance forever. She had to mellow sooner or later. Maybe if I keep cool and sweet her up a bit, she a go love me up again.

Women love when a man run them down saying sorry. And like my old lady said, I have to make the first move. I bought a one-way 'cause a man has to be optimistic.

Within twenty minutes I was walking out of Wolverhampton station, my heart beating like a lovesick yout'. I tried to calm myself by sayin' I'm a big rahtid man but my emotions wouldn't have it. The adrenaline was flowing like Victoria Falls.

It was only a short ride to Busby Road. I got off the bus and walked down Howard Avenue, a cul-de-sac of about twenty semi-detached houses. By now my heart was beating so hard I could see my duffel coat tremor with every beat. It was still freezing but I couldn't feel it, 'cause there was a rahtid fire in my belly.

Marcia's dining room light was on, so I knew she was up. As I pushed the gate, her neighbour opened her door to put her milk bottles out.

"Hello Marcus," she said, looking intrigued. "I haven't seen you around for a long time."

I nodded, in no mood to satisfy her lust for gossip.

"Yeah, me'd a work inna London, y'know dem way deh?" I replied, knowing that she wouldn't understand a word. I turned my back and as I rang Marcia's bell, I heard her closing her door firmly.

I drew in my breath as I saw Marcia's figure approach the door through the frosted glass. She opened up looking criss in a pair of jeans and black tee-shirt, pushed her weave behind her ear and let out a sigh. Her expression said the last person she expected to see was me.

"What are you doing here?" she said in a loud hostile voice.

Ah man! Thought she would've mellowed a bit, but she came straight at me like a tank.

"Me come fe see you and Charmaine."

"You know you're not supposed to be within a mile of this place."

"Listen, Marcia, me sorry fe tekin' t'ings out 'pon you. I shouldn't 'ave done it. Jus' loss me head. It nah 'appen again, promise."

I knew it sounded like I was begging forgiveness, but I didn't business who heard if it meant she would tek me back.

46

"Let me tell you something, Marcus. I've seen my best friend beaten black and blue by her man. Then he says 'sorry, I didn't mean it...forgive me...it won't happen again'." She moved her head around like she was a puppet on a string.

"And like a fool she forgives him each time. Then he starts again, only each time is worse than the last. She was on a drip in hospital last month. Did you know that?"

I shook my head. I knew Bobby roughed up Joan sometimes, but putting her in hospital...rahtid, that was low.

"You know I used to see the way he treat her and I promised it would never happen to me. But it did."

Her usually smooth black features became contorted with anger.

"Marcus, you laid your hands on me once, but you'll never get the chance again, y' hear me? I don't want you back in my life. Ever!"

I began to feel a rage building up inside me. Why couldn't she accept my apology? That night was the first and only time I ever raise my hand to her. And she knew how low I felt afterwards, especially after growing up watching the old man beating my old lady to a pulp. I felt sick to find the same in me...thought I'd inherited his poison; but it was a one-off. That's not what I'm about, and she knew that, but still she couldn't forgive. All I wanted was one chance to prove myself.

The fire behind her eyes told me I wasn't going to get it.

"Listen, Marcia, I can't blame yuh fe de way yuh feel, but yuh cyan' stop me from see me yout' I need fe see me yout'. Yuh cyan' understand dat? Lemme just see 'er for a few minutes, nah?"

"Oh no! Oh no! You're not using Charmaine to worm your way back into my life. Just get the hell out of here before I call the police."

She slammed the door in my face.

I motioned to ring the bell, but before I even touched it, something just let loose in me, and I end up kicking out the whole of the door window. When I heard the glass shatter, I realised what I was doing. I couldn't hang around for Babylon to come fly down 'pon me, so I headed out quick time. Within minutes I heard the sirens. I slowed down and strolled casually as two Babylon cars fly past me in the direction of Marcia's yard. The minute I reached the main road, I started to run and didn't stop 'til I reached the cab office. I got in the back of the car and slunk down in my seat.

'Take me to the train station," I told the driver, "but stay on the back streets."

4
No Man's Land

Andre was shaken out of a deep sleep by Jermaine and Josephine crawling all over him—and a slap much harder than any four-year-old should be able to deliver struck the side of his face.

"Daddy, Daddy, tell Jermaine to stop hittin' me," Josephine cried, her little face camouflaged by long plaits.

All Andre wanted was the two of them off his bed and out of his bedroom. Only he wasn't in his bed or his bedroom. He'd fallen asleep on the dining room sofa. His neck was crick, his back was in spasms and both legs tingled with pins and needles.

"Daddy, Daddy tell him. Tell him, Daddy," Josephine pleaded when her brother began teasing her.

Andre peeled himself up from his slouching position, rubbed his eyes and looked piercingly at his son.

"Jermaine," he said sharply.

The five-year-old, still in his Superman pyjamas, looked fretful.

"Yes Daddy."

"Haven't I told you not to hit your sister?"

Jermaine's eyes fell to the floor. Andre became impatient for an answer.

"Well, haven't I?"

Jermaine's eyes wandered around the room, as though he might find the answer in some far corner.

"Answer me!"

Jermaine jumped.

"Yes Daddy."

"So why do you keep disobeying me?"

"But Daddy, she..."

"No buts. If you hit her again there'll be hell to pay. You hear me?"

Jermaine began to sulk.

"Yes, Daddy."

He looked vengefully at Josephine, who was now perched on Andre's leg wearing a smile as wide as the cat who got the cream.

"And stop teasing him, Jo," Andre said—trying to even things up.

Then he heard Heather's distinctly fed-up voice bellowing to them from above.

"Go on, you two, your mom's calling you."

As they ran out of the room and up the stairs—still tussling and arguing with each other—Andre began to rock his head from side to side to get the circulation going and ease the pain in his neck. He stood up and looked down at his crumpled clothes. His tie hung loose, his trousers were creased beyond salvation and his jacket looked like he had slept on it—which he had. This was no way for a high-powered legal executive to start the day.

He'd taken care to open the front door quietly at three-thirty that morning, afraid that Heather would be waiting up to deliver her nightly helping of verbal abuse. To his relief he found that she had gone to bed. He had poured himself a large scotch and dug into his massive collection of CDs. He put on Wynton Marsalis' *Uptown Ruler* and pressed the repeat button.

Heather had left him a note that said his dinner was in the bin. The dot under the exclamation mark she put at the end almost ruptured the paper—no need to wonder what kind of mood she was in when she wrote it. But Andre was unconcerned; after all, he had Wynton for company and he could go without food for the few hours until daybreak. So he kicked off his shoes, sipped whisky and relaxed to the soft, mellow trumpet of his favourite modern jazz player. Marsalis was still working his magic now.

Andre wished he could improvise on court the way Marsalis did with his trumpet— but he couldn't; he'd never had Winston's speed, Calvin's agility, Marcus' authority. And that tore at his soul. He could shoot and sink the ball from almost any position, but he was unable to make his own killer moves or create his own no-look passes. He was always waiting for someone else to play God and deliver, while he just received like a good disciple.

It bothered him even more when some of the Warrior started calling him Birdman. Not because of his love of jazz and Charlie Parker, but after white former Boston Celtic player Larry Bird. Most ball players—black or white—would have felt complimented, but Andre didn't like it one bit. There was already too much that separated him from the homeboys on the team.

He was educated, married, had a professional job and lived in the suburbs. He even spoke differently—like a bourgie white boy, Winston kept reminding him. Comparisons with a white player compounded his belief that he couldn't hack it like the streetwise-educated homiez. If he was to be deified he wanted to be likened to Michael Jordan, Isiah Thomas or even Reggie Miller; anyone but a white man

49

with no improvisational qualities other than an ability to shoot the house down.

His romancing was accompanied by Marsalis playing *Truth Is Spoken Here*, and disturbed by Heather doing her town crier impersonation upstairs. He looked at the clock—6.45 a.m.. He'd only had about three hours sleep and his body felt it.

He decided he might as well face the truth according to Heather Beckford, and dragged himself upstairs. He'd have to get himself back to work inside the hour, so he couldn't put it off any longer. As he reached the top of the stairs Heather opened the bathroom door and the kids ran out screaming, with white towels around their waists, and disappeared into their bedrooms.

"Oh, nice to see you this morning, Mr Beckford. Will you be booking a further night?"

She leaned against the doorframe and looked at him with disgust.

"Oh, and sorry about dinner last night. Chef got fed up of slaving over a hot cooker and chucked it in the bin. Will you be requiring a meal *this* evening, sir? If you do, at least have courtesy enough to phone and let chef know?"

"Heather, I don't need this, okay?"

"Oh, I'm sorry. *Andre* doesn't need this. It's all about what *Andre* needs, isn't it? It doesn't matter that *the kids* might need you, or that *I* may need some relief from them. No. Andre Beckford's playing bigtime executive, so everything else is too much trouble."

"You're sounding more like your mother every day," Andre muttered, slipping past her into the bathroom and closing the door before she could say another word.

Her dark mood was running into its third day now. It had started with a row over Andre coming home in the early hours of the morning, then progressed to his untidiness, and then on to everything else under the sun. Heather was beginning to seriously get on his nerves with her constant bickering for bickering's sake.

Okay, she had a point about him not phoning, but that was because he knew if he phoned she'd throw a tantrum and wreck his concentration.

He had to work. Why his wife couldn't understand that that was what paid the mortgage and put food in their mouths, he would never know.

He wiped the mist off the mirror and peered at his reflection. His eyes were red from sleeping in his contact lenses again. He decided he didn't need a shave, which was good news. He'd save time, and

50

avoid the red pimples it always left him with; against his light skin, they looked like chickenpox. As he got into the shower, the jingle for the Warriors came over the airwaves.

"Sat'day is de nite de Warriors go gunnin' fe de Outlaws. De heavy-weight Midlands showdung between de area two big b-ball teams. Handswort' Warriors versus Wolver'ampton Outlaws. Tip-off eight-pee-em at Handswort' Leisure Centre. Tickets four pong adults and three pong con-ceshon. R-E-S-P-E-C-K."

The rap was backed by some heavy reggae beat that sounded cheap, but it was better than nothing.

A blast of cold air blew the plastic shower-curtain inwards and it almost wrapped around his body. The volume of the radio went down and he put his head around the curtain—saw Heather standing, staring, with her arms folded across her chest.

Now what? She couldn't even wait until he was out of the shower before she interrogated him.

"Do you mind?" he said, gesturing that he wanted the volume back up. She ignored him.

"Did you phone the school about registering Josephine?"

"Blast! I forgot."

"Typical! Andre, it's first come, first served. You know the trouble we had getting Jermaine into that school. But you couldn't care less, could you? Does your kids' education mean so little to you?"

"You know that's not true. I've been up to my eyes in work. I just didn't have the time."

"Look, Andre, this isn't good enough. It's all work, work, work...basketball, basketball, basketball...me, me, me, as far as you're concerned. I'm sick of you placing the kids last on your list of priorities."

"Why can't you do it?"

She gave him a long searing look.

"You're useless, y'know that? Why the hell did you bother coming home?"

He often wondered that himself. She left the room, slamming the door behind her and he turned the shower up to maximum so that jets of water bounced off his torso. After a couple of minutes he felt refreshed enough to call a halt. He dried himself and was about to put his lenses back in when the phone rang. *Blast!* He hoped it wasn't anyone from work.

"It's for you!" Heather shouted up the stairs.

"Who is it?" Andre shouted back.

51

"How the hell should I know?"

He stepped from the shower and wrapped himself in a towel.

"I'll take it up here!"

He picked up the phone in the bedroom and heard Heather drop the dining room extension with a thud.

"Hello."

"Yaow, Dre. Marcus."

Andre took a short time out—Marcus had never phoned him in the five years they had known each other. He didn't even know that Marcus had his home number.

"Look, Dre, me in some heavy duty trouble and me need some instant 'elp, y'know."

"What's happened?"

If this was anything illegal, he'd have to refuse.

"Me lock up inna Steelhouse Lane."

"Steelhouse Lane?"

"Yeah man! Babylon kick down me door early dis mornin'. Dem beat me up, den arrest me."

"Oh hell. What for?"

Andre only read about such occurrences in the paper.

"Cha man, is a long story, but basically me bruck de injunction."

"Marcus, man! You know not to go messing with the law, especially with the referee case coming up any day now...." Andre replied, like Marcus needed an advocacy lesson.

"Me know, me know, but listen up...dem only allow me two bloodclaat call and me already waste one 'pon dis fuck-up solicitor of mine. Anyway, me sack im and me wan' yuh find me a good law man who know 'bout these t'ings. Y'overstand me?"

"Marcus, you're putting me on the spot—"

"Nevah mind de spot y' deh 'pon. Yuh goin' help me or not?"

Andre thought about it.

"M-m-m-m...I don't know, Marcus. I'm in property, not criminal law."

Marcus kissed his teeth.

"Me know me shouldn't bother call unnu sweet bwoy, 'cause y'all de bloodclaat same. Is a comfy lifestyle y'ah look. Cha, me gone...y' hear?"

"No, no, hold on Marcus—I'll search out someone from my firm who's experienced in criminal law. Leave it with me, I'll see what I can do."

"Me know say yuh was one a we. Later." Marcus signed off.

Heather came into the bedroom.

"Nice to know you can jump when your friends call, but when I ask you to do anything it's too much effort."

Was this woman ever going to let up? "What's up with you this morning?"

"What's up with *me*? Andre, there's nothing up with me. Like I said, if your kids don't mean anything to you that's your lookout. I've had enough of your crap, so from now on you better just shape up or ship out."

"What's that supposed to mean?"

"Just keep doing what you're doing, Andre, and you'll find out soon enough."

Andre didn't feel like going any further down that road, so he got up, picked some fresh underwear out of his drawer and a clean shirt and suit from the wardrobe and headed to the bathroom to change.

"You can't be leaving that for me!" Heather shrieked, pointing at the mess Andre had made of the bed sheets.

He inhaled deeply, then turned around and fixed the sheets and marched back to the door again.

"Oh—and you can take Jermaine to school and drop Jo off at Mrs Madge today. I've got an early appointment with my boss," she said matter-of-factly.

He rubbed his hand down his face in total despair.

"Why didn't you tell me this yesterday?"

"I didn't *see* you all day yesterday—or the day before, for that matter. How am I supposed to tell you anything when I don't see you? You're out at the crack of dawn and back in the dead of night."

Yeah, Andre thought, *you see enough of me to argue, rant and rave, but not enough to give me a simple message.* He was riled.

"If you fulfilled your role of mother instead of taking this job, then maybe you wouldn't have this problem."

"Oh, you'd like that, wouldn't you?"

She came and stood between Andre and the door.

"Then you'd have a little housekeeper at home looking after your every whim; scrubbing your dirty collars, ironing your creases and cooking your meals three times a day just like your mother. That's what you're looking for, a replica of your mother."

"At least she knew how to give her family support when it was needed, instead of gallivanting around playing a glorified housing officer."

"Housing manager, thank you very much."

"There's a difference?"

"Listen, Andre, I only work three days a week. If you can't fit your big-time executive schedule around it then tough. I always said once the kids reached school age I was going back to work, 'cause I'm bored as hell at home. You think my life is complete just traipsing around trying to keep you lot clean and fed?"

"Oh I see, it's all about what Heather wants to do, and sod everything else."

"That's no more than you've been doing for years, darlin'. Time for me to get a life and for you to realise the two of us brought these kids into the world."

She went over to the dressing table and started combing her hair.

"You don't have to tell me about caring for my kids."

"Oh really? Don't make me laugh, they hardly ever see you!"

Andre couldn't stand it any more. He left the room without replying, changed in the bathroom and went downstairs.

For some strange reason Jermaine had put his pyjamas back on and was playing a Sega game. Andre couldn't be bothered to talk to him. He picked up *The Guardian* from the dining room table, went through into the kitchen and made himself a cup of strong tea.

He heard Heather shouting yet again for Jermaine to go upstairs and get ready for school. He paid more attention to Super Mario than to her; she stormed down the stairs and gave him a clip around the ear. He ran back up the stairs howling. She came into the kitchen and busied herself, slamming cupboard doors, rattling cutlery, and clattering pots to destroy his peace. Typical woman tactic; first the verbal barrage to soften you up like a jelly baby, then the silent treatment, like Japanese mental torture. But for the moment Andre was content for her to take her stupidity out on the kitchen utensils.

As he browsed through the paper, it occurred to him that her moods always started when her mother, Ruby, came to visit. The old battleaxe had been there the previous weekend, complaining that Andre left Heather too much to do on her own while he enjoyed the bachelor life. Ruby's idea of a solution was for Heather to dominate him the way that she did Heather's dad, Archie—a man now so confused and battle-weary that he just sat through her tirades without uttering a word in his own defence.

Heather was wrapping the last of the kids' sandwiches.

"Could you make them some Ribena in their plastic cups? The blue cup is for Jermaine and the pink is for Josephine."

I could have worked that out myself, Andre thought as he raised his

54

head from behind the newspaper. Heather turned to face him.

"Did you hear what I said?"

"What d'you want me to do—jump to attention?"

She stormed out of the kitchen. Andre got up and made the drinks, then went into the living room. He began to pick the toys up off the floor and place them in boxes marked with their names.

Once he'd finished, he looked through the living room window facing on to the back garden. Some of the leaves had fallen from the oak tree at the bottom of the sloping lawn. It was a true sign that autumn had arrived. The tree had grown in the five years that they had been living there. He remembered when they had bought the house—a wedding present to each other when house prices in Birmingham were ridiculously low.

Their marriage—built on so much hope—was now reduced to nothing but anger and frustration.

Heather marched purposefully back into the room wearing a black lambswool ankle-length coat and matching black beret. She looked at him as though he had no right to be gazing out of the window while she was rushing around like a headless chicken. *Working your balls off 'til three in the morning buys you that right,* he thought.

"Are the kids ready?" he asked her in a conciliatory tone.

"Funny how you always ask about the kids when everything is almost done."

"Oh Heather, please," Andre answered, frustrated. "Do you have to keep this up?"

"Keep what up, Andre?"

He walked past her to go up the stairs and check on the kids.

"You can finish dressing them," he heard her shout, and the front door slammed behind her.

He wondered if she even noticed that the extra fifty pounds a week child-minding fees, plus the petrol for her Vauxhall Astra ate up most of her salary. Or that she was more stressed now that she was working than when she wasn't. But who was he to point that out? Heather wanted to work, so work she must.

His meeting with his boss, Mr Pal, was scheduled for nine; by the time he finished dressing the kids it was ten to. He tried to telephone Tracy, Pal's secretary, to say he'd be late, but she wasn't at her desk.

He bundled the kids into the back seat. The car wouldn't start. He tried it again and again, until he finally succeeded in killing the battery. He couldn't believe that the car had decided to pack up today of all days.

"Daddy, why won't the car start?" Jermaine asked.

Andre didn't answer. He felt like dumping it on the nearest scrap heap. He was about to take the kids back inside to ring for a taxi, when help arrived in the shape of his next-door neighbour, Pete.

Pete—a die-hard Warriors fan and often the only white face in the crowd—was already kitted out in his West Midlands copper uniform. Andre was glad he never wore his uniform to a game or revealed his occupation; if the others knew he was friendly with a copper the cries of Judas and traitor would be louder than the roar at Villa Park. But as far as Andre was concerned Pete was alright...especially as he had the car running in no time.

Andre didn't reach his Hill Street office until almost ten-fifteen. He managed to find one of the last spaces in the car park allotted to his firm. He walked to the front of the building and through the revolving doors and waited for the lift to come.

Tracy strode towards him as though she was parading down a cat-walk. Andre held his breath; he couldn't believe that, even in such frosty weather, she wore a skirt that reached half way up her thigh and a flimsy white blouse that he could see her bra through.

Maybe it was more important for her to show off her figure than to wrap up warm; she revelled in being the office flirt.

Tracy stood beside him, holding a cup of capuccino and chewing on a chocolate croissant—the aroma set Andre's stomach rumbling. She spoke with her mouth full.

"D'you just get in?"

"Yeah, the car wouldn't start. Is Mr Pal in?"

"Yep—" she said, flicking her hair out of her face "—he was looking for you earlier. Said something about some case tomorrow."

Andre had spent the last three days and nights working on it, and though it wasn't complete yet it was in good enough order to let Pal see it.

The lift arrived. Andre pressed the button for the sixth floor. They emerged moments later in the large office, divided into sections by perspex panels. He shared office space with three white men; John Frogett, an overweight, middle class yob with a penchant for racist jokes; self-styled Italian stallion Michael Tuzzio, who thought every woman in the world was after him; and William Baines, who had had somehow acquired all the traditional public school traits and mannerisms without ever actually having been to one. They were all legal execs, and all studying to become solicitors one day.

Living in a predominantly white area and working in a predominantly white office were two distinctly different experiences for Andre. At home, behind his front door, he was in control. He felt insulated. Safe. But at work he felt uncomfortable, restricted in what he could say or do. And he couldn't—and didn't want to—relate to his workmates.

They were brought up in suburbia and had little or no contact with black people from any walk of life. They all expected Andre to have street cred, to come in to work rapping or bogling.

They were disappointed to find that he could rap no better than Vanilla Ice, and thought Snoop Doggy Dog was a cartoon character. Even the universal currency of sport raised difficulties. John loved to rap about the rugby union team he belonged to, William was forever on about his golf swing, and the only sport Michael was interested in was chasing women.

Since Andre had no interest in any of their subjects—and no desire to discuss basketball with them—it was never very long before conversation ground to a shuddering halt.

As Andre walked silently to his desk, John looked at his watch.

"Morning, or should I say afternoon, Andre?"

Andre took off his jacket and hung it up behind his seat. Tracy put her head around the divider.

"Andre, Mr Pal would like to see you in his office. Now."

William looked at him as if to say 'you're going to get it, son'.

Mr Pal was an African-Asian from Uganda and one of the firm's leading solicitors, but in Andre's opinion he had only got where he was by sucking up to the Jewish owners, Robert Goldberg and Steve Samson. Rumour said Pal was soon to be offered a partnership in the firm.

Andre knew that any promotion for Pal would be bad news for him. Pal enjoyed pleasant working relationships with all of Andre's colleagues, but made his lack of tolerance for him very clear. He watched Andre closely, scrutinised his work and second-guessed every decision he made.

Andre searched his desk for the file, then made his way to Pal's office. His door was big enough to drive a herd of elephants through, and his name was written large on a gold plate.

Andre knocked and entered just as Pal was finishing a phone call. The office was spacious—the kind Andre would like one day himself—and painted cream, with a brown leather sofa to one side and a large working desk on the other. Mr Pal was seated behind it. He put down the phone.

"I hope you've finished the background work on the Waterworks case."

"Good morning, Mr Pal," Andre said, and handed him the folder.

Pal took it, then gestured to him to sit down. Andre sat watching him for fifteen minutes as Pal read the entire file. When he finished, he closed it and placed it on his desk. After a moment's thought, he said:

"You were late again this morning. I waited over an hour to get this file."

He stared at Andre questioningly. Andre immediately rose to meet Pal's antagonistic tone.

"Something came up unexpectedly. It couldn't be avoided. Anyway, I was here until three this morning making sure the file would be ready."

"I think you need reminding that you are paid to produce work of the highest possible quality. Now, if you have to work the odd late night to achieve this, then so be it—there are no brownie points on offer here, Mr Beckford. Doing at night what others are doing by day does not entitle you to wander into work in the middle of the morning. We are one of the top law firms in the country. Only people of the highest calibre work here.

"You ought to acknowledge the fact that you are privileged to be with us and stop treating your position here like it's some clerical jaunt at the DSS—unless, of course, that's where you *want* to be."

Andre had to steel his nerves to keep from biting the bait.

"Do you have any comment to make on the file, Mr Pal?"

"When I do you'll be the first to know, Mr Beckford."

It was eleven fifty-five before Andre remembered Marcus. He rang Simon, a legal exec on the fifth floor who owed him a favour. Simon said a solicitor with a good track record had started the previous week. He said he'd let Andre know if he would take the case, and within five minutes he called back saying he had agreed. Andre was amazed, he hadn't held out any hopes that anyone at Goldberg and Samson would be willing to take on such a job, especially for a black man.

"Coming with us down the pub for a drink?" John called.

"Nah, I'll give it a miss. I've got loads to do," Andre replied without raising his head from his work.

"C'mon, just a quick pint..."

"I don't drink beer."

"Well a short then, whatever."

"Some other time, maybe."

Andre couldn't wait for them to just vacate the place. Why the hell would he want to go with them.

"Does that include never?" Michael asked. "What, we got fleas or something? You never come drink with us."

"I don't drink alcohol at lunchtime," Andre said, raising his head from his books for the first time.

"Are you Catholic or something?"

Andre went back to his work.

Time flew. Lunchtime came and went and Andre didn't have time to eat. Hunger pangs hijacked his attention. Just before four o'clock, his phone rang.

"Andre, it's your wife on line two."

"Thanks, Trace."

No grief, please God. He pressed two. "Heather—" he said cautiously.

"I'm going to be late. So can you pick Jo up from Mrs Madge? She leaves for her cleaning job at five, and Jermaine is at the after-school club."

"Wait a minute, Heather, I'm snowed under with work. I'd have to leave now to get there for five. I can't do that."

"What about my work...or doesn't that matter? Everything's always a big problem for you. Look, I'm on the other side of Birmingham and I have to go to Alum Rock next to inspect a property. The kids are closer to you. So I'll see you about eight."

"Eight? Heather, I've got training at six-thirty. We have an important game on Saturday."

"What's more important, Andre, your family or a stupid game?" She hung up.

Andre flung the receiver back on the hook. *Damn that woman!*

"Guess you won't be going to the ball, eh, Cinders?" John sneered from across the room.

Andre looked at him, then realised he was past caring what John thought. He gathered his files together and put them in his briefcase.

"So Andre, sounds like you having woman trouble there. Anything I can help you with?"

Michael thumbed his braces and grinned.

"I mean, I always wondered what these black women are like. Do they, y'know, give good sex? I heard that once. Is it true, Andre?"

Andre snapped his briefcase shut.

"I was going to ask you the same about sheep. I heard you knew. Is that true Michael?

"Y'know I've never wondered about white women like that. Then again, I don't have to. The brothas in the locker room provide all the sordid details. From what I hear, I don't blame you for wondering about black women."

He winked at Michael. Michael chuckled. "Oooh, looks like I've hit a raw nerve. Don't take it so personal. I was only kidding."

"Yeah, I know you were kidding," Andre said, putting on his jacket. "You'd have to be. Which sane black woman would take up with you?"

He turned to William.

"If Pal asks for me just tell him I'm out visiting a client, would you?"

William nodded.

"So. you gonna fix me up with one of your women, Andre? You must have one you can spare?"

John looked at him in disgust.

"Aren't there enough white women out there to keep you happy? What's the sudden fascination with black women?"

Michael shrugged. "You know what they say. Variety is the spice of life."

Andre walked across the office towards the lift. As he approached, the doors opened and out walked a crisply-dressed black man. He was about five-eleven and wore an Armani suit, silk shirt and tie. Andre thought he must be a client.

"You must be Andre Beckford," he said, just as Andre was stepping in the lift.

"That's right."

Andre shook his outstretched hand.

"I'm Theo Rutherford, the new solicitor downstairs. Simon told me to look for the only black face up here," he laughed.

Andre smiled back, surprised that Goldberg and Samson had employed another black guy. He couldn't wait to see Mr Pal's face.

"I've just been to meet a colleague of yours," Theo said, looking through some papers he had in his hand. "Umm...Marcus Codrington."

"Yeah, how is he?"

"Your friend Marcus has been a silly boy, but I managed to get him bail. His mother stood surety. I had to go to her home to persuade her."

60

"He told me something about breaking an injunction."

"That's probably the least of his problems. They've charged him with causing damage to property, assaulting police officers and resisting arrest. Anyway, I just came to put you in the picture. He can fill you in on the details. He said he'll see you tonight at training."

"Oh yeah, basketball this evening."

"You play basketball? Snap. It's my favourite sport. I played a couple of seasons for a local side down south, but I haven't played since I came up from London. We must get together sometime and talk—but right now I've got to dash. I'll see you around."

Andre sat in the changing rooms at Handsworth Leisure Centre rubbing down his legs with liniment. The Warriors had a hell of a game ahead, without doubt the toughest of the season; they were unbeaten so far, but the Outlaws posed a different problem.

They played with the same hard-nosed attitude as the Warriors, and neither side would expect much sympathy from the referees, who took a back seat when two black sides played each other. The rest of the team were already kitted up in vests or black Warrior tracksuit tops—but Andre had to go through his ritual of being the last one to dress. He sat in just his jockstrap on the long wooden bench, massaging his calves with oil and trying to motivate himself.

Coach Bailey read out some additional instructions, but Andre couldn't hear. His voice was drowned out by the eccentric Dr Music Master, PhD., resident MC for the Warriors' home games. The Master psyched the crowd up with music, raps and toasting well before the Warriors got on court; Andre thought he was worth an extra ten points per game to them.

He finally pulled on his vest and brushed the number thirty-three as it dropped down past his waist...then his baggy shorts—which always reminded him of the ones Stanley Matthews wore in his soccer heyday—then Andre sat down to put on his stockings and boots.

Winston was still on the hype, giving everybody lip. He came up to Andre as he sat, eyes closed, taking deep breaths.

"Whassup Birdman?"

Winston put his hand on Andre's shoulder.

"Word man, homiez have a tuff Yank at two...Axel or some shit."

"Yeah, I heard. Come across him out there?"

"Nope. Dude been goin' round da globe playin' pickup for decades. Some grandad, but shit can still handle da pill. Homie gotta stay honest today, man. Punk gonna try run de dozens on your buggie ass."

Andre was confused.

"Dozens?"

"Yeah, homie. Man gonna talk all kinda shit 'bout your mutha, your wife, your bitch, your sista, any shit to cancel your business out. Stay strong, Birdman and we'll pack dis sucka off to da shack for dead meat."

"Sure, man, sure," Andre replied.

Even though it was a big game, Andre didn't feel up for it, not like earlier in the season. Then he'd always been eager to get out there and shoot up the shop. Now he just felt flat. He was suffocating both at home and work and now even this—the only release for his pent-up frustration—was becoming a chore. His game was on the slide and he knew it. How much longer he could hold on to his starting spot depended on how long Coach would put up with his shooting slump. Adam was training every hour God sent. He had to be, because when he came off the bench he was like a microwave on fire.

In fact, recently Andre had been watching the 'minutes played' column on the stats sheet with a strict eye. In each of the last four games Adam had averaged more minutes on court than he had, even though Adam was coming off the bench. If he lost his starting spot, he would have failed, but he was determined not to let that happen...not on top of all the other things that were screwing up his head.

The Warriors' mascot, little Jonathan, came into the changing rooms.

"Half an hour to tip-off!" he called.

Andre pulled on his tracksuit as the team lined up by the doors. As club captain and assistant coach, Calvin led them onto the court.

"Dis is it, man," Roots called out.

There was a loud echo of 'yeah' down the short, hollow corridor to the gym. Everyone was well-psyched.

They heard Music Man revving up the crowd as they approached the hall and as they entered he turned up their theme tune, 'Warriors'. They always ran onto the court to the Marley record.

They straddled the court centre line before raising their right fists in a black power salute, then placed their arms across their left shoulders. The gesture sent the crowd wild and their opponents—particularly the white teams—into a state of panic. But Wolverhampton weren't about to be intimidated. One player shouted "Leggo dat, man" as the Warriors broke away and started to warm up.

62

There were about a hundred-and-fifty people in the hall but the echo made them sound like thousands. The Uh Huh Girls faced the crowd, encouraging them to sing the Warriors' theme tune. An attractive red-skinned girl was helping them; Andre had never seen her before. First Marcus, then Calvin leapt up with both hands above the hoop and dunked the ball through the ring. The fans called the home court the House of Pain: Andre could see why.

He looked at the opposition, who were dunking the ball with every warm-up shot. He knew most of them by sight since he'd played for six seasons now. He watched carefully as their American import dribbled the ball, to see which was his best hand. He would dribble then stop, set himself and then jump, releasing the ball in the textbook jump-shot position. Worryingly he scored from every angle, every time.

Before the referee called the starters there was one last ritual to perform. The Warriors gathered in a small circle around Calvin, who recited:

"I am because we are. And since we are, I am."

One by one the Warriors repeated each word, culminating in a loud cheer that had the crowd stamping their feet. The Warriors then shook hands with their opponents and settled into position for the tip-off.

The Outlaws' centre, Rufus Alexander, won the tip over Joni and deflected the ball to their American guard, Axel Johnson. Andre immediately went to him to try— as Winston had suggested—to stay honest, but with one quick step Axel was past him. Joni didn't close down the lane to the basket quick enough and the American laid the ball in off the backboard for two points.

The early minutes continued the same way, with Andre unable to handle the American. Luckily for the Warriors, Marcus and Winston were giving the Outlaw defence a tough time. It was war under the basket as both teams waited for rebounds. Joni was no match for Rufus, who was pushing and pulling him all over the place.

Five minutes before half-time the score was 36-33 in the Warriors' favour. Winston came down the court dribbling past his marker. He threw a one-handed pass to Calvin on the right of the Outlaws' key. Calvin then tried to beat his opponent to the baseline but was well cut off. He sent a nice pass out to Andre, who caught it with enough time to steady himself behind the arc, before sending up a shot that cannoned off the backboard like a brick. Rufus grabbed the rebound. It was Andre's third three-point attempt and none had so far hit the target. On the run back to defend Winston shouted, "Damn, Birdman, give up da shit if it's too hot! Give it up, man."

As Andre ran back to position he could see Coach telling Adam to strip off his tracksuit and get ready to join the action. Andre knew he had some defending to do. Axel Johnson faced him up again.

"Y'know, sucka, no wonder y' look like me, it's your mutha I've been screwing all dis time."

That cut into Andre like a knife.

"C'mon, your me bwoy, c'mon me bwoy," Axel shouted as he slowed the dribble in front of Andre.

Andre's anger got the better of him and he dived in, trying to steal the ball. Axel saw he had overcommitted, switched the ball through his legs and waltzed past Andre like he wasn't even there. Again there was little cover behind him as the American went in for an easy lay-up and two points. The House of Pain was subdued.

"Man, you're gettin' your butt kicked," Winston shouted at him as he collected the throw-in pass after the basket. "You better wise up or he gonna run da shit past you all day."

"Brotha, why don't you keep it closed? You're not callin' plays," Calvin responded in Andre's defence.

"Kiss my black ass, man, 'cause your play-callin' ain't doin' jack shit for da homie." Winston brought the ball on to centre court.

"We 'ave a game to win, t' rahtid," Marcus chipped in, vexed. "Wha'ppen to unnu? Jus' play nah, mon."

"We got em guys," Rufus shouted when he heard them arguing among themselves.

Coach Bailey called a twenty second time-out to try and pull the team back together.

The Warriors went out at half-time leading 40-38. Coach was far from happy. He decided to put Winston onto Axel and replace Andre with Adam on the second drive.

Wolverhampton were already on court when they came out for the second half. They warmed up for five minutes before the battle re-commenced.

Andre sat on the bench in his tracksuit top as the Warriors began to get to grips with the Outlaws. Winston was handling Axel's offence better than Andre had and Adam was sinking the occasional basket. Andre badly wanted to get back on the court, and every so often he'd look down the bench at Coach in the hope that he'd remember him. But the five on court were doing a good job and though Levi Lewis and Lemuel Wright came in to give Joni and

Marcus a rest, Coach Bailey's eye never met Andre's for the first ten minutes of the second half.

Calvin was playing well, leaping around as usual to out-rebound Rufus, even though the Wolverhampton man was taller and stronger. With five minutes to go, the Warriors were in control and leading by 88-72.

Axel threw a shot that bounced off the ring into the air. Calvin and Rufus jumped together. Calvin grabbed the ball, but as he came down Rufus wrapped his hands around Calvin's neck and pulled him forcibly to the ground. It was a deliberate violation. Marcus dashed off the bench straight for Rufus, pushing him him in the chest. Rufus retaliated by doing the same to Marcus. Marcus grabbed Rufus by the neck and held him in a headlock. By this time both benches had been cleared—Andre was on court trying to calm things, Winston was in a verbal battle with Axel, and Levi was mouthing off at their second string centre.

The referees finally managed to free Rufus from Marcus' lock. Coach then remonstrated with them to eject him from the game. The crowd were hissing and booing Wolverhampton.

It was five minutes before the teams finally settled back on the benches. Calvin hobbled to the sideline with some help from the new girl in the Uh Huh posse.

The Warriors won 102-87; Wolverhampton left warning they'd face repercussions at the return match later in the season.

The mood in the changing room afterwards was upbeat and happy. The Warriors had put in a good second-half performance, but there was still a long way to go.

Andre was already dressed when Calvin limped into the changing room after seeing the centre's physio about his injured hip.

"How's it, man?" he asked, as Calvin laid his bag down and lowered himself gently onto the bench.

"It's Okay, brotha man. Physio said it'll be sore for a few days but I should be fine for next weekend."

"Who's the woman?" Lemi interrupted.

Andre wanted to know who she was too.

"What woman, brotha?"

The whole changing room now tuned in.

"Da fine lookin' bitch who escorted ya long ass off the court," Winston answered.

"Brotha, when are you goin' to learn to stop referring to sistas as bitches? *Damn!*" Calvin went to stand up to confront Winston but the pain made him decide otherwise.

"So who is she then?" Andre asked.

Calvin smiled.

"The sista's name is Dawn, cousin of one of the Uh Huh girls, and she's nothin' to me. Just came to see the game, that's all."

"Yeah geezer," Selwyn said, as he walked dripping from the shower. "Pull the other one."

Andre wondered why Selwyn bothered showering, since he didn't even get on the court, much less work up a sweat.

"Brothas, straight up, you know I'm almost married," Calvin replied seriously.

"So you don't mind if I pop her then?" Levi shouted. There was laughter all round.

Andre and Calvin returned to their conversation.

"We'll definitely need you next week, you played a strong game." Andre told Calvin as he tied the laces on his second pair of trainers.

"Yeah, brotha. I was well up for dis one, man. I didn't want to lose. What about you, Dre, you weren't having a tight game?"

"Just couldn't get to grips with the American—and my shot wasn't there, y'know, just one of those things."

"Brotha man, you know if you want to talk, I'm always around."

Andre nodded. But he didn't want to air his problems in detail. He always felt uneasy discussing personal problems with male friends.

Men were supposed to deal with their business on their own. For Andre, divulging his problems—even to someone as close as Calvin—would be like surrendering some part of his male sovereignty...giving up the cool exterior that covered inner confusion and turmoil.

He just told Calvin that he was alright, and said he'd be back on song next weekend after some practice.

The sounds of Grover Washington Junior's *Let It Flow* were smooth and relaxing as Andre drove home. He pictured himself taking off from the top of the key and flying through the air for a spectacular dunk just like the legendary Dr J, who the track was specially composed for.

When he got home it was a quarter to midnight. Heather's mother, Ruby, flung open the door before he put his key in the lock. Andre's heart sank when he saw her face. He had been so concen-

66

trated on Grover Washington and the defects of his game that he didn't notice he'd parked directly behind their car. Ruby was on her way out, thank God, with husband Archie riding shotgun.

Before Andre could say a word, Ruby let off.

"Ahh, ahh, now yuh reach, when everyt'ing settle," she said, tying the belt of her lambswool coat.

"What's settled?"

"Never mind, son. Is alright," Archie interjected.

"Wha' y' mean is alright? If we didn't come, who woulda look after de kids?" Ruby shot back, glaring at him for even daring to speak.

"When I left, Mrs Parchment, Heather was here with Jermaine and Josephine."

"Yes, she was here, but she had to go out and you was nowhere to be found, as usual."

Archie shook his head and headed for his car, truly dismayed that his wife never tired of having this conversation. Heather came into the hall.

"I don't know how you put up wid' 'im," Ruby muttered, pushing past Andre to follow her husband to the car.

Andre went into the living room and dropped his training bag on the floor. Heather came in behind him and sat on the floor in front of the television.

"What was she on about, 'no one being around to look after the kids'?"

She kept her eyes glued to the screen.

"Heather."

Still no answer.

Andre went into the kitchen—not that he wanted anything, he just couldn't tolerate Heather's cold, silent treatment. When he walked back into the living room, Heather acknowledged his presence by cutting her eye before turning back to the television.

Andre went upstairs to check on the kids. They were asleep. He bent down and gave each of them a kiss on his cheek. He could have done with a long drink and some music to soothe his tired mind, but with Heather down there he decided his best option was to go straight to bed.

5

Against The Tide

"So, brotha Rashid, they gutted the whole centre?"

Calvin stood in his living room, holding the phone to his ear with one hand, and leaning against the wall with the other.

"Not quite, brotha," Abdullah Rashid told him. "The fire people got here just in time. Knuckleheads only managed to torch one room. Investigators said it was a petrol bomb thrown through the window."

"Is the safe damaged?"

"You're okay, brotha. Your valuables are in Fort Knox," Rashid replied.

"You know what I've been thinkin', brotha?"

"What?"

"This wasn't no right wing racist attack. We've been burnt out by our own."

"Brotha, I think you're on the ball. The X Centre's been here for almost two decades, no devil has ever come close, let alone throw petrol bombs.

"Now, after a march on drugs in the community, this. Brotha, it's definitely our community."

"We're upsetting brothas whose livelihoods will be damaged by our crusade against drugs and black-on-black violence."

"Brotha Calvin, they ain't no brothas of mine. They're worse than the National Front. Brothas don't peddle crap to children and vulnerable people. Hear this: if I get my hands on the perpetrator...well, let Allah be my judge."

"Rashid, we got to continue the fight. Can't afford to lose this battle."

"Brotha, we're comin' out stronger than before. You keep the temperature up on that youth conference and after that we'll organise another march on drugs." Rashid's voice was becoming angrier with every word. "Lets mobilise the whole community against them. Squeeze them so hard there won't be a stone for them to hide under."

"You're right on that one brotha."

"Salaam brotha."

"Go in peace, bro."

The thought of black brothas torching the X Centre was biting

Calvin. He didn't want to believe that dealers were trying to demolish a building that had given so much help and assistance to the community just because a few hundred concerned brothas and sistas had decided to march through Handsworth protesting the growth of the drug culture.

Maybe it was the TV coverage the march got, bringing the reality of inner-city life to millions around the Midlands.

Or maybe someone felt it gave the police a green light to harass any black person, or kick down any door on the pretence of a drugs bust?

But as far as Calvin was concerned, there was no alternative. Talk is cheap; action speaks louder than rhetoric. The young brothas needed help and, in his view, the pluses of the march far outweighed the minuses.

He walked across the room and sat down at his desk. He peered out of the window at what seemed—from so high up—an idyllic scene. His flat was on the top floor of a seventeen-storey council block in Hockley, a stone's throw from the centre of Handsworth. From here, he could see out over Birmingham.

It was the Saturday before Christmas and light snow had settled. All that was missing from this scene was Rudolph guiding Santa's sledge through the Birmingham sky.

It was mid-afternoon and the light reflecting off the snow brightened the room. He looked at the picture on the wall of Martin Luther King and Malcolm X shaking hands and pondered the sacrifices they had made for black people in America. No-one in Britain had yet paid that ultimate price. No-one he knew of, at least.

People here just consigned themselves to failure. They were too damned apathetic. Too willing to accept their circumstances as if set in concrete. They wouldn't lift their heads for fear of what they might see. In Britain, the plantation mentality went deep.

He was distracted from his personal political broadcast by Lorna entering the room. She was on holiday from Oxford, where she was studying Archaeology, and was staying with him until Christmas Eve, when she was going to her parents in Coventry.

"How's it goin', babes?"

She looked good in her Kente dress with big African earrings hanging from her tiny earlobes.

"Sista, they've torched the X Centre. I just can't believe it," Calvin said, looking at her pensively.

"No. Who?"

69

"Brotha Rashid thinks it must be the dealers."

"Desperate people do desperate things, honey. These people don't have a moral fibre in their body. No conscience. Don't care who or what they destroy so long as they can ply their trade. It's not even like they're making money. The fools are taking a five pound here, a ten pound there, while the importers are carting off sackfuls. And there aren't any black faces with their hands on the sacks. They're always someone else's foot soldiers."

"It's true, sista, and we're destroyin' our nation in the process," Calvin added. "Will you tell your dad?"

"Yeah, I'll phone him straight away. He'll be cool about it. It's not like he's running the place anymore."

"I know, but we still have 'nuff respeck for your old man. He started the Centre way back when they wanted to lynch a black man for renting a house next door."

"Yeah," she said with a smile. "I remember the first time you came down in your tracksuit, basketball in your hand, like you were comin' to teach us how to shoot ball."

"Mmm...little did I know that marchin' up to a supermarket counter with four cans of Grapefruit Tango was goin' to change my take on history."

"I still can't believe I did that. I could've got the sack."

"Sis, you were well on track. I just innocently put my four tins down on the counter and you were off." He began imitating Lorna's voice. "Why don't you use your black pound responsibly and buy Ting, that way you'll be helping the Caribbean economy.' First time I ever thought about the power of a African consumer. Y'know it had a real effect on me."

"Brings back memories. I remember thinking you were a cool brotha, especially when you took my advice and changed brands."

"Mmm—invited me down to the X Centre straight away," Calvin said, taking the dachiqui off his head.

"Yeah, but it took you three months to show your face."

"I know, sista, but I did the right thing in the end. Five years now and still going strong. You watch, the X Centre is goin' to come back with a louder voice than ever. We've got a hard-working, radical crew."

"How's Kwesi? I haven't seen him for ages."

"Brotha's still there. But something about him doesn't click with me. He's not as dedicated as the others."

"He's strange. I can't believe I went out with him for so long.

Anyway, how's the youth conference coming along, darlin'?"

"It's a nightmare, but I've managed to coax seven volunteers from the Centre to help me, so that should take some pressure off; and Abdul Rashid has said we can have some office space."

"That's great." Lorna squeezed into the gap between Calvin's seat and the desk. "When are you thinking of staging it?"

"I pencilled in a date around Easter." He handed her a rough outline of a leaflet promoting the conference. "What do you think?"

"It's a nice start."

"I'm gonna print up thousands of these and deliver them to all the schools round the area. Whether or not they come, they're certainly gonna know about it."

Lorna nodded.

"Youths round here certainly need some positive vibe, babes."

"Don't I know, sista? Only yesterday there was a stabbing not far from here. A sixteen-year-old critical in Dudley Road Hospital after a disagreement with his best friend."

"Yeah, I heard it on the radio. Imagine how his mother feels."

"Worse, in this very block kids as young as twelve are couriers for older drug dealers. Can you believe it—twelve years old?"

"What's the name of the ring leader again?" Lorna asked.

"Ganja Kid. The little brotha's controlling the operation. Sista, if we can reach the youth then things can change for the better."

"Well, like Whitney says, the children are the future." She gracefully manoeuvred out of the confined space." Would you like a coffee, darlin'?" she asked.

"Yeah, babes, thanks."

She went into the kitchen. Calvin started thinking how nice it was having a woman around the place, particularly one as knowledgeable as Lorna. He had nothing but admiration for her. From supermarket cashier to Oxford student was some move for a thirty-year-old black woman from Handsworth.

When she got fed up with life, instead of sitting and complaining she got off her backside and studied for 'A' levels on correspondence courses, getting A's in three subjects. The administrators at Oxford were so impressed by her determination that they awarded her a bursary to attend the university. She didn't much care for the lifestyle, but the Guild of Students had a functioning African Society and she knew it would be her passport to a better future.

Lorna was only tiny, but she was hard as nails. Calvin owed her a lot; five years before, she had introduced him to his history. Took him by the scruff of the neck, sat him down in the X Centre and virtually spoon-fed him knowledge from newspapers, books, magazines...anything she could find to wise up this long-naive brotha.

Calvin had even been thinking seriously about settling down with her, but he believed that, with another year to go at university, she already had enough on her plate.

He even had a ring in a safe place at the X Centre...waiting for the right moment.

Lorna came back carrying two cups of steaming coffee. She set them on the desk, pulled up a chair and began flicking through the rough sketches on Calvin's desk.

"Who are you going to have as guest speaker?" she asked.

"I'm not sure yet. Rashid was thinkin' Minister Farrakhan, but he might only appeal to the Muslim brothas. Then there's gettin' him into the country. Government's already stopped him from entering twice."

"I think we need someone with a profile from the States. Jesse Jackson? Nah, sixties man, won't carry any swing with the young brothas. We need a young radical brotha. What about someone from Public Enemy—Chuck D, maybe?"

"Safe idea, sis."

Calvin gently pinched Lorna's left cheek. "Better still, lets try and get some of the young gangsters over. Y'know, the ones straight outta Compton. They're the only ones who know the real deal. They'd have more in common with the brothas on the streets than any middle class rap group or ageing politician."

"You're right. I'll see what I can do."

"Thing is, it's going to take money to bring them over. We need to get sponsorship or something like that."

The phone rang. Lorna answered and said hello four times before she replaced the receiver.

"Strange, that's the second time today."

Calvin knew there was nothing strange about it. The Uh Huh girl's cousin, Dawn, was pestering him. She had got his number somehow, and she rang night and day to speak to him. Calvin had done everything he could to let her know he wasn't interested but now it needed more than a polite 'no thanks'.

The phone rang again and Calvin moved swiftly to answer it.

"Calvin? Coach Bailey 'ere."

72

"Oh—peace, brotha."

"Me jus' ah ring fe tell yuh we'll be leavin' for Manchester from Handswort' Leisure Centre at six instead of five."

"Okay, Coach. So you managed to get the funds out of Lindsey?"

"I don't know, is like tryin' fe get blood outta stone. 'Im a argue say we don't need to go up a day before de game. I tell yuh, I had to get raw wid im. Insist 'cause is a big game, we need to prepare proper fe it. Anyway, me manage to get 'im to put 'im han' inna 'im pocket and de radio station put in a lickle. So we alright. Only t'ing is, 'im book everyt'ing from de bus to de hotel, so y'know wha' dat mean..."

"Brotha's still putting the dollar signs before the welfare of the team," Calvin replied. "Any thoughts to the startin' five, Coach?"

"Well, me been t'inkin bout startin' Adam instead of Andre at two man."

Calvin knew this change was going to be on the agenda. Andre's game had deteriorated so much that he really shouldn't be in ahead of Adam, who had done nothing but improve—but Calvin still felt the need to defend the brotha.

"Coach, why change a winning formula?" he said hesitantly. "We're unbeaten in twelve games."

"Is trut' y'ah talk, but is Cheshire Cherokee we a play Sunday. Dem also unbeaten in twelve."

"Brotha, we gotta show confidence in Andre...give him time to let his shot come back. Y'know how it goes with pure shooters."

"Me not convince 'bout 'im fe dis game. Me feel we go need a lickle more mobility and a player wid more options at two man. Andre game too one-speed. Slow. 'Im nah get me enough points fe shootin' guard. Me was t'inkin 'bout givin' Macca 'im shootin' guard spot, wid Adam at point to give us more versatility inna de back court."

"Coach, we're winning. Drop Andre now and he may never regain his confidence. Adam can come off the bench early to replace him if things are not going to plan," Calvin suggested.

"Ow much 'im a pay yuh? Y' always a fight fe 'im. Mustn't let friendship get in de way of business. Okay, yuh win me over fe now. Let me ring de others."

"Make sure you tell Winston five o'clock. You know it's the only way to get the brotha's backside there on time."

"Is trut' y'ah talk. Anyway, later."

"Go in peace, brotha."

Lorna had gathered the cups and gone back to the kitchen by the time he came off the phone. Twenty minutes later he smelt something good coming from in there.

He busied himself putting the finishing touches to the leaflet, and his concentration was only broken when she came back into the living room and played Omar's *'There's Nothing Like This'*. Calvin looked up and watched her walk towards him clicking her fingers and miming to the song like she was performing on stage.

"What's for dinner, sis? It smells wicked."

"Me, baby," she replied, smiling.

She came round behind him and began to give him a shoulder massage. He pretended he was concentrating on his work, but her hands were beginning to seduce him. She kissed his neck and shoulder then pushed her hands inside his T-shirt and played with his nipples. Calvin tilted his head back so she could kiss his lips. She almost bit him as she gobbled them in her mouth. Then her hands travelled down to his groin. She unbuckled his belt and unzipped his jeans. His manhood was already as hard as a ramrod. As her hand fought its way inside his boxer shorts, he thought about his golden rule: no sex the day before a big game.

But, shit, how could he resist?

Calvin stood up and gently pulled her towards him. Her eyes were closed as he bent over to lavish kisses on her face and neck. In one movement he swept her up and carried her next door to the bedroom. He placed her on the bed and lay beside her. He began to kiss her hungrily, his right hand caressing her thighs under her dress. Then he rolled onto his back and watched her strip down to her sexy knickers and bra.

She sat on top of him, pulled his T-shirt up to reveal his bare chest, covered him with soft spine-melting kisses.

Soon she had stripped his jeans and boxers down to his ankles, then sucked, stroked and kneaded his entire body. He kicked off his trousers, gently eased her onto her back and peeled off her bra and panties. He softly massaged her small firm breasts, then took them each into his mouth as she held him in a tight clinch.

When he entered her body, it felt so good. Calvin didn't want to rush it. For twenty minutes or more he moved rhythmically inside her. Her breathing got heavier and her groans louder as she moved slowly towards a climax—then moments later he was shaking like a leaf in a high wind and Lorna was crying out as they simultaneously reached a climax.

Calvin placed his hand over Lorna's as she changed gear and

pulled into the leisure centre car park; she looked at him and smiled.

"Thanks for takin' the car, sis. I hate leavin' it here overnight."

"My pleasure. What time do you want me to pick you up tomorrow?"

"I'll ring and let you know."

Calvin got out, grabbed his bag, and gave her a kiss, which was greeted with cheers from the watching Warriors. Lorna waved to Andre before she pulled away.

The bus was a twenty-seater, and as he walked round to the door, he saw Joni stepping out of Mr Lindsey's Mercedes. As far as Calvin knew Joni was still living with the boss, and Lindsey's plan to get sponsorship for him had produced sweet FA.

So much for publicity, Calvin thought, boarding the bus—then Marcus nearly knocked him back down the steps. He raced past, trying to get Mr Lindsey's attention as he drove away...but the owner either didn't see Marcus, or didn't want to see him, and drove off into the dark at top speed.

Calvin walked down the aisle past Lemi, who was gorging himself with a French stick packed with tuna, cheese, salad and about a jar of mayonnaise oozing out of the sides.

"Brotha man," Calvin asked, "don't you ever give your stomach a break?"

"Never had no breakfast," Lemi replied, shifting his tank-like frame on the two seats he was taking up.

"So you thought you'd make an early start on tomorrow's, right brotha?"

"Get out my face, man. I need fuel to get me fit and ready."

"Fit for what though, Lemi?"

Calvin went and sat one row from the back, with Andre in the seat opposite and Winston directly in front.

"Don't believe you're on time, brotha," Calvin said to Winston, knowing he would flip.

"Damn, git outta here, man. That mutha told me five. Homie been standin' round freezin' his dick off waitin'. Nigga better not pull dat shit again or man, I'm history. Can't be doin' dat shit to yer franchise player. *Damn!*"

"So wha' time did yer get 'ere loike, Macca?" Benji thrust his hog nose into the discussion from the seat next to Winston.

"Homie touched down five-twenty five. Not a nigga in sight. Shit, thought you homiez had split on my ass. Headin' off to New Street station when dis big-ass bus pulls up. Then I knew Coach was fakin' my ass out."

"Lucky he fooled yer boy, 'cause otherwise yer would've been late again," Benji answered, a smile covering his face.

"Hey nigga, anyone ever told you what an ugly, black mutha-fuckin' shit you are?" Winston raged.

"No."

"Recognise, homie, I'm da first. Talkin' shit 'bout I'm always late. When y' can handle da rock like me then homie can start frontin' on my shit. 'Til then, quit trippin' on my ass, y' two-foot-two tar baby."

"Wha' yer goin' on about? Keep yer 'air on," Benji said, a little embarrassed by Winston's harsh comments.

Marcus came marching back onto the bus. He brushed past Calvin—almost knocking him down for the second time—before slumping in the middle of the back row, duffel coat buttoned to his neck, cursing.

"What's up, brotha?" Calvin asked.

Marcus kissed his teeth.

"De man jus' a avoid me."

"Who, Lindsey?" Andre asked.

"Cha man, don't matter. Me a sight 'im at de game tomorrow."

Marcus leaned back in his seat and closed his eyes. As soon as Coach was on board, the bus pulled out and headed for the M6 to begin the ninety-mile journey to Manchester.

Calvin's body was still feeling the effects of his afternoon delight with Lorna. He didn't think women enjoyed sex as much as men, but even when Lorna had dropped him off he could still see that the experience had moved her.

The atmosphere on the coach was loud as usual, everyone chatting and trying to listen at the same time. *The Daily Sport* moved from hand to hand accompanied by obligatory cries of 'Bloodclaat! What a batty!' as Warriors ogled the naked girl on the page. Levi reckoned she resembled the woman he had screwed the night before, and set Winston off giving details of some white girl he'd had before he left to catch the bus.

The two were soon joined by Adam and Selwyn, and all four began to discuss their preferences between black and white women. They all agreed that they had an easier time getting whatever they wanted from white women, who seemed fascinated by black men: forbidden fruit...and, like Eve, they couldn't resist a bite.

But there was all-round dissatisfaction with the sistas. Views ranged from 'too lippy' to 'not freeing up the goods without a world war, or ACAS-style negotiations'.

"Look, speakin' from experience—" Levi began, placing his hand on his heart "—there's no difference between black or white 'oman. Underneat' dem both have de same equipment."

"Homie seconds dat, man," Winston chipped in.

"And you should know, geezer," Selwyn said to Levi. "How many women yer have now?"

"Eight, innit, and twelve kids."

"Lawd, talk 'bout population explosion. Dis breddah trying to create him own world!"

"Thirteen now," Levi said, proud as a lion. "Me forget fe tell yuh, me new t'ing gimme another son two weeks ago."

"Shit, homie! Where d'ya find da time to perform on da black-top?" Winston asked.

"Geezers, I'm taking a book on Levi's next kid." Selwyn called. "Ten-to-one three months. Evens tomorrow."

Everyone laughed.

"Man gotta do what he's been put on earth for, to reproduce. I ain't breaking no law. Women are willing. I'm just providing a service," Levi replied, taking high fives from the other three.

"How many of da bitches white?" Winston asked out of interest.

"They're my queens like, not bitches," Levi answered, trying to be politically correct. "Half and half. Four apiece. Man ain't got time to discriminate, like."

"Snap, homie! As long as da hoochie can deliver da snaps on a regular basis she's got da part. Jus' happen dat white chicks supply da dead presidents without a damn FBI investigation."

"So wha'ppen to the red girl you was movin' wid?" Adam asked Winston.

"Still waxin' dat regularly, homie. Bitch 'n' moan at times but come dick time she's under a homie's control, no fear, cuz."

Calvin stopped listening after a while. He felt the brothas needed educating, but he wasn't about to start one of his lectures on the bus today. He looked across to Andre who sat, eyes closed and motionless, with his head tilted towards the air-conditioning outlet. Calvin deliberated over whether or not to disturb him, then asked:

"How's Heather, brotha?"

Andre didn't open his eyes.

"Heather? I suppose she's alright."

"Suppose? Don't you know, brotha?"

Andre turned his head to look at Calvin. "These days I don't

77

know what she's thinking or feeling. All I get is a lot of noise in my head."

He turned away and gazed out of the window. Calvin took this as a cue that he didn't want to talk.

The bus had made good ground and was already past the Stoke-On-Trent turn-off. Calvin leaned back in his seat and closed his eyes. He must have dozed off, because when Andre nudged him thirty minutes later they were passing the Stockport turn-off.

"The youth conference, how's it going?" Andre asked.

Calvin gave Andre a progress report; Marcus tuned in with interest.

"De problem wid de yout' today," he interrupted, "is dat dem a grow up widout no father to teach dem discipline."

"True," Calvin agreed. "We need to bring the extended family back into our community. Fathers need to be around. If you listen to the brothas down the bus you realise what the problem is. They don't behave responsibly towards their women or their kids."

"Cha, dem foolish, man. Me would love to be a proper father to my yout', but fe dat bloodclaat woman."

"As long as the father cares for his kids, he doesn't need to be with the mother," Andre said.

Calvin was surprised to hear this, because it went against Andre's usual opinion.

"I don't agree wid dat," Marcus said, leaning forward from his slouched position. "There's certain t'ings a woman cyan' teach a bwoy, like how to be a man. Is trut' me a tell yuh. Hard as she try, my mother couldn't teach me a t'ing 'bout manhood. An' if yuh wan' proof, how come is de bwoy and not de gyal dem causin' so much bodderation? Tell me dat nah, Mr Intelligence?"

Andre sighed.

"All I'm saying is a man can be a father to his kids, boy or girl, whether he's with the mother or not. And my mum taught me as much as my dad about being a man."

"Cha, but you is one of dem middle-class black people. T'ings don't go so 'pon de ground."

"That's crap and you know it!"

Marcus kissed his teeth.

Calvin saw they were each bringing their own recent experiences into it, and the discussion was becoming tangled. Just then, Coach Bailey rose from his seat and made his way down the aisle.

"Look, I sorry to haffe tell unnu dis but everybody 'ave to pay eight pound toward de cost of de hotel."

"When was this decided?" Adam asked. "No one told us that."

"I am not even going to get a bloody game and the geezer wants eight quid—" Selwyn added, "—you must be jokin', geezer."

"Anybody see me laughing?" Coach asked, looking harshly at Selwyn. "Me jus' look at de receipt and it say VAT still outstandin'. Mista Lindsey pay. So we haffe pay it or we a sleep inna de park tonite. So everybody haffe pull together and dig into dem pocket. Please!"

"Dis shit's way outta line," Winston told him. "Man, homie gotta pay for his own crib. Damn, mothers don't pay enough as it is."

"Macca, yuh should be de last fe open yuh mout'!" Coach turned and made his way towards the front of the bus.

They arrived at eight-thirty and, as they expected, the hotel was nothing to write home about—a Victorian building on the outskirts of Moss Side. Then they discovered they'd be sharing single rooms because Mr Lindsey was too tight-fisted for them to have one each.

Calvin shared with Andre. They drew lots to see who would take the bed. Andre won, but when Calvin looked at the length of the bed he realised he'd better off on the floor anyway, since he'd have to bend himself like a Z to fit in it.

After they had settled in they met Marcus and Roots in reception and went to find a pattie shop. Twenty minutes later, after walking around Moss Side and asking every black person they saw, they finally found what they were looking for.

Lemi had beaten them to it. As they were going in he was leaving with two large brown bagsful. John Nettlesford came out beside him, stuffing a pattie in his mouth.

"Look like yah a buy out de shop, Lemi," Roots said.

"Just me first course, man," Lemi replied, tapping his stomach.

On the way back to the hotel, the aroma of stew chicken and rice 'n' peas wafted out of the container Calvin was carrying, and made him quicken his pace.

"Eh, anybody know this car yah so?" Marcus asked.

Calvin turned to see a car trailing them, adorned with so many spoilers it looked like the Batmobile. None of the others recognised it. The car stopped beside them and the tinted window came down slowly. Calvin saw four black guys aged about seventeen wearing blue bandanas across their mouths.

"What the fuck you doin' on our turf, man?" the boy closest to the window said menacingly.

"Wha' de raas? Dis is a free bloodclaat country," Marcus said, taking a step towards the car.

"Come any closer and I'll blow your fuckin' balls off," he said, producing a semi-automatic pistol.

"Marcus, back off man!" Calvin told him.

"Yes, Marcus, you be a good little nigga and back the hell off," the gunman said, squinting through one eye like Clint Eastwood.

Calvin could see Marcus brimming with anger, but for once he took the commonsense option. They stood in silence on the deserted street.

"We're goin' to circle and if we find you lot here when we get back we're goin' to have some target practice."

They pulled away, laughing.

"Me a stop right 'ere 'til dem come," Marcus said. "No lickle bloodclaat bwoy goin' talk to me so and get 'way wid it. No bumbaclaat way!"

Calvin had no intention of becoming a statistic on tomorrow's news.

"Look, those idiots are serious," he pleaded with Marcus. "They had *guns*. Think about it, brotha."

Roots backed him up.

"Easy, Terminator, is best we mek a move."

Marcus stood, fists clenched, staring in the direction of the car. Calvin could see he didn't want to quit and knew exactly how he felt. Powerless—and in front of brothas almost young enough to be their sons. But he also knew that sometimes you have to put pride away. A young boy's effort to prove his manhood was not worth losing your life over. He took Marcus by the arm. "C'mon, man."

Marcus reluctantly started back in the direction of the hotel, but he didn't say a word 'til they got there.

Reality had hit him. The reality of inner-city Britain.

"Here we are people, Steady Eddie on BPRL bringing it to ya just the way you like it. This one is to cheer up the Warriors after their heavy, heavy duty defeat this afternoon. The House of Pain men caught nothin' but pain on the backboards as Cheshire Cherokee beat them 118-74.

"Ouch, it hurts to say it, brothas and sistas out there in Birmin' of ham; the worst beatin' for the people's choice in four years; big Marcus 'The Terminator' Codrington limited to eleven points. What? Yeah, I'm comin' correct, eleven points. Well, guys, records are made to be broken..."

In his semi-comatose state Calvin reached across his bed and turned the volume down until the DJ's voice was nothing but a memory.

His body was tired with exertion, his voice was hoarse from shouting and his mind was shattered after the humiliation of losing to an all-white team.

When Lorna came to pick him up from the centre she could tell she was in for a night of not asking him about anything, not insisting he eat the rice and chicken she had made specially, and not even mentioning she had a great idea to raise money for the youth conference.

All that would have to wait. The half-hearted peck on the cheek he gave her when he got in the car told her that they had lost, and that she had lost him for the rest of the night, to a sulk.

For Calvin, top-scoring with twenty-one points didn't matter; seeing Joni play his best game since his arrival didn't matter; neither did seeing Marcus have his worst game in five years at the club.

It was losing, that was the problem. He hated it. It hurt his manhood and attacked his pride. Worse still, he disliked the way the team disintegrated into squabbling—like in the bad old days. No unity in defeat for the Warriors. Every man was out to save his own ass from catching the blame. Coach had benched Andre, then shouted in the changing room that Adam would definitely start the next game. And he was right to do it.

But even that didn't matter now, as Calvin lay sideways across his bed in pitch darkness. Alone.

It must have been around eleven o'clock when he heard the phone ring. He waited for Lorna to answer it. He could hear her talking and assumed it was her mum or dad. Then she put her head round the door. "Honey, it's Heather."

He walked to the dining room and picked up the receiver.

"Heather?"

She was crying.

"What's wrong sista?"

"He's gone," she said, her voice cracking.

"Gone? Sista, you mean, he's working on a Sunday evening?"

"No, I mean really gone. He's left me and the kids. We had a row when he came back from Manchester and he just packed some of his things and stormed out."

"Do you know where he went?"

"No...I thought he might be with you."

"Haven't seen or heard from the brotha since we got off the bus."

His mind started racing. *Where would Andre go?*

"Calvin, can you come over? Please? I don't know what to do."

She sounded desperate and he could hear the kids crying in the background.

"Don't worry. Just see to the kids. I'll be there in about twenty minutes."

Calvin wondered what the hell Andre was playing at; he and Heather were going through a tough time, but to up and leave like that, that wasn't him. He remembered the conversation on the bus. Looked like Andre had already planned his little escape.

He felt Lorna's eyes burning a hole in his back. He turned around.

"What's up, sista?" he asked.

"He's got another woman, hasn't he?"

"I don't know what's going on with him."

"He's your bosom buddy and you don't know if he has another woman? Who are you tryin' to kid, Calvin?"

Calvin recognised Lorna's 'we sistas are together' tone.

"For a very intelligent woman you can sometimes be very stupid," he answered.

"Don't you dare patronise me!" she shouted.

"Look, all I know is that Andre and Heather were having a few problems—and I only know because *she* told me. Andre hasn't said a word to me, okay."

"Okay, okay. I'm sorry."

She went over and gave him a hug—then pulled back and squeezed his cheeks, hard. "Calvin, if you ever cheat on me I'll kill you."

"You don't have to worry about that, sista," he replied, confidently.

"Do you want me to go with you?" she asked.

"No, I think it would be better if you stay here in case Andre phones. I'll be back soon."

6
Free At Last?

It was six in the morning when Andre arrived at Goldberg and Samson. On occasion, he left the office a couple of hours early, but never in his life had he arrived at this time.

As he made his way to his desk he could hear Mabel the cleaner—one of the few black faces to be found at the company—hoovering away in Mr Pal's office. It made him feel slightly better that somebody else was working at this hour.

He got a black coffee from the vending machine and walked back to his desk, giving thanks for the empty office; it was a relief not to have to perform for his workmates like an out-of-work actor looking for his big break. Today he could sit down at his desk without John, Michael or William gawking at him as if he were a Martian...but in his mind he could still hear faint echoes of the inane conversations he usually had to put up with each morning.

His thoughts soon turned to Heather and the kids. He had booked himself into a hotel, and then stayed awake all night wondering if he had made the right decision. At the time it wasn't a matter of right or wrong; he just had to get out. He felt he was in a straitjacket. Heather, the kids, work, basketball, they were all getting to be too much. He had to take time out.

Now, although his family still dominated his thoughts, the pressure was off. It was as if the time bomb that had been ticking in his head had at last been defused.

He knew Heather would be saying *'How could he? How could he leave Josephine and Jermaine? How could he run out on them less than a week before Christmas?'* The more he thought about it the more he felt like a bastard. He'd be judged, for sure; and he knew better than to expect anyone to understand the way he felt. He had every intention of meeting his responsibilities towards the kids, but it was far too early to know whether he had left Heather for good.

They were married too young. Twenty-three was far too early to take on so much. But at the time they had thought it would work; they were madly in love—at least he had been. They had been dating since they left school. Calvin used to joke that they were joined at the hip. Then Heather became pregnant and her mum virtually ordered them to get married. Andre hadn't got off the rollercoaster since.

It came at a particularly sensitive time for him too. His parents had been killed in a car crash two years before. On the way back from visiting his two older sisters their car mysteriously flipped over at high speed on the M6. No one knew exactly how it happened. His mother was killed outright—his father spent three days in intensive care before he also died.

At first playing happy families was just what he needed. But after Josephine arrived, things started to deteriorate. Heather became dissatisfied, and condescending with it. Her moods lasted too long to be post-natal. She said that she was frustrated, that her life had stopped. She hadn't achieved her goals or fulfiled the ambitions she and her mother had visualised.

At twenty-six, she found herself tied to the kitchen sink with only two screaming children for company day and night, while Andre still pursued his career, still went drinking with his mates and still travelled around the country playing basketball.

He felt her resentment towards him. She would bitch about him not pulling his weight at home, knowing full well the stress he was under with all the crap he experienced every day at work.

She said she needed to work to put some meaning back into her life. To an extent he sympathised, but it was hard to adjust to such a fundamental change in someone he knew and loved.

He tried, with little success, to get thoughts of Heather out of his head. He had a mountain of work to do, particularly on the Lighthouse Company case. It was the largest case he'd ever worked on and the one thing that was keeping him sane in this place—since when he switched on to it everything else around him paled into insignificance.

He made a start, but soon had to stop reading because his eyes were burning. He had forgotten to pack his cleaning solution, and had to sleep in his lenses. When he woke up, his eyes had been as red as the devil's.

Mabel came in to dust and hoover. She had on a pink overall and a woolly ski hat. She was overweight, but moved with the speed of a woman four stones lighter. She reminded Andre a little of his mum, only Mabel was much darker.

"Oh God, y' frighten me. I t'ought y' were a ghost," she said, clutching her heart.

"Sometimes I wish I was, Mabel. I could just drift away into thin air and not have to answer to anyone."

84

"You don't t'ink dat. Such a lovely boy with everyt'ing to live for."

Would she say that if she knew what he'd done to his wife and kids, he wondered.

Mabel liked to talk but she could see Andre was up to his eyes in paperwork. She began dusting down the desks while humming a tune, but eventually succumbed to her need to chat.

"So how come yuh in dis early?"

"Just thought I'd make an early start...lots to do," Andre replied, distantly.

"Den how come everybody don't start early? Every morning I see a pile of papers 'pon your desk and nothin' on de others?"

"We just have different ways of working," he replied, unconvincingly.

"Oh, and here I was t'inkin' it had somet'ing to do wid de colour of y' skin."

Andre looked at her. She had said what he'd been feeling for years, but never once whispered inside the office.

It was so encouraging to at last hear someone speak the truth about the situation. Even Mabel—whom everyone in the office, Andre included, viewed as just a simple charlady who laughed loudly and had no views on office politics. For that, he felt ashamed.

"Mabel," he said hesitantly. "When you're the only black in the department and one of only three in the company, you know you have to be three times, sometimes four times as good as the others."

"It a shame," Mabel said, parking her considerable backside on the corner of Michael's desk. "Why dem don't just judge people 'pon dem merit eh?"

"I guess life isn't like that. Not only do I have to work harder to get the same recognition, I can't fail either—because I'm representing the whole black race. No white guy has to put up with that constant pressure. If he fails they'll surely get another white guy in as soon as he's out of the door."

"Me know, son. Me know," Mabel said sympathetically.

For a moment Andre felt like he was talking to his mum. He felt comforted. Knowing someone was listening, and really cared, made a big difference.

"You know, I think if I'd failed my exams, or had any black mark against my name, they wouldn't have taken on Theo Rutherford two months ago. I feel like I paved the way for him."

"Dat bossy one on de fifth floor?"

Andre nodded.

"I can't tek 'im. Too smooth for my likin'. Like 'im have 'im head in de clouds...not down to eart' like you."

"He's okay, Mabel. You just have to try and understand why he is the way he is," Andre replied—even though he had certain reservations about Theo, too.

"Anyway, baby, I goin' leave you. I won't mek no noise wid de hooverin'. I'll do it tomorrow; dem will never notice. And listen, don't let dem buggas get y' down, y'hear? Yuh is de first black person me see in 'ere for de twelve-and-a-half years me been workin' here—and I wan' retire in four years time and see you a head dis organisation!"

She let out a shriek of laughter.

"Thanks, Mabel."

Andre was thinking he had more chance of becoming Prime Minister.

When he next looked at his watch it was eight forty-five and other people were arriving. Tracy was the first to stick her head around the partition.

"Oh, Andre, good morning," she said, surprised.

"Hi, Trace, how was your weekend?" he asked, eyes still fixed on his files, trying to get the formalities out off the the way as quickly as possible.

"Oh, a bit depressing. I didn't do much. How about yours?"

"Very eventful, to say the least."

"You comin' this evening?"

"Coming where?"

"The Christmas party!"

"Oh, that—" He'd completely forgotten about it. The office was glittering with tinsel, but he wasn't exactly in a festive mood, "—I don't think so, Trace."

"Why?"

She came and sat on the corner of his desk, her dress near enough to the top of her thighs. Andre tried his best to keep his eyes off her legs and on his papers.

"You've got to come," she continued. "I'll miss you if you don't."

Andre laughed uncomfortably.

"I don't know. Maybe. I'll see how I'm fixed."

She grinned suggestively.

"You won't regret it, I promise."

The morning passed quite quickly, mainly because Andre told

Tracy to take messages instead of putting any calls through to him; and that included calls from Heather.

She had called five times in one hour. Tracy said she sounded frantic and asked whether she should put her through if she phoned again. But Andre just couldn't take another tongue-lashing today, so he said no.

Mr Pal was on the warpath, too. He was shouting and ranting at everyone—including the other guys in the office, which made a change. Andre got a roasting for looking scruffy with his top two shirt buttons open and tie dangling like a limp dick. But how would Pal look if he had spent the weekend the way Andre had?

Andre went to the bathroom, washed his face and straightened himself up, then hurried back to his desk to continue work on the Lighthouse case. Then *bang!* A box of CDs landed right in front of his nose, closely followed by the wedding ring he'd bought seven years ago in the Hockley jewellry quarter. Heather stood before him, livid.

"You'll be needing these, you bastard," she shouted—then she left as suddenly as she'd arrived. Everyone in the office peered over the partition. Andre looked around, reeling with embarrassment.

William and John looked away and buried their heads quickly, but Michael burst into fits of laughter.

"Who's been a naughty boy, then?" he said bitingly.

Andre's shame reached a level he'd never felt before. He thought that was embarrassing, but there was more to come. She came back into the room with another six loads—handfuls of clothes, tapes, law books...everything she could find that belonged to him and would fit in her car.

Andre stood up and paced around the room, hands on his head, as Heather piled a mountain of his belongings in front of him. If he opened his mouth, she would make a bigger scene, bawling their business around the office. She was in no mood to be placated; and he didn't know what he could say to even try. *Damn this woman!* When it seemed everything he owned was piled up around his desk, she made one last trip...and came back holding Jermaine and Josephine by the hand. The children looked frightened and confused.

"Oh God! Heather, don't be silly! You can't do this."

She left them by his desk and walked out. Andre told the kids to stay put and ran after her. He caught her at the lift, and shrieked:

"Damn you, Heather, what the hell you playing at? This is my office!"

"Fuck you and your work!" she screamed back. "You wanted a

clean break. Well, now you've got one. But don't think I'm going to sit at home going through that single parent shit, waiting for the social cheque to drop. For once in your life you can face up to your goddamn responsibilities."

The lift arrived and Heather walked in. Andre followed. She pressed ground and looked up at the ceiling as if he wasn't there.

"Heather, we need to talk about this."

"Oh, Andre wants to talk, does he? When you decided to piss off and leave me with all the responsibility you didn't want to talk then, did you?

"Or when I tried to phone your wotless ass ten times this morning. All I got was excuses from your bitch of a secretary. So *now* you want to have a deep meaningful discussion when the shoe's on the other foot? Go to hell, Andre. I've got to get to work."

Andre couldn't believe what was happening. "And what am I supposed to do with the kids?" he asked, as the lift doors opened.

Heather looked at him.

"Whatever it was you expected me to do with them. See yah."

She pressed six and stepped out of the lift with a triumphant smile on her face.

The doors closed.

Andre took a deep breath, leaned on the wall of the lift and tried to compose himself on the way back up to the sixth floor. *What the hell was he supposed to do now?* When he got back, Tracy was playing with the kids. Immediately, they fired question after question at him.

"Daddy, where's Mummy?"

"Is she coming back?"

"Why did we come here?"

"Are we staying with you today?"

"Is this your work?"

"What's this for?"

"Can we have McDonald's for lunch?"

"Daddy, what's wrong?"

Andre slumped behind his desk trying to work out what to do. Mrs Madge, according to Josephine, had gone to a hot place for the Christmas break. He phoned all his friends and relatives hoping to find someone to look after them until evening.

As a last resort he phoned Heather's parents. Archie answered. He agreed to have them and, since Ruby had the car and would be gone for hours, he told Andre to drive them over straight away.

An hour later Andre was back at the office, putting his belongings in Mabel's store room. He was just about to get down to work when Mr Pal stormed up to his desk.

"I'm givin' the Lighthouse case to Michael, so get the file together and and pass it over to him, please, Mr Beckford."

Andre went into shock.

"But I've almost completed it. I've just got a couple of days work to do then it's—"

"Andre, I'm not going to argue with you. I've made my decision; I want this transition completed by the end of the day."

He stormed back out of the office. Andre watched him go in a state of bewilderment. Even Michael looked too stunned to gloat. So, Pal had finally gathered enough rope to hang him with.

He had a good idea what was coming next. Whatever Pal had planned, Andre knew it would be another major and humiliating blow to his career.

He spent the rest of the day tidying up the case before handing it to Michael. Tracy gave him his messages just before five-thirty...two from his sister, one from Calvin and fifteen from Heather's mum. He didn't want to speak to any of them. What he needed now was a quiet drink and to rest his mind.

The city centre was packed with shoppers and Andre was jostled by parents doing last minute Christmas shopping and their screaming kids. The viciously cold air made him feel like he'd been caught in an avalanche.

He stopped off at Boots to buy some Hydrocare and a night container for his lenses. In all the things Heather had dumped on him, she'd forgotten to look in the bathroom cabinet. He joined the queue in front of a nice-looking black cashier.

"Yaow, Birdman!"

Andre swung round to see Levi a few places behind him in the queue, dressed in his Palisades security uniform and laden with bags full of presents. He waved at Andre, then said something to an old lady behind him before disappearing down a nearby aisle. Andre was wondering what he was up to when Levi returned carrying a box of Milk Tray.

The sly grin on Levi's face and the way he eyed the cashier told Andre exactly what he was thinking. Sure enough, soon Levi's mouth was chasing after his wandering eyes.

"So baby, where we going tonight?" he asked as she bagged his goods. She took the money and handed him the bag without a word, but a smile crept slowly across her face.

"Sweetlips, I can show you a good time, wine and dine, or maybe spend some time in my jacuzzi—"

Her smile grew bigger.

"—sipping champagne by candlelight."

She giggled.

"Just say the word. Your wish is my command."

Andre shook his head. Levi was such a smooth operator when it came to sweet talk, and with his good looks—like a cross between Les Ferdinand and Linford Christie—he had an easy time with women. Levi was supremely confident. He handed her the chocolates.

"These are for you, sweet thing," he crooned.

"Thank you. That's really sweet," she blushed.

Levi then leaned over the counter to speak confidentially.

"So what time you finish, cris' biscuit?"

"Seven-thirty," she replied, smiling broadly.

"Okay, I'll pick you up outside, New Street, seven thirty."

She nodded and straightened her face to serve her next customer.

"How do you do it, man?" Andre asked, once they'd hit the street. He wished he could melt women into submission like that.

"It's the one in ten thing," Levi told him.

"One in ten?"

Once again Andre felt out of step with the street vibe.

"Yeah, man. Out of every ten women you approach at least one's gonna bite. Works every time."

"Yeah?"

"Yeah, she was my eighth chat-up today, and the first to bite."

"So how often you do this?"

"Every day I'm on duty. There's always a woman wanting her bag carried or wanting directions. Got to be alert, y'nah. Never know when you gonna hit. But cha...dis one nah see me tonight."

Andre was astonished. "You're not meeting her?"

"Nah man, that's just a bit of fun. I have to go home and wrap my kids' presents—dat good fe tek me two days t'raas. Plus, I have to see a couple of me woman as well."

"But she's going to be waiting."

"Well maybe one day I'll go back in with some flowers and make my apologies, sweet her up again. But even if I don't, she got a box of chocolates out of it, didn't she?"

Andre couldn't argue there.

"Listen I have to go. You just reminded me I've got Christmas presents to buy. Might as well do it now."

Now I've got pure time on my hands, he thought. *No work, no family and no practice tonight.*

"Yeah, see ya later," Levi said.

After he'd gone Andre realised Levi had been a welcome distraction from all his troubles.

After two hours of traipsing around toyshops and department stores, Andre ducked into the first bar he came across. He didn't even know its name—he didn't need to know. He just positioned himself at the bar and downed three large scotches in the space of an hour.

"O-o-oh, the hokey cokey! O-o-oh, the hokey cokey!"

The sound of the singing outside of the lift made Andre want to press ground again and head straight back out of the building. But the doors opened and everyone seemed glad to see him.

The party was in full swing. From the warm welcome he'd received, he could tell they'd already had too much to drink. People were prancing around the normally sober sixth floor wrapped in tinsel and wearing Santa Claus hats. Andre spotted Mr Pal whispering in a secretary's ear.

He got a strong urge to punch the bastard, but Tracy intervened. She whipped out some mistletoe, held it over his head and gave him a long hard kiss on the lips. He had hardly recovered before she grabbed him and pulled him into the melee of people.

He wasn't in the mood for this. He could feel them all whispering about what happened with Heather. And he had to put on a brave face...make it look like a lover's tiff. Forever acting. That way he could still seem like one of them, despite this mad black woman in his personal life.

Michael came up to him and introduced his wife, a tired Greek-looking woman in an off-the-peg blue dress. He also apologised for what Mr Pal had done. Andre assured him it wasn't his fault. They shook hands and Michael wished him a Happy Christmas.

Just then, Theo came out of the lift with an elegant brunette on his arm. He looked immaculate, as ever—in an olive single-breasted suit and a black tee-shirt—but she was wearing a little too much make-up, spoiling an otherwise beautiful face. As soon as Theo saw Andre he came straight over.

"Andre, meet my wife, Rachel. Rachel, this is my colleague, Andre."

She shook Andre's hand and he noticed a massive diamond ring on her finger. Theo pulled Andre slightly to one side.

"I heard what Pal did to you today—" he shouted over the music, "—and what your lady did...I tell you, these black women are out of control."

Andre wasn't surprised that the news had travelled so fast. But the fact that Theo felt free to talk to him on a personal level caused mixed feelings.

"Don't worry; you're better off without her sort. Just keep your head low for now. I may have something in the pipeline for you."

Andre was about to ask for more detail when Tracy bounded out of nowhere and kissed him again, this time on the cheek. She handed him a yellow Post-It note with 'Call Calvin—urgent' written on it. Andre looked at her strangely, hoping she wasn't going to pass all his messages on like that. He told Theo, Rachel and Tracy he'd be back soon and went to his office to make the call.

"Hi Lorna, it's Andre," he said, cautiously. Lorna knew Heather well, and he knew women always stuck together when it came to such matters.

"Oh, it's you," she said.

"Can I speak to Calvin?"

As she handed the phone over, he heard her say: "Sounds like he's enjoying the single life already..."

Calvin came on the line.

"Brotha Dre, man, what's goin' on?"

Andre sighed.

"It's a long story. A hell of a long story."

He didn't feel able to dredge it all up for Calvin's sake.

"Where are you? Heather's worried stiff."

"Don't kid yourself. She paid me an unexpected visit this afternoon. And let's just say she left an indelible mark."

"Listen, I'm in a hurry, I have to get to work. Where are you?"

"At the office do."

"Look I'll try and get an hour or so off and meet you somewhere."

"Okay—I'll be in Ronnie Scott's around nine."

"Right. Go with peace, brotha."

As Andre put the phone down Tracy came in with two glasses of champagne in her hand. She looked the worse for drink. "Andre, you're missing all the fun."

"I'm just not in the mood," he replied.

"What's wrong, want something more spicy?" she pouted. She sat down on his lap, took the glass from his fingers and wrapped her arms around him.

92

"Tracy, you're drunk. Get off me."

"I'm not drunk. I'm perfectly sober and I've been meaning to do this for a very long time."

She pushed her body up against him and kissed him passionately. Andre almost let her get the better of him, until she began to force her tongue in his mouth. He came to his senses suddenly and pushed her off him. "Get off me!"

As she almost fell to the floor, she grabbed at his shirt. He heard the seams burst.

"Jesus, what's the matter with you?"

She pulled herself to her feet.

"There's no wifey-wifey to take care of you now, so why not let racy-Tracy soothe your sorrows?"

She pulled in close again, running her hand along his thigh.

"Come on, you know you want me really."

"Tracy, you're the last thing I want."

Her mood changed abruptly.

"You bastard."

She snatched up his glass and emptied the contents in Andre's face.

"Hell hath no fury..." he muttered, taking a hanky from his pocket to wipe his face. She swung her hand to slap him but he caught it.

"Don't even try."

He pushed her away and she turned and fled, cursing him and promising that he would pay for what he'd done.

Andre decided he'd definitely had enough of this party and these people. He left without saying goodbye.

He felt a bit tipsy driving the short distance across the city centre to Ronnie Scott's. To tell the truth he couldn't care less right now. He had had a bastard of a day, that's all he knew...the rest didn't matter.

When he entered Ronnie Scott's, he headed straight for a phone to ring Archie and check that the kids were okay. Ruby gave him an ear lashing before confirming they were fine. She left him just ripe for another stiff drink. He took a seat near the window.

Local sax player Alvin Davis was releasing some live mellow tunes. Andre listened intently, sipping at his scotch. Occasionally he gazed around the room. There wasn't another black face in sight. He could never understand why jazz had such a bad reputation in the black community. After all, they had started it, but a local cool cat like Alvin Davis could churn out the beats without a black face present to share it with. Andre thought about what might have been if he had continued to play the sax his father gave him for his seventh birthday. He watched Alvin's key changes like an eager learner watching a seasoned driver. When Alvin played *'Someone To Love'* Andre forgot about the fingerwork, becoming totally immersed in the melody.

Three scotches later he was disturbed by a tap on the shoulder. He looked around to see Calvin behind him, looking just like a bouncer in his black suit, white shirt and black bow tie. He pulled up a seat.

"Hey, brotha, want a drink?" Andre asked.

Calvin refused but Andre ordered another scotch on the rocks anyway.

"So what's the SP, Dre?" Calvin asked. "Been having fun, brotha man? Look at you, lipstick on your collar. Shirt all ripped. Man, look like you been playing hard."

He flicked at Andre's jacket. Andre didn't respond. He just stared at the band like he hadn't heard a word. A full two minutes passed before he mumbled:

"It's over man."

"Damn brotha, you've been moving too long to call a halt now."

Andre looked at him.

"I've had it with her up to here."

He tapped the top of his head.

"No more *'do you have to work tonight?'*, *'how long you going to be?'*, *'brush your teeth before you go to bed'*, *'stop wiggling your toes under the sheets'*. No more ear-bashings and tongue-lashings. No more Heather. Glory to God!"

"Brotha man, things ain't that bad. You can work it out."

"Don't be offering advice until you've lived with a woman full-time," he warned Calvin. "You don't know the crap a man has to put up with on a daily basis. Getting it in the ear from first thing in the morning 'til last thing at night."

Andre was getting agitated just thinking about it.

"I may not have had a regular at my pad but I know one thing, brotha Dre."

"Yeah, what's that?"

"At a time when African people should be pulling together, uniting around a common goal, we're moving further and further apart. It bugs me big-time to see a loving couple talk about separating when times get a little rough."

"You don't know what you're saying. The sea isn't just a little rough between us. We're whirling around in a damn tornado. I can't take it any more."

"What's going to happen to the kids?"

Calvin looked concerned.

"What do you think I am? I'll always see my kids are taken care of. I just got their Christmas presents."

"Man, its going to take more than Christmas presents. Brotha, can't you see you could be destroying them? Jermaine's going to need your guidance into manhood. Who's he going to learn from, some street thug?"

"Look, don't lecture me on looking after my kids. You're no child psychologist."

"Brotha, I don't have to be to see that boys just slightly older than Jermaine are strung out on drugs, stealing cars and disrespecting their elders. And every one of them involved in this madness has one thing in common; he's fatherless."

"There you go again, Calvin—moralising! Look, Jermaine is growing up in a three-bedroom semi in Handsworth Wood, not some run-down council block in Hockley."

"Brotha, this thing is spreading like a cancer and kids are going to need strong black men around to guide them through the right channels. They have all this racist nonsense to deal with as well. Brotha, my father didn't teach me how brutal this place can be. I had to find out alone. No child should ever have to do that. We can't expect the sistas to handle everything on their own..."

Andre seized on his words.

"Don't go thinking you have a monopoly on experiencing racism."

"Brotha, I didn't say that."

"You think that 'cause you read some books on the subject you can come and throw it in my face like I'm some bourgeois, middle-class black guy who don't know what's happening in the world? Remember I came from the same street as you. Shopped at the same shops, kicked the same footballs.

"You think you know about racism. I like to see you put up with working in my office day in, day out. I have to deal with it at the cutting edge, the personal level, every damn day.

"You and your radical friends can confine yourselves to the X Centre, but you're not in the real world; I am."

Andre gulped down his scotch. Calvin remained cool.

"Brotha, I know your history. The question is how do you and we as a people go forward to the future?

"Separately—man and woman at each other's throats and dividing our families? Or together in harmony, leading our children into adulthood. That, brotha, is the choice. And that didn't come from a book. It's my gut feeling. Think about it, 'cause I have to get back"

"Yeah, you go on like Mr Righteous about men and woman being together as one. But all those words didn't stop you cheating on Lorna twice. I didn't cheat on Heather, not once. So don't tell *me* what is morally right or wrong."

"Lorna and I ain't married, brotha Dre...neither do we have kids. But you're right, we are together and that shouldn't have happened. I've regretted the two occasions that my strength wasn't what I thought it was. But my failings shouldn't stop you from doing the right thing. Anyway—" he stood up and patted Andre on the shoulder, "—I've got to get back to work. Go in peace brotha."

"Thought you were a friend," Andre muttered. "You sound worse than Heather."

"Brotha, if I didn't care deeply about the two of you I wouldn't be here."

Calvin left the club.

Andre ordered another scotch, quickly sank it and left soon after Alvin Davis had finished his performance.

As he drove away from the club Andre couldn't get Calvin's hypocrisy, Heather's behaviour and the kids' future well-being out of his mind. It wasn't until he got out of the car and slammed the door that he realised he'd driven home to Handsworth Wood.

He looked up at the front bedroom. The light was still on. Heather must be getting ready for bed. He fought with himself, half-inclined to follow Calvin's advice...but visions of Heather humiliating him in the office this afternoon flooded back.

Then the bedroom light went out, and with it any enthusiasm he'd had for disturbing his family.

He was driving up the Walsall Road to his hotel when he saw the flashing blue light in his mirror. *Blast, the police.* They drew up alongside him and signalled for him to pull over.

He stopped the car, knowing that all the scotch he'd drunk that night had put him way over the limit...and that a drink-driving conviction would put his law career on the line...

7
Man Talk

I have two vexations in life at the moment, the weather and Marcia—and not necessarily in that order. It was pissing down with rain and cold as ice, and Marcia was still biggin' up herself against me. My worst nightmares did inside me head a mess 'bout.

Christmas Day came and went and I never even noticed. What the New Year had in store, Jah knows.

All I wanted for Christmas was to see my yout'. I even spent my last Brown on a little black doll for her. But I don't feel she will ever get to see it.

I could've sent it by post. But that don't feel right. What's she gonna t'ink when her father can't even hand her a present face-to-face? Anyway, knowing Marcia, she'd probably tell Charmaine the present come through the chimney with Father Christmas rather than say it was from me.

Cha. It was eating at me not being able to see Charmaine, and—in a way—not seeing Marcia vex me too. I was burning inside to take a trip up to Wolverhampton, especially since it was New Year's Eve. But Theo told me I'm done if I break the injunction while I'm on bail. Moretime since I've got a criminal record now.

Six month suspended sentence is what them give me for boxing the referee at the game last season. Theo and the barrister fought a solid line and I didn't have any previous, so the judge warn me 'bout my future conduct and send me on my way. All the Warriors and some of the team we played against back me up in court; that was crucial to my case. They made the jury understand t'ings were done in the heat of the moment. I feel that persuade the judge to go easy on me. Cha, if only Marcia could do the same.

Anyway, that's more than I can say for Bigga. The two of us went to court in the same week. It almost broke my old lady's heart. One day she was hugging and kissing me like dem clear me of murder, and the next, she down 'pon her knees in tears when Bigga got seven years.

When they read out verdict she start, shouting:

"My boy is innocent, you cyan' do dis. You cyan send 'im a prison."

I can picture her now. But the Krays would have stood a better chance of walking. The old lady forgot that is she pressure Bigga to give himself up to the beastbwoy. I noticed no emotion passed through the big man when the judge gave sentence. Like 'im did know he was going to do a long stretch.

He's still in Greens at the moment, but they plan to move him somewhere far soon and mek it impossible for me to go see him. Without shekels or transport, Greens is about as far as I can afford to go. The old lady still won't visit him. By the time he's released I don't t'ink she'll even recognise him.

It was impossible to pull my duffel coat any tighter, but the wind was turning my body to ice. I had been waiting over an hour for the barber, Skipper. He was the best shears man in Handsworth. Moretime people would come from all over the Midlands to his shop. But to get a cut in regular hours you had to leave home with the blasted milkman.

I reach here eight-thirty and there was already two people queueing; a brotha with a toad-like face and one gyal and her yout'. He didn't seem partial to the winter elements.

Skipper suppose to open the shop at nine. It was now twenty to ten. Since I been coming here he never turn up on time once. And he don't give a blouse and skirt about the customers neither. He knew he was large in the area, no other barber came close to him, so he could take his time. Once, I got so fed up waiting I went to another barber a few streets away.

Him butcher me so bad I had to wear a hat for a month.

Everybody cuss 'bout Skipper, but dem know seh if you want the job done properly, yuh have to wait for the man.

It was ten past ten before Skipper pulled up in his shiny grey Saab. He was making corn, his car proved that.

"Morning, gentlemen," he said, smiling at his frozen customers.

"Is wha' time you call dis, boss?" the toad-face brotha shouted. "I've been here since bloody eight o'clock!"

Skipper pointed at the opening hours on the door.

"Wha' time dat say?"

"Nine 'til six."

"So wha' yuh come at eight for?"

"Skip, it's ten fifteen. You still woulda been late."

"But if you did come at nine you woulda only wait one hour instead of two."

Skipper opened the shop door, and turned on the lights and heating. The rest of us couldn't bother argue, we were too glad to get out of the cold. Skipper disappeared into the back and come back ten minutes later, sipping black coffee. He really couldn't give a rahtid, no man was goin' to hurry him.

Skipper's Salon was one big room of a renovated house. Its large windows looked out onto the busy Soho Road and the walls were covered with full-length mirrors. The old hard chairs scattered around the room were Skipper's way of making sure nobody got too cozy.

People would just come in and spend the whole day chatting, without getting dem hair cut. My father was one of dem man. Skipper never partial during the slack period, but he didn't like to see a customer stand while a freeloader sat. Last time I was in here, 'im just haul an' pull one a 'im closest idren out of a seat to let a customer sit down.

There were two cutting stations in Skipper's place, but whenever he employed someone to help him, almost every man in line would say the immortal words "Me a wait fe Skippa," leaving the help redundant.

More people piled in the shop over the next ten minutes; some of them just looked at the queue and marched straight back out.

Skipper took his time to clean his tools, and change out of his street shoes and into his slippers, so it was another half hour before he called his first customer.

A middle-aged man suddenly leapt to his feet and craned to watch a girl walk by. "Watch de batty 'pon dat nah!"

All heads turned to the window.

"Lawd!"

"Jeeeezum peace!"

I couldn't resist a peep. I just about caught a glimpse of her in a black bomber jacket and tight leggins', swinging her big backside past the shop window.

The man who'd first noticed her got up and walked to the door, watching her every move.

"She mus' a paint dem t'ings 'pon dat backside," he said. "Yuh ever envy a paintbrush sa?"

Everyone in the shop saw the funny side except the gyal with the yout' sitting a few seats from me. She just shook her head like she was disgusted. But she should know better, barber shop is no place fe a gyal.

The shop at last warmed up enough for me to take my coat off. I pulled the Christmas edition of *The Voice* out of my pocket and started to read, but I found my eyes creeping over the top of the paper to size up the gyal. She was big, but a sweet biscuit. Her round face was partly hidden by a long fringe, like Mary Wilson's when she was a Supreme. I think she have Indian blood in her 'cause her hair was black and natural...just like the hard-on I was getting looking at her. I wondered what she'd look like naked. I measured her up to all my woman fantasies. Kym Mazelle without the fake hair...nah...more like Chaka Khan, but with a more wicked smile.

My dirty mind games were disturbed when I sight my old man a limp past the shop like him leg bruck. But last time me see 'im, 'im body look firm and good. I shrunk in my seat 'cause I never want to deal with him today. He stood looking over the road like 'im ready to cross. Then he changed his mind and carry on down the road on the same side. Typical, the man still don't know where 'im going.

"Can I borrow your newspaper?"

I was so engrossed in watching the old man, I didn't notice when the gyal put her son in Skipper's chair. Now she was begging for my *Voice*.

"No problem," I said without hesitating. I folded it and gave it to her.

A sweet smile appeared as she said thanks. She had on a black woolly jumper and trousers and judging by the way her breasts bulged under her jumper, I could see she had outgrown her Playtex. She sat back down and crossed her legs.

I reached for the *Evening Echo* on the table. The place was very quiet. Maybe it was 'cause of a woman di'deh, the regular chat just wasn't happening. I flicked to the job section and a vacancy immediately drew my attention: *'Cook wanted in New Year'*.

But I had applied and been rejected without an interview so many times that the good feeling only lasted a few seconds.

A middle-aged man came through the door. One of the resident chair-warmers. He sat down in the spare barber's chair next and started swinging from side to side, trying to get Skipper's attention.

"So wha'ppen, Skippa. Yuh cyan' say nothin'?"

"Wha' y' want me fe say, Balu?"

"How y' mean? I walk in 'ere, y' suppose to greet me, y' miserable ass."

The man looked for support from the other clients in the shop. Not even a nod came in his direction. So him turn back on Skipper and kiss 'im teeth like 'im mout' a suck egg.

"Balu, hope you nah come a me shop fe mek up noise?"

Balu kissed his teeth again. "Cha man, y'know say me get rob today?"

Skippa laughed. "How y' mean. Somebody mug yuh?"

"Mug me? Yuh mad? Me ready fe any a dem teefin' bwoy out deh!"

"I hear a couple of the Indian jewellry shop get rob yesterday," the man with the patch interjected.

"So me hear 'pon radio. Say dem a look fe two black man," Skipper said.

"Never mind dat!" Balu sounded frustrated that he was being eased out of the limelight. "Me pardner money was suppose ta come through and de woman tell me I haffe wait 'til next week. Why de ass dem cyan' gimme me money 'pon time?" Balu kissed his teeth for a third time before rubbing his hand through his silver coloured beard.

"It serve you right." Skippa said, pointing the scissors at him.

"Wha' y' a talk 'bout?"

"I tell you nah fe get involve in dem pardner foolishness."

I was interested to hear this 'cause my old lady always save in a pardner. Come to t'ink of it she said her hand was coming up. So she was well happy. She could afford to buy a new outfit for church and go shopping with Charmaine. The old lady was well vex that she don't see her grandchild. Keep pressuring me to bring her down. Blasted Marcia have plenty to answer for.

As I returned to the conversation, a cold draught from the door opening brush my neck. I look round and see Shorty bopsing through the door. His head was already peeled closer than a potato so I know it wasn't a fresh cut he wanted.

"Wha'ppen, sa?" Shorty greeted everyone in the shop before sitting down next to me. "Hey, me hear Bigga gone dung fe seven years," he whispered.

"Yeah, man," I replied, thinking Shorty should have gone with him.

"Cha, dat sad, man. Look, me 'ave somet'ing fe you. Check me down me mother yard dis evening. Some big corn inna it fe you"

"Listen, Shorty, me nah inna no wrong doings."

"Easy nah, man, yuh don't know wha' me a deal wid."

"Shorty, me don't wan' know. Yuh already let me brother tek de rap fe you. T'ink say me nah know dat?"

"Easy, man, easy 'pon dat talk. Is Bigga tell yuh dat?"

I gave him an eyeballing that told him not to test me.

Shorty turned his attention to look at Skippa. "So 'ow t'ings, sa?"

"Busy, busy."

Balu butted in again. "Is not stupidness. Pardner is like a bank. Me a save me money."

"It is not like a bank," Skipper said, he stopped cutting the boy's head momentarily and looked around the shop to get everyone's attention. "If it was a bank you'd be gettin' interest on wha' y' put in. How many times y' draw your hand a year?"

"Twice," Balu replied, sensing he was being set up for a big one.

"Two times a year. How much y' put in?"

"Ten a week," he replied cautiously. "Wha' y' wan know fa?"

"Ten a rahtid week. Dat's..." Skipper looked up to the ceiling to do his calculations, "...forty pound a month and four hundred and eighty pound a year. Yuh see de problem is yuh put in four hundred and eighty and get back four hundred and eighty so you not better off. If you did put dat money in de bank you would get interest 'pon it."

"Is true," Shorty said distantly. His eyes fixed on the window like he was waiting for something.

"If black man did run de pardie right and each man invest dem hand like de Indian man have, Skippa and Mr B and de man who own de bread shop wouldn't be de only black businessman on bloodclaat Soho Road. Yuh check it," the middle-aged man said.

"There's no unity between black man," Shorty added, looking at me like he was trying to make a point.

"Uh huh."

"Is true."

Balu tried to argue another line about the bank being to blame for the lack of black business but he was on a losing wicket.

"Yuh 'ave a point, Balu 'bout de bank not givin' black man loans," Skippa conceded. " 'Cause I've been tryin' to get one to renovate dis place, and dem gi' me nothin' but excuse. But there's enough black people inna Birmingham to join together to start a little t'ing, and when dat tek off buy another one and so on."

"Dat nah happen. Black man too craven," Balu said.

"If black man was too craven, how come 'im did runnin' de pardner system from time?"

Shorty suddenly jumped up. "Hey Skippa, yuh 'ave a back door?" Then he charged across the room and through the door.

Skipper stop cutting the little yout' head and started after Shorty. "Wha' de raas a go on?"

Before I could get to my feet three white man in suit and tie burst through the door. I know dem was beastbwoy. They charged through the back door pushing Skipper out the way. Everyman was now on his feet trying to look through the door.

"Sit back down nah, man," Skipper pleaded.

But he would have needed a machine gun to get dem to miss this action.

"I wonder wha' 'im do," one said.

"He mussa teef somet'ing, de little crook. Me know me see 'im face somewhe' before," Balu said.

Within a few minutes seven Babylon came back with Shorty hand in cuffs bend up behind his back. He was in pain and screaming out:

"Aargh. Me hand, easy nah, man."

The beastbwoy just push him through the door.

"Yuh don't haffe hold 'im like so," the patch-eye brotha said.

"Shut the fuck up before I nick you as well," a big-face beastbwoy warned.

All the man move to the front door. There was a hum of disapproval at the way the beastbwoy were treating Shorty but no man voice his concern louder than a whisper. The fuss soon died down but the shop continued to let off on the topic. Out the corner of my eye, I could see the gyal raising her eyes from the paper, looking bored as the discussion went around in circles...from Shorty being a big time crook to mistaken identity to police brutality and back again.

Suddenly the gyal jumped. "Shabba's comin' to Birmingham!"

I looked across to see she was talking to me.

"I must get a ticket," she continued excitedly, then started to sing Shabba's tune, 'Wicked in Bed'. I didn't care too much for him—then again, not many man did. I used to hate the way Marcia would wind up herself to 'im record like she really in bed with him. Anyway, how can a maaga fart like that be wicked in bed? Rahtid fraud. Just then, the same tune came over the radio. Talk about blasted coincidence; I must be cursed.

"So what's your New Year's resolution?" she said to me as the DJ cut in on the record to make a request.

I didn't want to expose myself by telling the truth.

"Well me jus' wan' good health, y'know...wha' 'bout yuh?"

"Well, I want to lose some weight," she said, tapping her thighs. "And make some money."

That lined me up. I remembered that I was still short on shekels. Mr Lindsey had been avoiding me for the best part of two months

103

and took off to Jamaica for the New Year without even mentioning the little pay rise we reasoned over.

"So what do you do?" she asked. "You look like a boxer or some kind of athlete."

"Me play lickle basketball, but me is a chef by profession. Me in between jobs at de moment. In fact me jus' sight a job inna de paper dat me a go apply fa."

I sat beside her to show her the situations vacant page, and she told me what I should write on my CV and covering letter. As the conversation got deeper I learned she was a careers liaison officer, who visited schools in Handsworth advising children on their job opportunities. She had her work cut out, 'cause if there were any jobs in this place somebody was keeping them secret.

Last week the Job Centre had three jobs on offer and all a dem was for janitors.

Our conversation was interrupted when Skipper started to brush down the little boy with talcum powder. She got up, took out five pounds and paid Skipper. After putting on their coats she pulled a card out of her bag and handed it to me.

"If you're not doing anythin' tonight, come down," she said, flashing that criss smile again.

"Nice, nice," I replied as I got up to take my place in Skipper's chair.

"And don't forget to bring a bottle."

"Seen...Yvette," I replied, reading her name off the card. "Me name Marcus by the way."

"Okay, Marcus. Hope to see you tonight."

It was still raining when I left Skipper about midday. I was hungry like a lion but the readies was in short supply. They refused to give me unemployment benefit, saying I hadn't paid enough contributions, and even my supplementary was cut to the bone when they found out I left work under my own steam.

'Nuff time I trod up to the dole office to complain that I don't have enough to live on and the same feisty gyal tell me say they can't do raas 'bout it. Rule is rule. But dem cyan' expect a big rahtid man to live on thirty-three buff a week. If the Babylon never grab Shorty I woulda t'ink seriously bout him offer.

And since we've gone two weeks without playin' I won't even get my weekly expenses from the Warriors.

The last game we played was when we got our arses kicked by

Cheshire. I still think the referee was racist. It's my game to play physical and when the man keep blowing his whistle for pussy fouls, me game gone. One t'ing though, I never lick him, 'cause it would definitely have been the end of my basketball career. And I couldn't take that.

I let my clean head catch some rain as I made the ten minute walk from Skipper down to Beresford's. 'Mr B' cooked the best Caribbean takeaway food this side of the West Indies...but like Skipper, he was on BMT. Fortunately the miserable wretch only work in the evening, so his wife was on duty when I got there. She was nice, reminded me of my old lady with her head tie. Is like all the nice Caribbean women marry fuck up man.

Beresford's had a large and varied menu on the wall but very few of the dishes on the menu were ever available. I always jest with him to employ me and mek me change up his menu. But 'im say his recipe is secret and no ragga going to come in and rip him off.

I ordered a breast of deep fried chicken and a strawberry Nurishment.

I sat down on the stool facing the window and was tearing away at the chicken when I felt a tap on my shoulder. As I turned, cleaning the grease from the side of my mouth, Mr B stood over me with his big hair sticking up like Don King.

"Yuh pay ta eat in?" he asked, knowing full well I didn't.

I smiled.

"Rasta—"

"Don't rasta me," he cut in. "The comfort of inside don't come cheap. Fifty pence extra."

"Cha Mr B, yuh' a tek liberty."

"Liberty? Liberty? Yuh know 'ow much it is fe sit inna McDonalds?"

I dug into my pocket for the fifty pence and gave it to him.

As I finished my chicken I saw a sweet bwoy pull up in a bright red Porsche. When he got out I realised it was Theo. He crossed the street to a vacant office, with a white man at his side like some lackey. Sometime I wish I could work with the white bwoy like him and Andre. It seem the secret to success. But me nah able fe do that. Cyan' play that game. Even Calvin, with all him black t'ing, get on with them. I don't know, it just don't feel consistent.

I was going to hail him but decided against it. Theo was too white-boyish for me. He was doing a good job on my case though, hoping to get me some visiting access to Charmaine.

Anyway, he'd probably feel a way if I shouted him while he's on business.

Evening approached fast and I was watching the box as usual and getting more and more restless. I wasn't sure if I was going to Yvette's party. I don't really like house parties 'cause dem always full with bwoys who wan' act like big man. Pint ass raggas who want to cut you for stepping on their shoes. Also the spliff messed with my breathing system.

But with no basketball and the gym closed for the holiday I needed to release some energy. I thought two hundred sit-ups and a hundred press-ups would do it, but my body was in need of more excitement. I went for a five-mile run and came back for a shower. I still never feel right.

In the end I realised that I'd been living like blasted Howard Hughes since I split with Marcia, and I decided to go and shake a leg at Yvette's. After all, it was New Year's Eve. I went to the wardrobe and pulled out a pair of black Farah pants and my white Pierre Cardin shirt. Lucky my only pair of good shoes were black, t' rahtid.

It was ten-thirty when I remembered that I had to bring a bottle. I threw on my jacket and rushed down to the off licence, but he had already closed. Rahtid. I never wanted to turn up at Yvette with me two long hand so I waited half an hour for a bus to take me to The Star Club—the only place I could get a bottle this time of night. Yvette's yard wasn't far from the club, so I could just jog round well before midnight.

When I got to the club I was surprised to see Mr Lindsey's car was in the drive. I thought he was still on holiday. At the door the bouncers nodded and let me walk straight in. Made me feel big in the area 'cause enough people did ah queue to get in. The New Year's Eve party was in full swing. Yuh should see the over-fifties shuffling in the New Year.

I knew the gyal behind the bar so I managed to get some white wine for quarter of the price down and pay the rest later. As I was about to move out I sight Mr Lindsey leaving his office. As soon as our eyes made four he turned and hustle back to his office. Cha, me nah let him get 'way this time. I followed him down the corridor and opened his door without knocking.

"M-M-M-Marcus. Nice ta see you here at our New Year's Eve party."

"Me nah stay," I replied. "Yuh know somet'ing, yuh never did

106

mek dat decision."

"W-w-w-hat decision dat, Marcus? Me mek hundreds a day. Me is a busy man. Y'know me 'ave to see to dis place, me house, me car and...and de basketball, a-a-and...."

"Missa Lindsey, me a talk 'bout me raise. Times tight, y'know? You say yuh was goin' see 'bout payin' me a extra twenty buff a week."

I was trying hard to keep my cool. He came towards me and placed his hands on my shoulders, that had begun to stiffen with the after effects of the press-ups.

"Marcus, y'know de Warriors fightin' fe dem financial life. Dat Manchester trip cost me a packet. Where yuh t'ink de money come from? Ou-ou-outta my pocket. Look, if unnu win de league and den promotion me 'ave plans fe a big sponsorship deal. We a go play inna dat new National Arena up town and everybody a go get a pay rise. Until den, no money inna de till."

I had heard all this talk before. And that's all it was—talk.

"Missa Lindsey, me cyan even eat proper food. Me been the club's leading player for five years. Me deserve lickle more."

"Look, I already give you five pound more than Calvin and Andre and yuh get de same as Joni."

"Bloodclaat Joni!" I had to let off. "Ow come 'im get de same as me? Dat nah right. Man cyan' even tie 'im bootlace properly."

"Anyway, Marcus—" Lindsey interrupted, "—de way me see you play in dat last game, I don't t'ink you inna position to be criticisin' or askin' fe a rise."

I decided to play my trump card.

"Well, yuh know, Missa Lindsey, me nah play fe de Warriors fe de rest of de season. Then next year me lookin' a new club. Wolverhampton already a size me up."

I know Lindsey wasn't going to let his rival Mr Brown take away his best player after already poaching his assistant coach. They played golf together, but they couldn't stand each other. I'd have to step over Lindsey's dead body to go to Wolverhampton.

"Y-Y-Yuh cyan do dat, Marcus, yuh sign contract fe de rest of de season. I'll sue you."

"Listen here, Missa Lindsey. Me officially injured. Yuh gwan sue me 'cause me injured?"

I turned to leave knowing he would call me back, as sure as night follows day...

"W-w-wait, wait Marcus! Okay, I'll give yuh an extra ten quid a

107

week."

"Twenty, is wha' me a look fe..."

"Okay, okay. Fifteen, and I'll make the first payment now."

Before I had even agreed Mr Lindsey took the fifteen buff out of his wallet.

I took the money.

"You've got a deal. It's a pleasure doin' business with you."

Lindsey mumbled somet'ing 'bout bankruptcy and followed me out. But I know Lindsey never pays what he can't afford. So I didn't feel no way 'bout taxing him. The man haffe learn he cyan' run a basketball team on the cheap.

I jogged all the way up to Yvette's yard. I could hear the music from half-way down the street. From the number of cars parked in odd positions, I could tell the place was well ram.

Yvette lived in a downstairs flat in a large, old-time house. When I knocked, a big fat geezer push him head 'round the door.

"Ticket?" he said, his face trembling in time to the reggae baseline.

I searched my pockets—I had left the rahtid t'ing in my duffel coat.

"Me forget me ticket, boss."

"No ticket, no entry."

"Yvette invite me, sa. Look, me 'ave bottle."

"Look, 'nuff man turn up with bottle and no ticket and dem had to go. There's no exceptions."

"Okay, call Yvette," I pleaded.

"Look man, wha' wrong wid you? You can't hear? No ticket, no entry."

"Who's that?"

I was sure that was Yvette's voice.

"Some fool," he muttered.

She put her head around the door. She had on a low-cut dress and I got two eye full of breasts.

"Oh, it's you!" she said, with that bright smile. "I thought you weren't comin'. It's Okay, Tiny, I invited him."

I could just about squeeze past the fat mess on the door, and as I did he try to eyeball me. I returned the compliment. I wasn't going to back down.

"Stop it, you two," Yvette said. "Men always have to get this macho thing going."

As expected, the place was packed with a decent crowd. Y'know,

108

the type that don't stamp out cigarette ends on your carpet or piss in your bath when there's a toilet right beside it.

"What do you want to drink?" Yvette asked.

"Jus' a Coke or somet'ing soft," I replied, handing her the bottle of wine.

"Coke! This is New Year's Eve. Have something stronger."

"Nah, me don't drink strong stuff."

"Ooh, that's different. A man that doesn't drink alcohol."

She disappeared into the kitchen.

Looking around I got the feelin' that it was the kind of party that I would like. The ratio of gyal to man was about two-to one, and they were fine-looking fillies. I was standing amongst a group of women butterflying to Buju Banton—each of them dressed to the nines, hairstyle immaculate and body fit, nah raas. I wiped my mouth in sheer anticipation, then felt someone next to me and turned to find the same feisty gyal from the dole office smiling with me.

"Fancy seeing you here, Mister Codrington."

"Bwoy, me cyan' get way from unnu people."

"That's right. We're everywhere," she laughed. Is then I realise that all the gyal in front of me was dole office people.

Yvette came back with a plastic cup full of Coke.

"Oh, so you know Veronica then?"

"Yeah we know each other," Veronica said. "We have a regular meeting every two weeks, and it's not a pleasant exchange."

"Oh, really?" Yvette replied, her face dropping.

"It nothin', me jus' sign at she station each two week."

I wondered why I was defending myself when me and Yvette had nothing. She laughed.

"Oh, I thought you were having a deep thing with woman upstairs."

Bloodclaat, I thought. She live upstairs, to rahtid. That's all I needed.

The lights around the set dimmed and Yvettte came to stand close to me.

"So where's your partner?" she asked, gazing up into my eyes. I got the feelin' she wanted to make me hers for the night.

"Wha' partner?"

I know she was checking out my availability. I wondered should I come straight or play hard to get? Gyal love mysterious man.

"Me a live an independent life," I told her.

"What does that mean? Your woman can't tell you what to do...or

109

you're single?"

I smiled, but didn't answer. She moved closer to me. I could feel her breasts on my arm. They were soft and warm. I moved my arm slightly and it seemed to disappear among the soft tissue.

"So, whe' yuh man de?"

"What man? I don't have one."

We both smiled.

The MC fling down Beres Hammond's 'Tempted To Touch' then let rip with Frankie Paul's 'Could It Be Love?' My arms took the cue and wrapped themselves around Yvette's waist. Yvette held on to me tight.

"I don't have a man. Justin's dad ran out on us two years ago and I haven't seen him since."

The story had a familiar ring to it. Man a run away from their pickney, but me wan' see my yout' and can't. T'ings in life was mess up.

Just when things were getting cozy, we were interrupted by the MC shouting ten seconds to 1993. The whole party joined in the countdown and when we reached zero Yvette turned and planted a kiss on me. I didn't argue, I just gave as good as I got. We spent the next hour in each other's arms, only breaking when she had to go and dish out the curried goat and rice.

When she was away, I spotted Levi Lewis from the Warriors. Even though the New Year was only seconds old he was probably already with his tenth girl of the year. I managed to push my way through the crowd to talk to him. He was still feelin' a way over the Cheshire beating but I came to the reasoning that the game might have been the best thing that could happen to us.

We were too confident and needed the kick up the backside. This year I promised myself that nothin' was going to stop us winning everyt'ing.

As we talked, I glanced into the crowd and couldn't believe who I saw. Rahtid Marcia, standing there like she had no problem in the sequinned dress I bought her last Christmas. Dress cost me two hundred notes. *What the hell was she doing there?* She was close to some ragga bwoy I recognised as one of Zorro's men. *What the fuck was she doin' mixin' with them kind of people?*

I left Levi and pushed through the crowd. I never care who I was knocking aside or whose toes I was steppin' on. All the things Theo told me not to do I felt like doing. She had her back to me, rubbing down with this roughneck.

I tapped her on the shoulder. When she turned around, she was surprised to see me.

"I wan' talk to yuh," I demanded

Her eyes grew wide with rage. "No—I'm here to enjoy myself. Who do the hell do you think you are, anyway?"

The bwoy she was with tried to put his hand between us. I pushed it out of the way.

"Tell him to ease off unless 'im wan dis dance fe done right now?" I said, ready to rip his head off his shoulders with one lick.

She whispered something in his ear. He nodded and then tried to stare me out. But I stood firm and militant. Nah mek no pussytail bwoy a look down on me.

Marcia followed me outside, the wind felt like it was blowing right through my skin.

"What the hell do you think you're doing?" Marcia asked.

"So wha'ppen, yuh seein' dat bwoy?"

"Marcus, it's none of your business who I'm seeing. We're finished."

"Dat fool is a waster. Why yuh nah grow up?"

"You're tellin me to grow up? You, who lashes out like a spoilt child whenever you don't get your way? Anyway, if he is a waster he's no worse than you."

I felt a rage coming over me.

"Look, me don't give a rahtid 'bout wha' you wan' do, but me haffe t'ink 'bout my yout'. Whe' she deh anyway, when yuh a party wid yuh idiot bwoy?"

"Don't you dare accuse me of neglecting my daughter!"

"Our daughter. She's mine as well."

"Really? If you behaved like a human being then I wouldn't have to look for a babysitter on the few occasions I do want to go out."

That was the limit. I slammed my fist into the brick wall. Marcia jumped like someone had sent two hundred volts through her body. Blood started to pour from my hand, but I ignored the pain. "I don't wan my yout' callin' every bwoy 'pon de street Daddy. I'm her Daddy, and she haffe know dat."

"So that's it, Marcus. You frightened another man might take your place? Well, tough. You should have thought about that before you started throwing your fists around. Sorry, I've got my own life to lead now."

She pushed past me and went back into the dance. I followed her. My hand was covered in blood. She walked straight back into his arms. He whispered something in her ear and they started giggling. My heart was burning. The bwoy was looking straight in my face as he scrubbed down with Marcia, as if to tell me there was nothing I could do. He was messing with the wrong man.

It was about thirty minutes before he made his way to the door, leaving Marcia alone in the room. I hurried out after him. He went into the bathroom. As he was about to shut the door I ran up and forced it open, then I pushed him inside and bolted the door behind me. He shaped as if he was going in his pocket for a weapon, but before he could make a move I sent a right hook upside his head with my blood-stained hand. He screamed like a woman, before collapsing in a heap on the floor.

I picked him up by his throat and held his head over the toilet bowl. I wanted to flush his whole nasty body down the bog.

"Let me tell yuh somethin', is best you don't see Marcia again, y'hear? 'Cause if you hurt one fuckin' hair on her or my yout's head, you're a dead man. Yuh hear?"

He mumbled something, and when I was satisfied he'd got the message, I let him slide to the floor.

As I made my way to the front door, the doorman eyed me like he suspected something was wrong—but before he could say a word, I slapped the fat fucker across his face. He wobbled back trying to keep his balance, but I didn't see what happened next.

I pulled the door open and left.

8

Badness Around The Corner

Helen was the kine of babe a homie felt down with.

The bitch had class. She was a looker, had brains, laughed when a woman supposed to and she had a bank like a homie's never seen. Bitch was buyin' up shit like Getty. Dollars no object. Kept a homie in the manner he was supposed to be kept.

We'd been hangin' since the Cheshire game and kicked in the New Year Beverly Hills style. She chauffeured me down to London, and we had lunch at the Savoy, feastin' on caviar and all that million dollar shit, then went on to a theatre. Homie couldn't tell you what play was on stage, 'cause we were gettin' busy in the balcony. Spent the rest of the night bumpin' and grindin' away in some phat ass West End hotel. Bitch couldn't get enough of my black ass.

Helen was takin' care of business. Anything a homie wanted was mine; gold chains, sweet kicks, hoochie even put a thousand pound system in my wheels.

Damn, she was so easy-goin' as well—a homie's delight. Only commitment she booked in from tip off was that she be given the three point treatment under the rim. She had her little white stock-broker fiance up in Manchester and was due to get hitched in the summer, but that didn't stop her bringin' her ass to be serviced by me.

Since she was cool with me I let her know that I was hangin' steady with Cheryl. Shit didn't make a dollar of difference. Straight up. In fact the honey got off on our stolen nights of the wild thang.

Cheryl couldn't understand why I didn't want to spend part of the Christmas vacation with her and her folks down in Bristol. But hell, homie was in no mood for that separate bedroom thing, and goin' to midnight mass wasn't high on my entertainment agenda. I had to make some bull excuse about needin' a complete rest to recharge.

The only way she could talk to me was when I phoned her ass, 'cause her pops had put the brakes on her making long distance calls after Cheryl made half a dozen to me when I was in the States. The old man classed Birmingham as foreign territory.

Three days into the New Year, Helen was still pining for me. We were in bed down at my shack until mid-morning, then Helen gave my crib a clean-out. Honey did a five-star job, could see the reflection of a homie's dick in the wooden floor. Place was spotless apart from the empty bottle of Chardonnay and a five ounce draw of weed, the only evidence of our night of passion.

"What do you want for breakfast, Winston?" she called from the kitchen area.

Homie paused for a moment. I didn't even know what was in the cooler. Before she left, Cheryl had packed it tighter than it's ever been. Said she didn't want me getting skinny while she was away. Fine chance, baby. I was goin' a la carte and that beat muffins from Sainsbury's. No danger.

"You're da man," I shouted back. Helen was looking in the fridge. She had on one of my Delaware College tee-shirts and no panties. As she bent over, her cute little booty caught some fresh air. It was an opportunity not to be missed. Homie slapped her full on the rump. Shit wobbled like jelly mama used to make.

She re-surfaced from the cooler with a pack of bacon and a box of eggs in her hand and homie planted a smoocher on her cheek before heading for the shower.

Helen had already sorted afternoon breakfast by the time I came out, and was sitting on the floor in front of the TV watchin' the seasonal James Bond movie.

Unlike Cheryl, Helen had few inhibitions. She sat with her tee-shirt half way up her butt and her legs spread so wide an Inter-City 125 could travel through.

I sat down beside her, but she didn't even try to cover herself. Just sat there munching on a bacon and egg sandwich like she was alone in her own place. She not only kept her shit open but the invitation to my homeboy was as green as grass.

"So when's your girlfriend coming back?" she asked, eyes still peeled to Roger Moore waxin' some blond stuff.

"Tomorrow."

"Ah..." she said, popping the last piece of sandwich into her mouth. "I've only got one more night to fuck your brains out then."

"Well, I can come up to Manchester if yer wanna continue dis episode."

"No. I promised my fiance I'd spend a little time with him."

She finally closed her legs.

"But you can come the following weekend if you like."

"We start shootin' ball for real that weekend, but we'll sort it."

114

She smiled, took her plate to the sink, then went off to shower. As she sang 'Young, Gifted and Black' under the spray, I started comparing her with Amanda. Helen was better looking. Her shoulder-length brunette hair and grey eyes gave her the look of an innocent schoolgirl. But you couldn't beat Amanda in the sack.

Unfortunately the bitch couldn't keep her big mouth shut. Made a sorry ass move by mentionin' what happened between us to a friend, one of Zorro's homegirls. And when you let another ho know your business, shit gonna spread faster than a California bush fire. When Zorro finished beatin' on her, her face was worse than Frank Bruno's when Tim Witherspoon finished with him. Homie heard she needed serious surgery.

The only good shit to come out of it was Five-O coaxed her into filing against Zorro, so he's now on remand Greens awaitin' sentence. Shit sounded like NWA to a homie's ears. Man knows, if the G had set sight of my ass...*Damn!* Would've been a cripple. Probably finish my whole b-ball career over one dumb-ass bitch.

Helen came back into the living area naked. Her backside and 34C titties wobbled as she walked to the bag of underwear and tee-shirts lying on the bed. She didn't hang with any clean clothin'—hoochie just bought a load of gear when we were kickin' in London, then sacked them in the garbage after wearin' them once. Said her closet was already packed with enough clothes.

Time was against me again. Damn, it was already four-thirty. We planned to go to the cinema to see *White Men Can't Jump*. Seen the movie three times but Helen wanted to watch it again. Bitch wanted to eye up Wesley Snipes in them tight ass pants. Then she'd go on sayin' the punk looked like me. Bitch even wanted me to reverse my cap like Billy Hoyle! I told her that shit went out with Afrika Bambaataa. The phone rang. Helen went to answer it but I pipped her to it by a Carl Lewis vest.

"Stop trippin', Helen, it could be Cheryl!"

"I thought she couldn't phone you."

"Shit, there's call boxes in Bristol."

"She really believes you spent Christmas by yourself? She can't be that stupid."

"Cheryl ain't stoopid. Just chill da shit out," I replied, feelin' pissed at her.

It was only Marcus calling, wanting to hi-jack some of the NBA basketball tapes I copied from Screensport. I told him to hurry if he wanted to collect them 'cause I'd soon be history at the crib. We moved quickly on to chattin' about the Cheshire game. Brotha went through every false move he made. Sounded like he was hurtin' bad. The humiliation was total and the whole league knew about it.

The only place Marcus could hide was up his own butt and the homie was talkin' like he had already made a reservation for a one-way ticket there.

But Marcus' game was the only one I respected on the roster. He's quick off the wood with a vertical leap that's not supposed to come from a man his size. Brotha played with heart too, and for that homie had his back each and every time.

Helen, now fully clothed, came and kneeled in front of me, put her hands down the front of my sweats and started pumping away on my pride. My breathin' got heavier and heavier. To Marcus, shit, must have sounded like I'd just finished a race with Linford Christie. Then the bitch tried to get her mouth round my homeboy, but none of that lips shit was goin' down in my parlour. I called time on Marcus and pulled her head out of my pants. Marcus would soon be here for the tapes. Anyway I was into marathons, not short sprints.

I had over a hundred b-ball tapes arranged in rows around ten high on the floor by my bed. Most of them were on the Yankee system and not worth shit to me 'cause I couldn't play them here. I selected three, hoping Marcus would be satisfied.

Helen and I were playing the Sega b-ball game when the bell rang. As usual, Mrs O'Farrell was out quicker than lightning to answer it. Within a minute there was a knock on my door.

"Whassup, homie?" I said, about to give him a high five. I held back when I saw his hand in plaster. "Whadda shit happened ta yer, man?"

Marcus walked into the room. "Me get a lickle carried away, y'know. New Year celebration and t'ing," he shrugged.

"What's da damage, bro?"

I took a closer look at the plaster.

"Doctor say is a hairline facture so is gonna be 'bout three weeks before I can tek it off, and another week before me can flex it again."

"Shit, Marcus. Dat's six weeks off da blacktop. Coach must be trippin' on yer ass."

"Me don't even mention it to me modder, let alone Coach. Me a go past down trainin' by de end of de week and see wha' im a say."

"Not to worry, man. I gotcha back. Pick up da void and shit 'til yer git back," I said, faking a jump shot with an imaginary ball.

"Me know say y' ready. All me wan is to be fit fe dat return wid

116

dem rahtid white bwoy."

When Helen joined us, Marcus quit dissin' white people.

"You remember my babes, Helen?" I said, placing my right hand around her sweet little waist.

"No wonder you did ah breathe so hard fe on de phone jus' now." We all laughed.

"We met at that hotel in Manchester," Helen said. "You had a mean look on your face. It scared the shit out of me."

Marcus could just recall being introduced to her.

"Oh yeah. Me did jus' 'ave a nasty ordeal. Don't read too much inna it," he replied apologetically. I left Marcus and Helen talking and went to put the tapes in the bag Helen had taken her undies out of.

"Watch da Chi-Town-New York first," I said, handing him the bag. "Dat's a bad li'l game. Jordan, man, he's da man. Pulls dis dope 360 on Starks, shit wuz da livin'." I spun in a circle and performed a slammin' action. "Watch for da dunk by Ewing over Pippen. Awesome!"

Marcus was just warming to my DIY commentary, when there was a knock on my door. I opened the door and froze. Cheryl was standin' there with this nice-to-see-you smile on her face.

"I thought I'd surprise you and come back a day early," she said, sniffling her red nose at me.

Damn! this shit was for real. I stood there like the Statue of Liberty, dumfounded, motionless. A hot flush went through my body. My mouth was jammed. I managed to finally jar it open.

"I...er, I didn't hear the bell, babes," I stuttered.

"Your landlady was cleaning the doorstep when I arrived. She sent me straight up."

Damn you Mrs O'Farrell. I told you never to let anyone past who hadn't rung the bell. Shit, man gotta have some warnin' if he's about to be buried alive.

"Well, aren't you going to let me in?"

I held the door open and she walked past me. I squeezed my eyes shut, wondering how the hell was I going to retrieve this scam.

I closed the door and placed my finger to my lips, indicating to Marcus and Helen not to voice a thing. There was a deafenin' silence. Cheryl sensed there was something wrong. Homie had to add some authenticity to the crisis.

"Ah, Cheryl, yer down wit' my homeboy Marcus?"

"Hi," she replied.

"And this is his girl, Helen."

Marcus screwed his face as if to say *'Man this is your personal shit, don't include me'*.

"Say hello to my babes Cheryl," I continued.

It was the best live shit a homie could come up with. They completed the formalities and Cheryl went to sit on the sofa. Helen sat beside her and Marcus just stood behind them not knowin' what the fuck to do. Homie wished he would just loosen up and go with the flow.

"Ah, Marcus and Helen are jus' collectin' some b-ball videos," I said, watching the two women.

"Yeah, I love basketball," Helen told Cheryl. "Especially that Mark Jordan. Wow, he's a stunner."

"Michael Jordan."

I couldn't help but put the fool straight 'cause even Cheryl knew who Michael Jordan was.

"Of course, silly me," Helen said, giggling.

Cheryl asked about Marcus' hand, and Helen dived in before he could answer with some bullshit story about how Marcus saved her from a bunch of thugs. I could see she was enjoying herself. While she was giving Cheryl the lyrics, I went around to the bed and kicked her clothes under it. Marcus left the discussion and came to join me.

"Yuh a live a dangerous life y'know, sa," he whispered.

I looked at him, smiled and gave him the rest of the plot. I could see Cheryl looking over her shoulder at us but as far as she was concerned we were just engaging in homiez talk. Marcus had had enough:

"Helen, it's about time we were leavin'."

"Oh, are you sure, darlin'? It was just gettin' interesting talking to Cheryl."

"We've got to get to the theatre in thirty minutes," he continued. He was heading for an Oscar...but he was comin' dangerously close to overdoin' it. *Which homie goes to the theatre?*

Helen got up from the settee.

"Let me just get my bag, darlin'," she said.

I saw them to the door and down the stairs. When we passed Mrs O'Farrell she looked at Marcus leaving with Helen, then at me, shook her head and retreated to her room. Outside I gave Helen a kiss and told her to ring me on my mobile tomorrow.

Then I remembered I was skint and begged some dollars from Helen. She had no change and threw me a fifty pound note.

When I came back into the room Cheryl was staring out of the window. I slammed the door to get her attention. She smiled and gave me a hug a grizzly would be proud of. I closed my eyes and grinned, knowing I had pulled off a bigger strategic operation than Colin Powell in the Gulf.

"I thought Marcus not long had a baby with a black girl from Wolverhampton?" she said as she released me and made her way to the kitchen.

"Had ta give her her P45."

"Well, it looks like he's landed on his feet. The white girl must be rich. She wears Coco Chanel and it was the perfume, not no eau de toilette. Must have cost a bomb."

I always thought Cheryl should moonlight as a prospector 'cause she had a nose that could sniff out oil buried thousands of feet underground.

"And I saw her get into a Mercedes," she continued.

"Yeah man, homeboy said he was attracted to da phat wallet."

"You black men are so money-orientated. White girls only have to flash their cheque books and you all come running like dogs on heat. Anyway, things can't be all that great between them. He left on foot."

"Straight up? Wonder what's da real deal. Shit ain't what it seems."

I came up behind Cheryl and held her around her waist.

"So...how we gonna kick in da New Year?"

We decided to stay in and drink some of the wine Cheryl had bought before she left for Bristol. It seemed ages since we had sat and talked like that. Most the time I'd see her after ball on weekdays or after home games at the weekend. On days when I wasn't trainin' Cheryl had gym classes, so we very rarely got time to do anything apart from the nasty. She was her normal beautiful self in her red and black Nike tracksuit and Reebok trainers. She wore light make-up, although a face like hers didn't need it.

We got tight on the settee. We munched away on little nibbles and got through a second bottle of wine. She had a fresh body smell that was completely different from the white girls I've been with. Not that the white girls I've had a piece of stunk—wouldn't catch a homie treatin' them like roses if they had—but for me black girls had a more subtle and invitin' body smell.

Cheryl rested her chin on her knees, which were tucked up close to her chest.

"Where did you spend Christmas Day?"

"Right here in my crib," I replied.

"Didn't you see your mum?"

"Nope."

"Why, Winston?" she asked, as if I'd committed the worst sin on earth.

"Mama's only gonna come wit some shit 'bout why I didn't finish my studies or get a career. Wasn't in da mood for it, man. I dropped her a line and wished her all da best."

"So you spent the whole day on your own. Here?"

"Da Inspecta turned up," I replied, wondering' if she was going to ask what I had for Christmas dinner.

"Oh...I see."

I know she had a beef with it.

"What about Janet, when did you last see her?"

"I was wit' her on Christmas Eve, dropped off some presents. Why?"

"I'm getting really worried about her. She stays in that flat all the time. She doesn't go anywhere and when I saw her before I left for Bristol she'd lost a lot of weight."

"Mama said da same shit on da phone. Homie jus' put her weight loss down to da supermodel vibe. You females always tryin' ta git skinny."

"Winston, I think it's deeper than that. Do you think she's recovered from what happened to Joseph?"

"Dunno, babes, but does anyone git righted? Shit, one second life's a ball then, bam, It's ripped from yer, jus' like dat. Janet doesn't deserve dis shit."

"She doesn't. It's a real shame. She was full of zest when we were at the Beeb together..."

My mobile rang, cuttin' her in full flow. I got up and went over to the table by the bed to answer it. *Damn!* It was Helen, sayin' that she'd just got back to Manchester and was looking forward to makin' our next episode a full length feature.

Cheryl could hear my every word.

"Okay, nice to link words again. Say yo to all da homiez up north and next time yer in da vicinity, touch my digits. Bye."

I ended the call then went and sat back down next to Cheryl.

"Some punk ass sucka I met after the ball game in Manchester. He wuz in da hood over da Christmas vacation checkin' out some cousins and I hooked up wit his sorry ass. Man jus' talked a load of bull."

"That'll teach you to go out without me," Cheryl laughed, moving closer to me. "Winston, did you miss me?"

Homie paused. The question sounded like something skiers hear before an avalanche. She was testin' me with one of them no-victory numbers.

No matter how a homie answers he ends up in the slammer. But I had to put my shit up to get it blown down.

"S'pose I did..."

"Only suppose? That doesn't sound too hopeful."

"Damn, whadda yer wan' me to say? Shit couldn't happen widout yer? Nites were so wack, I couldn't git no shut-eye wit 'out yer by my side? Dat my very existence depend on you hangin' wit' me?"

"No"

"Yer feelin' insecure, ain't yer?" I said, pushing her shoulder.

"No, it's just..."

"Jus' what, Cheryl?"

"Do you love me, Winston? I mean, *really* love me."

Cheryl had gone for the big money shot. Never once thought about this love thing. Shit never sat right with me. Why bitches so hung up on this love thing, anyway? Don't mean shit.

"You don't, do you?"

Shit like this could mess up a phat evening. "Of course, Chez, babe. Y'know I'm down wit 'yer."

I said it with such tenderness that she fell for it, and I didn't even have to mention the word love.

Why did hoochies have to make a distinction between sex and love? Shit, if you love a bitch you bone her and vice versa. No big deal. No emotional, philosophical or deep shit about it.

The doorbell rang and, like clockwork, Mrs O'Farrell was out to answer it. Soon there was a heavy bang on my door. Cheryl told me not to answer it, and I didn't want to spoil the atmosphere, but whoever it was must have known I was in 'cause Mrs O'Farrell let them in.

I answered the door. Shit, it was Hector the blasted Inspector. What a time to disturb me.

"Wha'ppen, star!" Hector said, grinning to reveal a gold-capped tooth. He told everyone it was solid twenty-four carat, but if it was, he would have wrenched it out with pliers to pawn to the highest bidder by now.

"Me never know yuh had company. Wha'ppen Cheryl, long time no see."

He raised his hand, as if expecting Cheryl to give him a high five.

She didn't even acknowledge him. Cheryl dissed Hector and all he stood for. But homie knew it was because she tripped on me drawin' back the blunts. Since Hector was the man that supplied it, he got the bad vibes.

"Hey, is wha' me do wrong?" he asked, drawing closer to me.

"No need to front, man, she down wit da programme."

"So wha'ppen to de white piece?"

"S-s-s-c-h-h, cool bro," I said, looking quickly at Cheryl.

She was raising the volume of the TV as if to drown out Hector's voice.

Hector put his hand in the pocket of his infamous cream mac, which was black with dirt around the collar and cuffs, and pulled out a transparent polythene bag of weed the size of a thumb nail and asked me how much I wanted. Homie looked at him and laughed.

"Wha' so funny, man?" Hector asked.

"Nothin', dude, nothin'."

"Look me had a busy bloodclaat nite and dis is all me 'ave lef'. You lucky me t'ink 'bout you and never sell it to another client."

"How much snaps, homie?" I asked.

"Gimme a blue. And dat's a bloodclaat bargain."

"Look homie I'll settle later. Only gotta fifty dollar note."

"Hold on deh, me might 'ave some change." Hector searched around in his pockets tryin' to look for what he didn't have.

"Cha, man, yuh expec' credit now?"

He took a small red notepad and a piece of lead out of his inside pocket and licked the tip before marking something down.

"Y'know, dat goin' cost yuh three pound interest."

I laughed but agreed to the trade 'cause I didn't want to raise a discussion.

"Nice, nice," Hector said, completing the transaction. Mutha then pulled out some silver foil wrapped in a ball.

"Y' sight dis before," he said, opening the foil. Inside were five white lumps. I knew what it was instantly because a couple of the players at college was heavily into it.

"De finest crack inna Birmingham," Hector announced. "Y'wan try some? If y' did t'ink Christmas Day did anyt'ing, tek some a dis and yuh be floatin' 'pon a cloud."

The dude was out of it. Blunts was one thing but crack, shit! Homie knew the damage one dose of this could do. The whole of inner-city America is littered with niggaz walkin' around spaced out on this shit.

"Lose it, punk. Don't wanna see da shit in my crib again."

My voice raisin' above a whisper but still not loud enough to disturb Cheryl.

"Okay, okay," Hector said, quickly putting the foil back into his pocket. "If yuh change yuh mind y'know where to find me."

A second after Hector left, my mobile rang again. It was Helen again, asking to set a date to meet. This bitch was beginning to get on my case.

"You've got the wrong number!" I shouted then ended the call.

I eased up beside Cheryl and put my arm around her. She smiled until she saw the bag of weed in my hand. I knew she was ready to trip, but I didn't want to get into any deep shit about whether or not I should be gettin' high on the stuff, so I immediately set a new agenda.

"Lets go and hang wit Janet—cheer up her and Uriah," I suggested, not really wantin' to disturb the evenin' further.

"Okay," she said enthusiastically.

I grabbed my Delaware jacket and we left.

I didn't phone Janet to tell her we were coming because I knew she'd spruce herself and the place up.

I wanted the real McCoy. I wanted to see her as she was, not some stage-managed act. If something was troublin' her, I wanted to hear. If she was starvin' herself, I wanted to see if I could ease the shit and help her out.

We arrived about ten. The same little homiez were kickin' around outside again. Cheryl stared at them as we got out of the car.

"Where are their parents?"

"Probably out playin' too."

Cheryl shook her head; I know she wasn't down with this crap. Had more sense than to get herself pregnant with all her life ahead of her. She must know that I ain't down with that programme. Homie being a father freaked me to shit out.

The lift was out of order so we walked up the stairs.

"Who is it?" Janet shouted when she came to the door.

"It's me, sis."

"And Cheryl."

She gave me a bitch look for forgetting we were an item.

Janet unbolted the door and hugged us both. "I just phoned you. I thought you had gone partyin'."

"So yer knew she'd be comin' to da 'hood a day early?" I asked.

123

"Yeah, she wanted to surprise you. Don't you think it was romantic?"

I looked at Cheryl. She stared back, waitin' for the right answer.

"Yeah, yeah, it was cool."

Janet was looking a lot better than when I last saw her. She was smiling and full of bounce.

"What did you want to see us about?" Cheryl asked, as Janet took my jacket.

"They're tryin' to assimilate Joseph back into the community," Janet said. She sat on the floor opposite us.

"Wha' yer sayin', sis?"

"Well, they're going to let him come home on a short-term basis to see if he can adjust to life away from the hospital."

"Damn, yer comin' correct, sis? Yer told us da homie's head is on another planet."

"Why do you always have to frame things in that language?" Janet said, looking sharply at me.

"Sorry sis," I replied quickly, not wantin' a battle on this.

"Anyway, he's improved since then. When he's had his proper medication, he's fine."

"What about Uriah?" Cheryl asked.

"I've taken him to see Joe a couple of times to try and get him used to seeing his daddy again, and tried to explain to him what has happened...but he's still too young to really understand."

"Can yer handle da pressure, sis ?" I asked.

"Joe's mum is going to help out. But I want him home so that I can look after him."

Damn, didn't know what concern to voice. I didn't think Janet realised she was making a false move. When a man is one player short of a full roster, can't know what tactics he's gonna come up with next. The dude wasn't in the nuthouse for nothin'. He was sick and needed a doc. And Janet was no medic.

We sat for over an hour listening to Janet tryin' to convince us, but by the time we were ready to make a move, the shit had reached stalemate.

Before we left I handed Janet the fifty pound note I had taxed off Helen. Man, she was gonna need every dime she could get.

By the time we got down the stairs to the war zone they call a car park the little foot soldiers had finally called a ceasefire.

Shit, it was so dark I could scarcely see my wheels. Then it hit me like a wave of bullets. I had forgotten to fortify my wheels. Homie hadn't switched on the alarm. I ran around to the cockpit side. The window was shattered into a thousand pieces. They had left the door open. The white leather seats were rubbed down with shit and my thousand pound stereo and four hundred pound speakers were now someone else's Littlewoods pools win. The punks even left a callin' card in the front seat. Sheet of white paper had NEXT TIME PAY YOUR BILLS AND DON'T FUCK WITH US FOOL scrawled on it.

"Muthafuckas!" I shouted at the top of my voice. "Yer gotta come out one day. Then your ass is mine. I've gotta contract on each of yer punk asses!"

"Winston, shut up, there's people sleeping," Cheryl said.

"*Damn!* Look what da punks done ta my wheels."

"Well, shouting's not goin' to solve it, Winston."

"I'm gonna cap their muthafuckin' asses when I catch the li'l bums."

With Janet's help we spent the next two hours cleanin' and patchin' up the motor. We covered the missin' glass with cardboard and tape; damn thing is going to cost a fortune to fix.

On the drive back to my place Cheryl wanted to pick up some food from Beresford's. Man, I was too angry to even think about refuelling my body.

I just wanted to go stake out those little punks and smoke each and every one of them. I took a detour into downtown Handsworth.

There were a couple of brothas waiting in line when we got to the shop. Mr B was behind the counter with his usual miserable face. When it was my turn I said:

"Gimme two vegetable pattie."

"Is wha'ppen, y' nah have no manners?" Mr B asked.

"Please," I replied, knowin' the man was on an ego trip. Old-timer always wanted to mess with you in front of your bitch. Gave him some kinda kick. If he was in the States, I woulda put a cap in his ass.

"Please, wha'?" he shouted.

"Please, two veg patties."

"Me nah have no vegetable pattie, jus' run out."

"It's alright," Cheryl said. "I'll have a curry pattie."

"Straight up, gimme two curry patties and one dumplin'. Pleease."

"I don't serve one dumplin'," he replied.

"Man, you doggin' me or what? I want a dumplin' wit' my shit, homie."

"Listen, yuh don't use dat kinda language inna dis shop y'hear? And, like me say, me don't sell one dumplin'."

"Man, yer need a hearin' aid. I said two curry patties and a dumplin' wit' it?"

"An' me seh me nah sell one dumplin'. Me nah go argue wid you. If you don't like my rules, tek yuh business elsewhere."

Cheryl interrupted. "We'll just have the two patties, please."

Damn. Whatever happened to that 'the customer's always right' shit? Mr B wanted to get some skills in talkin' to people.

While the food was in the microwave I remembered I didn't have any dead presidents.

"Hey, Chez, yer got any dollars?"

"Winston, you never have any money."

"Had some business to take care of. I'll pay yer back, babes."

She shook her head. I knew she was thinkin' what a low-life I was. As she searched through her bag two homiez with white chicks came into the shop. Didn't pay the dudes no mind, but homie's eyes was playin' havoc with the tits of one of the bitches. Things stuck out like she had Mount Everest and Mont Blanc on her ches...

"Is you, yuh lickle bloodclaat!"

Suddenly Zorro was standing in my face. Homie's body started to tremble.

"You t'ink dat little whore could testify 'gainst me? Dem had fe let me go. Yuh see, me is Zorro."

He slapped himself in the chest like King Kong.

"Yuh see you, y' fuck one of my gyal and never pay. Now you haffe pay wid interest."

Cheryl took a step back, looking confused.

"Look, bro, yer got da wrong nigga. Shit don't know what yer on about," I said, trying to look innocent to Cheryl and chill Zorro out.

"Fuck you, yuh don't 'ave yuh lynch mob now—"

He reached inside his leather coat and pulled out a ten-inch blade, looking at me like a crazed butcher ready to cut the gibs out of a chicken.

"No!"Cheryl screamed, and tugged at the arm Zorro was getting ready to carve my face up with. The blade dropped to the floor as his homie slapped Cheryl across the face.

I tried to defend her, but Zorro grabbed me around the throat. The pressure was like he had me in a straitjacket; I was paralysed. I could hear Cheryl screamin', then heard a crash. Zorro's boy had slapped her down to the floor. I tried to struggle but he had this vice-like grip. His big, red-stained eyes rollin' in his coal-coloured face said the homie was highly charged on something. Mutha was enjoyin' watching me choke to death. I was suffocating. I became faint. My whole shit flashed before me. Then suddenly, like a blessing from God, the pressure around my neck loosened. I fell to the floor coughin' up blood.

I looked up and saw Mr B pointing a double-barrel shotgun at Zorro's head.

"I don't need yuh custom tonite or any other nite fe dat matter, sir," Mr B said. He meant business, and Zorro knew it.

"Carry on yuh nastiness elsewhere. Me run a decent and honest business 'ere."

Zorro had his two hands in the air like something outta some damn John Wayne film. "Okay Pops, okay, me leavin'."

Mr B followed them through the door and waited while they drove off.

Cheryl was standing by the counter in tears. She had severe red bruising on her right cheek from where she had been slapped. I got up and went over to her. I held her, she was breathin' heavily and tremblin' like a leaf. There was a small cut on her lip.

"You okay, Chez?"

Tears started to flow like Niagara Falls. She laid her head on my chest and I held her close.

Mr B was back behind his counter, with the gun under it.

"Yuh wan' me call de police?"

"No," I replied quietly.

Mr B wrapped the two patties and passed them to me.

"Tek these on de house."

I thanked him and helped Cheryl to the car. I didn't know where the hell I was steering; I must have stalled the car at every junction. Homie's legs were wobbling like a drunk's. We drove for about fifteen minutes in total silence. Cheryl kept her eyes fixed on the road, like she was hypnotised. Suddenly she looked at me.

"Why didn't you call the police?"

"It was all a misunderstandin'," I said, trying to play it down. "Shit gonna blow over..."

"Winston, I've heard about those guys. We could've been killed in there. And all for a misunderstanding? If it was a mistake, let the police sort it out. They can't go around beating up innocent people just because they bloody feel like it."

She had regained her full faculties, but she was still trippin'.

"No Chez," I said. "Jus' let it ride."

"No. You're seem to be forgetting that I was involved in this. It's not you who's going home with blood all over your clothes and all battered."

"You'll be okay, babes."

I went to place my hand on the side of her face with the bruising. She slapped it away. "What did he mean when he said you had one of his women without paying?"

"Da homie's demented, Chez. Yer saw da look on his face, he's a nutter. Don't wanna listen to a word fake-ass G's like him say."

She started hitting me violently upside my head. Homie had to step on the brakes in an emergency stop. Cheryl was thrown forward, and bounced back into her seat.

"You're a fucking liar," she screeched, throwing clenched fists at my head. I was protectin' my shit with my two hands so she pierced her finger nails into my face, diggin' deep into my flesh. I managed to hold her arms and calm her ass down.

She sat in silence for the rest of the journey. When we arrived at her house, she got out without a word and slammed the door.

I didn't want to push it. I sat outside her house for an hour just thinking. I knew this shit would burn itself out eventually. But God knows, I'm no firefighter.

When I arrived home I looked in the mirror. Cheryl had made a good mess of my face. I tried to clean the cuts with water, but the real wounds were more psychological than physical.

I dried my face, built a blunt from the weed I'd bought from Hector earlier and went and lay across the bed.

9

The Last Straw

"Who's the fastest sprinter in the world?" John whispered in Andre's ear.

"Go to hell, John," Andre whispered back.

He was standing so close to Andre they looked like Siamese twins. John giggled. "An Ethiopian with a luncheon voucher. Get it, Andre? Get it?"

Andre ignored him. He'd never appreciated John's dry, racist humour. And now, at the presentation for Mr Pal's promotion to partner, Andre had totally lost his sense of humour.

He was beginning to think that if there was someone up there watching over the human race, they must have a real beef with him—because Mr Pal was moving up to the tenth floor. If Andre had his way he'd be flying Concorde first class to Hell, crash-landing in brimstone and fire and surviving just long enough for Lucifer to plunge his horns through his heart.

Where the move would leave him, he couldn't tell. Over the past two months Pal's behaviour towards him had become increasingly malicious. He wasted no opportunity to remind Andre that his private life was out of step with what the company expected of a professional man—and that the company wouldn't tolerate it for much longer.

Now, with Pal pulling strings at a higher level, Andre felt he would have to jump before he was pushed.

Everyone on the sixth floor had gathered outside Mr Pal's office, each holding a glass of Moet champagne. Their faces had become so familiar that Andre took them for granted. In fact there was a sameness about everything around him, except the Cheshire cat smile on Mr Pal's face after his ten-minute acceptance speech. He shook hands, first with Mr Goldberg then Mr Samson.

"Cheers to a long life for the new Goldberg, Samson and Pal," Mr Samson shouted, raising his glass. Everyone except Andre raised a glass to toast the man that only he knew as a brute. Then Mr Goldberg closed the ceremony and ushered the flock back to work.

On the way back to his desk Michael approached Andre.

"What do you think?" he asked.

"Of what?"

"You know, Pal getting his partnership."

Andre hesitated, wondering whether to speak the truth or play the diplomat. Up to now he had never shown his true feelings in the office; a survival mechanism in a hostile environment. People noticed there was animosity between them, but they didn't hear it from his mouth. He decided it was time for a change. If he was going down he would go with guns blazing.

"If that bastard sacks me I'm going to have his ass up on race discrimination charges," he rasped, not caring who heard him.

Michael's mouth gaped open with surprise. "Sack you? Race discrim...what you on about?"

Andre knew any energy spent trying to explain it to Michael would be energy wasted. Andre said no more on the topic. Michael would never understand the pressure he was under.

"Hey, you know what I've heard?" Michael said, looking around the office as if the whole floor had their ears cocked for his exclusive revelation. In fact, no-one except Mr Pal cared two hoots what he had to say. "I heard that Pal's father offered the company a six-figure sum for Pal to become a partner in the firm. You hear that? Six figures."

Michael looked at Andre expecting amazement, but Andre wasn't about to tickle his ego.

"Well, you know what they say Michael; money talks and all else walks. Sorry, I've got work to do."

Andre went back to his desk. As always, it was crammed with files, staring at him as if to say 'fix me, Andre'. But like everything else in his life, they were in total disarray.

"I say, Andre," William called. "Did I overhear you saying you're going bring a discrimination case against Mr Pal."

"You may have done, William."

"Well to be quite honest, I can't see how that's possible. I mean, you're both black." William pushed his glasses up his nose and stared expectantly at Andre. Andre sighed heavily and told William to go consult some of his law books. He sat down behind his desk and looked across at John. For once, his head was buried in his files. There were exams again in a couple of months and the four of them had permission to leave early in the evenings for revision purposes.

But since the company's generosity didn't stretch to reducing their case load, they all had to come in earlier and earlier if they wanted to complete their work and catch the central library before closing. Not that it worried Andre—he was always in at the crack of dawn and tended to do the bulk of his revision in the last month before the exams. He found he retained the information better when he crammed it in.

Most evenings when he left early, he headed straight for the gym to practice shooting. He had lost his starting place in the team to Adam and it freaked him out. It was as great a blow to his dignity as Mr Pal taking the Lighthouse case from him.

Sitting on the bench waiting for Adam to make mistakes before he could get on the court wasn't what he was in the game for.

Andre got off the bench twice for a total of seven minutes last Saturday in the return with Wolverhampton, as the Warriors annihilated the Outlaws 101 to 83. When the team won and he didn't even get time to tighten his laces it didn't feel right. It felt like reaching the destination without going on the journey.

The Warriors hadn't lost since Cheshire beat them in Manchester and, though they had already qualified for the play-offs, they needed a victory by a clear ten points over Cheshire in the return on Saturday to clinch the championship and give them home court advantage throughout the play-offs.

Saturday's was the biggest game of the season for the club, because home court in the play-offs would mean increased revenue; and Andre was to be a bench-warmer for the occasion. But still, if he *was* called upon he'd give a performance that would make it impossible for Coach Bailey to drop him for the crucial play-off games.

He had given up trying to match his more athletic team-mates' aesthetic grace and concentrated on what he knew best. Shooting. He had to match the time Adam was putting in on his game. So some evenings he would hire a court at at any leisure centre and just practice shooting from all angles and positions, over and over again.

Once, he would have asked Calvin to come down to give him some competition, but their relationship had soured. They still talked, but not as often. The camaraderie had gone.

Calvin didn't say as much, but Andre knew Calvin was still judging him for leaving Heather and was waiting for him to swallow his pride and run back to her. But there was little chance of that happening. He had moved out of the hotel and rented a one-bedroom flat in Sandwell Road at the top of Handsworth.

He visited the kids often, partly to prove Calvin wrong about them not having a father figure around. But Heather refused to talk to him unless it was absolutely necessary. Andre had thought it was just a phase she was going through, but it looked like one New Year's resolution that she meant to keep.

Andre's thoughts were interrupted as Tracy strutted into the office. Since the incident at the Christmas party she had refused to speak to him other than to say good morning and goodnight. He had also learnt that she was feeding Pal little bits of information about his working practices. Although they had nothing solid on him yet, Pal was still keeping a close eye in the hope that they would soon. Tracy would drop hints in front of Pal when Andre had a long lunch, and would purposely misinform people about his whereabouts.

Like most people around him at the moment, Tracy was hellbent on making Andre's life difficult.

As usual she had on a figure-hugging dress. Both John and William raised their heads and eyed her up as she went to get some paper from the cupboard.

Even though Andre didn't fancy Tracy, she made him think about sex. He hadn't had any since leaving Heather; he was as horny as hell, but then again, he wasn't sure he could put up with a relationship right now on top of all the other crap he was going through. And he wasn't a one-night stand or a hit-and-run kind of man. He liked to romance a woman...fatten her up before the kill. But that took time and time was the one thing he didn't have.

Just as Tracy was returning to her desk Michael gave her a wolf-whistle. She smiled, coyly. Rumour had it that she'd had better luck with Michael at the Christmas party. Apparently he'd knocked her off in Mr Pal's office and his wife had been so tipsy, she didn't notice he was missing for over an hour.

Andre's phone rang.

"Hello."

"It's your wife—or should I say ex-wife—on three," Tracy said, with a touch of malice, but Andre was used to it now. It sounded strange hearing Heather referred to as his ex-wife. He had never thought about making it official. He didn't even know on what grounds he could make it official; he wasn't up on family law. But if nagging came under unreasonable behaviour or mental cruelty, it would have to be one of those.

He was happy with things the way they were, but if he ever met anyone else, that would come up for review.

He took a deep breath, wondering what she wanted now.

"Heather, how are you?"

She totally ignored his greeting.

"What time are you coming to pick up the kids this afternoon?"

"I finish here at about three-thirty, so I'll be over about four."

"Well, I hope this time you keep your word. It's not good building up their expectations, then dashing them."

"Heather, you know what happened on Saturday. I've explained to the kids."

"D'you really expect kids to understand that their dad wanted to play basketball instead of taking them to McDonalds like he promised?"

"You know the game was rescheduled at the last moment. I told Jermaine and Josephine that I would take them today and I will."

"But you didn't have to put up with them crying their eyes out on Saturday afternoon, did you? No, you left that to me."

She just had to subject him to emotional blackmail every time the kids came on the agenda. She was using them as a weapon to beat him with; trying to make him feel guilty. He knew she had a point over his no-show, but why blow it out of proportion?

"Like I said, Heather, I'm taking them today, okay?" he replied, in a tired voice.

"You think I don't know you're only taking them today because training's been cancelled? Anyway, you said three-thirty."

She put the phone down before he could correct her.

"I said four," he insisted, putting the phone down.

How did she know that they had switched practice to tomorrow? Then again, it didn't really matter how she found out. If it wasn't for the kids, Heather and her bloody mother wouldn't see him for dust.

It was lunchtime. He put on his coat over his blazer and waited for the lift. Tracy came to wait too. He felt like taking the stairs, but, stayed where he was twiddling his thumbs.

Andre looked at her and she looked at him; if looks could kill he'd be joining Charlie Parker six feet under. The lift arrived and they got in together.

"Ground?" Andre asked pressing the button.

"Yes," she replied sharply.

The door closed.

"I see there's been no kiss and make up yet," she remarked, as though she was commenting on the weather. Cow just couldn't resist a dig. But Andre wouldn't give her the satisfaction of a reply.

"No divorce yet," she continued to goad. "So she hasn't taken you to the cleaners yet. But she will. Soon. I've heard about these black women. Very materialistic. Want every penny a man's got in these divorce splits."

Andre was riled. "Listen, you little cow. Keep out of my business or you're going to wish you were never born."

"Touchy, touchy! Did I strike a raw nerve?" she said, smiling. "Don't worry...if you need a shoulder to cry on, mine's still available." She blew a kiss at him.

"Thanks, but if I want a bitch for comfort I'll get a mutt."

"You'll be sorry you ever refused me," she fumed, red-faced.

"Now, now, you don't want to threaten a man in the legal profession. Could be very nasty."

"It's not a threat, it's a promise, you bastard," she spat.

The lift opened and he allowed Tracy to leave first. She wiggled her backside over to the revolving doors. As he followed, Theo came running up behind him, breathing heavily.

"Saw you get the lift and wanted to catch you," he gasped. "Damn, I'm so unfit. I don't think it was wise to take the stairs."

Andre laughed. "Was it urgent?"

Theo rested his hand on Andre's shoulder, still fighting to get his breath.

"Yeah, I just finished with my boss and was coming over to ask you to lunch. It's a long time since we had a chat."

"Okay, what do you want, a sandwich job or something more substantial?"

"Let's go to Henry's."

The pavements were still white with the overnight frost and the frozen vapour that came out of their mouths was thick enough to rival a steam train.

On the short walk to Henry's, Andre noticed a confidence about Theo that he wished he had; he liked the man's authority. He had money, of course, had it coming out of his ears. The Porsche, the Armani suits, the expensive gifts for the woman. This man, Andre thought, had made it legitimately. He was someone to look up to, someone to admire, someone who could give Mr Pal a run for his money...and he was black.

At Henry's they had to wait a couple of minutes for the waitress to clear a table. Theo took off his beige cashmere overcoat to reveal another Armani suit, this time in steel grey. He brushed some specs of dust off his coat before putting it on a hanger, then adjusted the cuffs of his silk shirt and fingered his tie before sitting down.

Andre hoped Theo was going to tell him about these great plans he had mentioned at the Christmas party—plans that had mysteriously gone off the boil over the last two months.

He remembered Marcus saying he saw Theo go into an empty office in Handsworth. Theo was a solicitor—he could have a thousand reasons for being there—but Andre's mind was working overtime. Maybe he was looking for premises to set up his own practice.

"Have I got some news for you," Theo announced, as he browsed through the lunchtime menu.

"Is that right?" Andre said casually, praying it would be something that would release him from his misery at Goldberg, Samson and Pal.

"Now that bastard Pal has gone upstairs, guess what?" Theo said.

"What?"

Theo placed the menu on the table.

"Pal's old job is vacant. And my boss has recommended me to the partnership."

Andre wanted to pick up a knife and slit Theo's throat. He'd thought this man was a mover and shaker, a man with so much energy, vitality and get-up-and-go that corporate Britain could never hold him. He had admired Theo.

Now he was listening to him getting excited about filling someone else's shoes at a racist two-bit law firm. Andre felt his hero was as institutionalised as himself and the rest of the black men he saw sitting in the bar with their fancy suits on, playing the game.

Before he could think of a reply, the waitress came over to get their order.

Andre had a club sandwich; Theo ordered Buffalo wings. Andre watched him order, and could see his little two-faced persona shining through.

"Also I'll have three potato skins and a large cranberry juice," he told the waitress.

"So, you'll go for Pal's job, then?" Andre asked, once she'd gone.

"Well, I told my boss I wouldn't be applying, but if he put in a good word to the right parties, I'd be interested if it were offered to me."

"What's he sayin'?"

"He reckons I'm far ahead of the competition in terms of experience and ability, although I've only been at the company for three months..."

The glow in his eyes said he was home and dry.

"He said you don't find many black men like me...you know, no chip on the shoulder; no sob stories about how racist Britain has done them bad. He said I could be in the room and people wouldn't even notice I'm black.

"I took it as a compliment, because you don't want to stand out. Take that incident with your wife, for instance. That was bad for your image. You can't have some lunatic fitting you like that.

"Take it from me, Andre. The best way to get on in this world is not to wear that blackness on your sleeve. Anyway, think about it. It will be great for you when I get the job. No more Pal to bother you, and me as your boss."

"That will certainly make a change," Andre replied, wondering *do you really have to sell out to get on in the world? Or, more to the point, have I sold out?* He decided to change the subject.

"How's the case going with Marcus?"

He immediately wondered why Theo had taken on Marcus' case so eagerly if he was trying to neutralise his blackness.

"Not very well at the moment. Marcus is not being very helpful, but I've got it under control. You see, I need to build a reputation up here. This could be the case to establish me."

The waitress returned with the order and set their food before them.

"We'll clear up his access rights to his daughter without going to court. I have a meeting with his common law wife and her solicitor tomorrow afternoon to settle it."

"What about assaulting a police officer and resisting arrest?" Andre asked, tucking into his sandwich.

"Assaulting *an* officer?" Theo asked, his mouth full of potato skin. "I wish it had been just one. Seems your friend Marcus doesn't do things by halves. They charged him with assaulting four officers. Between you and me, with his current suspended sentence, he's going down unless I can work a miracle."

Andre was anxious that Theo should conjure up something—any-thing—to keep Marcus from eating porridge for the next five years.

"What are the chances?"

"That's top secret at the moment," Theo replied slyly, "but believe me, when I deliver it I'm going to be the best known solicitor in Birmingham!"

They split the bill and went back to the office. The afternoon passed quickly, and before long Andre was heading out to Handsworth Wood to pick up the kids and take them to McDonald's.

The drive from the city centre was pleasant only because of the sounds of Wynton letting off his original brand of trumpet. Andre was engrossed, even though he had heard the tracks from *'Uptown*

136

Ruler' countless times. He purred to *'Prayer'* and swayed from side to side with *'Harmonique'*.

Even the fact that traffic made him forty minutes late didn't bother him until he pulled up outside the house. He walked up the driveway to the house; the front garden was in a mess. No man, no gardener, he thought. He had to ring the bell, since Heather had changed the locks without informing him. He found out when he turned up one day in January and couldn't get his key in the door. If a policeman had come past he would have had a field day. A black man, in the dead of night, fiddling with a door in suburbia? Must be a fair cop. Heather opened the door, then turned around and headed back in, leaving it wide open. Andre was about to step inside when he heard his name being called.

"Andre, just a minute."

He was glad to see his neighbour Peter bustling up the path in his full West Midlands Constabulary regalia. Andre walked down the drive to meet him.

"Hi, Pete. Sorry I haven't had a chance to thank you properly for not breathalysing me at Christmas," he said, offering his hand. Peter had pulled Andre over, and told him to leave his car parked and get a taxi the rest of the way home.

"What night? I don't know what you're talking about. Did I miss something?" he laughed.

"Listen, Andre, you didn't hear this from me, but there's talk all over the nick that your mate Marcus is going to be fitted up. There are officers fed up with all this crap over corruption and abuse of power within the West Midlands force and we're trying to make a stand— trying to bring back public confidence in the police.

"I know one of the four officers giving evidence against Marcus is a weak link. He's ready to spill his guts, if we can get to him. I'm going on duty now and I'll have more info tomorrow morning. I'll let you have the full details then. It's about time we got rid of this hooligan element in the force. But keep shtum about it," he warned.

Andre wondered if Theo knew anything about this. Maybe that was his secret. He decided to wait until tomorrow before getting too excited for Marcus. Tonight he had more pressing problems on his mind, like Heather.

Crash!

The sound of Heather slamming down plates in the kitchen sink shuddered up Andre's spine. He hadn't been in the house five minutes before she had dropped the A-bomb, and Andre had taken it about as well as the folks in Hiroshima.

"Heather, damn it, you're not being logical about this," he said, his face stony.

"Logical? There's nothing more straightforward, honey. The white slut said she's been having an affair with you for the last twelve months. That is, *eight* months before you decided you needed a break from your wife and kids. That's adultery in my book, baby."

"Adultery? Heather, get serious."

"I'm as serious as a heart attack. You're not going to get off lightly, like you have up 'til now.

"I want everything above board. Maintenance, mortgage, Jo's nursery, bills and every other goddamn expense. 'Cause honey, you're going to pay for the day you ever crossed me for some piece of white junk."

Heather threw down the last plate and stormed across the kitchen almost running Andre over.

"You're being silly," Andre pleaded, following her as she slammed pots and pans into the cupboards. "Nothing has ever happened between me and Tracy."

"Damn, Andre, you've become so deceitful, you'd sell your own mother to save your ass."

Her words hit him. He placed his hands on her shoulders to stop her Speedy Gonzalez routine around the kitchen.

"Don't talk about my mother! She's nothing to do with this."

Heather shrugged herself free.

"Take your hands off me. You have no rights over this body, baby. I must have been so stupid. All these late nights away, early morning arrivals, no phone calls. Telling me shit about being at work and all the time you were out screwing your tramp secretary. I bet you were having a good laugh on me. You were, weren't you? Weren't you?"

"For the last time Heather, I have not slept with Tracy—or anyone else for that matter."

"Save it for the judge! I've had enough of your lies. It's time Heather Parchment had herself some fun."

Andre knew enough about family law to know that he would have to give his consent in a quickie divorce. But the law didn't seem to bother Heather...she was acting like she wanted it tomorrow.

She walked briskly through to the stairs and shouted: "Jermaine and Josephine, hurry up and get down here!"

She came back into the living room and stared at him like he was some adulterous Casanova who had no right to be in the house.

138

"Heather—if you stop for one moment and hear me out, you'll see all this is a mistake. But no, you want to believe it. I bet you never even considered that she could be lying."

"Lying, eh?' Heather looked straight at him. "Why on earth would she be doing that, pork-checker?"

He shrugged.

"I don't know, but she is."

"Andre, she told me live and direct on the phone this afternoon when I phoned to check what time you were coming for the kids. Only you were out on a l-o-n-g lunch. That's when the bitch spilled her guts. Givin' me all the tears about what a rat you are now you've dumped her. Slag's lucky. It only took her a year to find out."

"You have to believe me, it's not true," Andre pleaded.

"I suppose it's not true that you had her lipstick all over your face and love marks on your body at Christmas?"

"What you tryin' to say?"

"No, Andre, what are you sayin'? 'Cause the truth is, I don't believe a word you say nowadays. You're just like all the other wotless creeps out there that can't keep their dicks inside their briefs."

"I've had enough of this stu-"

"Daddy, Daddy, tell Jermaine. He keeps throwing my shoes away."

Jermaine and Josephine came running in the room, Josephine was in tears as usual.

"Jermaine, behave!" Andre shouted, and raised his hand to clip him around the head, but stopped himself before he took his frustrations out on the boy.

Andre stood almost in a trance as Heather bent down to button Josephine's coat. Why did it bother him so much that Heather had gone to see her solicitor about a quickie divorce? He was first out of the blocks wanting to end the marriage, so how come Heather had become the pace-setter?

And who was filling her head with all this 'lipstick on your collar' crap. If he could get his hands around Tracy's neck right now he'd wring it full circle.

Josephine tugged at his trouser leg. He smiled, then lifted her up and planted a kiss on the side of her face.

"Daddy, I want a Big Mac."

She looked like a Smurf with a woollen pompom hat covering her head, which was itself no bigger than a Big Mac.

"Yes, beautiful. You will have a Big Mac."

"Just get her an ordinary burger," Heather butted in, pushing Jermaine's baseball cap on his head. "She can't eat one of those big things."

She ran her hand over Jermaine's face, making it shine like her mahogany table.

"But I *can* eat a big one, Mummy," Josephine complained.

"You'll eat what I say. I'm not having you throw up all over the place, 'cause Daddy won't be here to clean it up."

She took Josephine from Andre and gave her a kiss before handing her back.

"We need to talk," Andre said as they left the house.

"I've got nothing more to say, Andre."

Jermaine was racing down the driveway to the car.

"Just make sure they're back by eight. They've got school tomorrow."

"I know that, Heather."

"That's a surprise, considering you were hardly ever here to put them to bed at night."

There was no let-up with this woman. He shook his head and got into the Rover.

"Dad...Dad...Dad...*Dad!*" Jermaine shouted, each time with greater intensity.

Andre woke sharply from his trance.

"What? What, son?"

Jermaine pointed across the McDonald's table at Josephine.

"Look."

"Josephine, what an earth are you doing?" Andre exclaimed.

Her red coat had a blotch of vanilla milkshake straight down the front of it. Andre picked up some paper flannels and began to clean off the sticky, creamy mess.

"Mum's going to kill the both of us, now."

"Sorry, Daddy, I didn't mean to..."

She started to cry. Andre pulled her out of her seat and hugged her.

"Don't worry—it's alright, baby. It's alright."

He looked at his watch. It was quarter to eight. Damn, Heather would flip if he got them back a second after eight o'clock. Cow probably had a stopwatch timing his backside.

"Come on, time to go home. Jermaine, you haven't eaten any of your burger."

"I don't like it."

Andre emptied their leftovers into the flip bin.

"Since when have you disliked burgers, son?" he asked.

"Uncle Calvin said they're bad for you. Is it true, Dad?"

"Only if you eat them every day," Andre said, absently. *Calvin has told my kids not to eat burgers? Damn, he's got no right.*

It was below freezing when they left McDonalds, but he'd parked close by. They set off and he put Alvin Davis on low, and when he next glanced at the back seat, Jo was asleep. As he cruised up Constitution Hill towards Handsworth, he suddenly became curious about what Jermaine had said.

"Jermaine, are you awake?"

"Yes, dad," he replied, in a sleepy voice.

"When did Uncle Calvin tell you you shouldn't eat burgers?"

"Ahm...can't remember."

"Was it a day ago or two days ago, or longer than that?" Andre asked, so Jermaine could get the gist of what he was saying.

"I think it was last week when he took me and Josephine to school."

"Does Uncle Calvin often take you to school?"

"Only when he makes us breakfast."

Andre's mind was going spare. *What the hell is Calvin doing at my house playing Delia Smith in the early hours of the morning?*

He didn't want to jump to conclusions, but this didn't smell right.

"Jermaine."

"Yes, Dad."

"How often does Uncle Calvin make you breakfast? Once a week, twice a week or more times a week."

"Ahhhh...about three times."

The bastard. Andre's mind started to run riot as he cruised across Hockley Flyover. *Damn, he's having an affair with Heather.* His foot went down on the gas like Damon Hill at Monza.

No wonder she wants a damn divorce. It must have been music to her ears when Tracy filled her head with all that nonsense. She knew it could take years for a divorce to come through if it was due to desertion, but with adultery the damn cow could be free before we could sign the papers.

As they approached the junction between Hamstead Road and Villa Road, Andre wanted to jump the lights so he could get an adult explanation of this Calvin crap in quick time. He watched impatiently, tapping the wheel.

"Come on, come on."

The lights eventually changed to red-and-amber, then to green. He moved off slowly, only to be blinded by the headlights to the right of him. Some reckless idiot who'd jumped the lights was hurtling towards the Rover.

He tried to get out of the way, but it was too late. The car skidded and slid into him at speed.

Andre was flung sideways and his head crashed against the side window.

Everything silent and black.

When he came to, the pain in his head was excruciating.

"So you're awake, Mr Beckford..."

Andre was seeing six of everything. He couldn't make out who was speaking or where he was.

"You've just got a little concussion. You're lucky...could have been much worse."

Andre gathered his senses enough to realise he was in hospital, then suddenly, on a reflex, he shouted:

"Where's my kids? *Where's my damn kids?*"

Things came slowly back into focus. "They're okay. Your kids are fine."

Andre realised that the man speaking was a doctor.

"Where are they? I want to see them. I want to see them!" he shouted, struggling to get up.

"Sir, trust me, they'll be okay. They're with their mother. Just lie down and get some rest."

10

Me Against The Rest

As far as I was concerned, my rehab was complete. I'd played in the last two games and now I was fit and ready to smash dem Cheshire bwoy.

Last time they didn't give me time to settle, they abused me. But Sat'day they going to find out the real Marcus Codrington can play ball. I ready to shack out.

I sat in Yvette's front room. Nothing else was important in my mind today. Not Yvette, not Marcia, not my blasted money problems, not even my court case. What I was going to do in less than two days time took up all my head space. I had given Yvette's yout' Justin a second-hand basketball for his sixth birthday, but this evening it was my pickney as I caressed it, occasionally leaping off Yvette's grey leather sofa to fake a shot, shooting the ball straight up in the air almost hitting her ceiling, with some wicked back spin.

"Me cyan' wait fe get 'pon dat court," I said, looking at Yvette as she lay on the floor, a mountain of books around her.

"Y'know dem bwoy limit me to eleven rahtid points last time. Lowest total inna me history. Dem nah do it again. Ever."

"Is that so, Marcus?" Yvette replied.

"Well you go out and show them who's boss," she said, taking the piss.

But I never care what anyone had to say—I was getting psyched for this t'ing. Believe me.

"Too blasted right, when Sat'day come me gwan bury some bwoy."

I finally sat back down and watched Yvette scribbling away on a note pad. She had on another of her long jumpers which covered her backside and a pair of baggy pink jogging bottoms.

T'ings between us have been tight for the last two months or so. She was what I needed, and though her yout' could never truly replace my Charmaine, I loved to ramp with him and teach him to play basketball—somet'ing I was never able to do with my own pickney.

Cha. It's been over five months now that I haven't seen her and at times it jus' burn me so much, I feel like going out in the street and punching the first person that eyeball me. If it wasn't for b-ball I don't know what the hell I'd do. It kept my mind moving, it kept me focused.

"What you looking at?" Yvette asked.

I realised I'd been staring directly at her round face, in a day-dream.

"What you thinking about?"

"Me jus' 'ave dis match inna me head."

"I don't understand you men. Marcus, you've got an interview tomorrow morning and an important meeting with your solicitor in the afternoon, and all you can think about is a bloody basketball game. I don't get it."

I gave her a wicked stare...how she could call it just a basketball game. This was the championship match. My pride was at stake. This was more important than any blasted interview or solicitor meeting.

"Cha, 'oman never overstand," I replied, looking at her puzzled face.

"It just seems to me that your priorities are all mixed up," she said as she got up off her front and sat directly in front of me.

I was trying to keep my mind off this stupid interview. They've been messing me about, anyway. I filled out the application since December and is just now dem a write me 'bout interview. Anyway once dem see I'm black I'm not getting the job.

"So, Marcus, how have you prepared for the interview tomor-row?"

"Prepare? Me nah even know if me a go yet."

"What do you mean, you don't know if you're going?"

She looked well vex.

"It's a blasted waste a time," I replied shaking my head. "Listen 'ere. Since October me apply fe hundreds of jobs. Me only get six interview. Most dem employer jus' look 'pon me post code and decide dem nah employ me. Even when me get interview dem see me is a big rahtid black man and get 'fraid, say dem goin' write me nex' day. Me still a wait fe dem letter fe drop."

"It might be your interview technique," Yvette said, snatching the basketball out of my hands and placing it on the floor.

"Technique? Rasta dat 'ave notin' fe do wid it. Me is a black man and no white bwoy gwan gimme a job that fe 'im people can do. Is like 'im feel dat if 'im gi' de black man de job 'im a go tek over and start run t'ings. Dem bwoy well 'fraid."

"That's stupid," she said, coming to sit beside me on the sofa. "I

144

know only too well the racism that's out there, but you can't let it stop you doing what you want to do...or going to an interview for a job you are qualified for."

I wasn't convinced in the slightest. I didn't see the point of a man judging you on things that have nothing to do with the job you're going for. It was humiliating to walk in a room for an interview and sight the white bwoy just taking the piss out of you. I'm not into that anymore.

"Look Marcus, you've got to go out there and do the best you can. You've got to fight against this kind of thing. If our forefathers and mothers didn't fight against it, we'd still be in chains today."

"Me see dat," I replied, warming slightly to her argument.

"You feel good in yourself if you do the best you can. They may not give you the job because of your colour, or because they feel they can't control a black man."

Yvette held my hands tight like she was squeezing out her pickney at delivery time.

"But you must put yourself in that position and make them question their conscience. If you don't, there's no hope for the likes of Justin and Charmaine."

I sat with my eyes fixed on a picture of Tiye, the Nubian Queen of Egypt, 1415-1340 BC. I only knew that because it was written in bold type under the image of the queen with a backdrop of pyramids. Calvin talked the truth 'bout our heritage, I thought. We had a solid history that we didn't know anything about.

If we had the knowledge to build pyramids then, how come black people are struggle just to exist now?

It's about time I started to pick up some of those history books instead ah the ones that said blasted Columbus found the Caribbean.

"So what are you going to do, Marcus?" Yvette asked, placing her hand on my cheek and turning my face towards her.

"Me goin' go and find out wha' dem a say."

She smiled, and pulled me forward to kiss me on my lips. Raas, the t'ing switched me on. I tried to position myself better to get my arms around her, but she pulled away.

"We've got work to do," she said.

For the next thirty minutes Yvette took me through interview technique.

It was the first time ever anyone had taught me anything about preparing for an interview. I always just turned up on the day and let t'ings take their course; but Yvette told me what to wear, showed me

145

how to sit and suggested questions to ask.

She even had me walking in and out of her living room and greeting her like a rahtid idiot—but I saw that, as she said, first impressions were very important.

"You've got that now?"

"Yeah, Miss Malcolm," I answered, like I was at primary school. "I got it now."

The two of us laughed before she headed for the kitchen.

"You want a hot drink?"

"Nah, me cool."

For the entire time she was in the kitchen I thought about all that she'd said, and I was ready to hit the interview man with some new lyrics.

She came back with a cup of coffee and a half packet of chocolate digestives. She offered me it and I pulled a biscuit out. She sat down beside me and placed her cup on the floor between her feet.

"I know I shouldn't," she said as she thrust her hand into the packet. "I'll have to start my diet again tomorrow."

I looked at her and smiled. Yvette was a big girl, but not messy like some of those mampy gyal. Yeah, she could do with dropping a few pounds but even so, in my eyes she was nice and cuddly. She always talk 'bout how she was slim before she had her yout'. Then her weight just took off out of control. She said she wasn't going to have another pickney in case she start to favour Big Daddy.

"So what about the solicitors tomorrow?" she asked.

"Cha. Me nah know wha' a go 'appen. A de first time me goin' see Marcia since de New Year rave."

"You mean my party, that you left so abruptly after wreaking havoc with two guys' faces?" Yvette replied, flashing that boom smile. "We had to get the paramedics to revive the one in the toilet and a crane to lift Tiny off the floor."

I laughed. We agreed that the two of them was a test me to the extreme.

"I didn't even know that Marcia was your baby mother," she said, sipping her coffee.

"Yuh wasn't fe know," I replied. "Anyhow, tomorrow is judgment day. T'ings a go sort out one way or de other."

"Despite what you've done—and no way do I condone it, it's a sin for a man to hit a woman in my book—I don't see how she can refuse to let you see your own flesh and blood."

"Is true," I said. I can't undo the past; the most I could do was take

146

care of the future. But my future was looking bleak.

"Justin's dad is a no good so-and-so, but if he came back tomorrow I'd have no problem letting him see Justin, because a kid should know who his father is."

"Me wish Marcia could t'ink like you."

She smiled briefly.

"Marcus, I've been thinking, you ought to see a psychologist about controlling your temper. That inner rage you have needs to be controlled before you cause some serious damage to someone. I mean the party...Marcia. You could...well, you know..."

"Cha, man, yuh a joke?"

Yvette shook her head. She wasn't jesting.

"I know a good one. Black guy in Dudley. He helped the son of a friend of mine who was going through problems at school. I'm sure he could help you."

"Me nah mek nobody work dem head 'pon me. Me nah mad."

"No-one's saying you're mad. He just makes you understand more about yourself."

"Me already know all me haffe know," I said, getting vex. I wish I didn't tell her what happened between me and Marcia now. Some t'ings are best left unsaid. She probably afraid I might rough her up too.

But she kept pushing it.

"This guy's good, Marcus."

"Yvette, don't mek a fuss. Me nah go, and dat's it."

"Okay, calm down," she replied, backing off.

She offered me another biscuit. I refused but she insisted. I think she only did that so as not to feel guilty about taking another one herself. I looked at the clock. It was quarter to midnight. I stood up and stretched my limbs.

Yvette sensed I was getting ready to make a move. She stood up and wrapped her arms around me. I could feel her body pressing against mine. It felt soft and warm—made me feel like staying 'til morning. I kissed her. But this was not any old kiss, it was one of those 'I might never see you again' kisses that go on forever. She looked up at me and her eyes told the whole story. She was ready for it. She must have seen the same thing in mine.

"We can't, Marcus...not when Justin's in the house. I don't want him finding his mother in bed with the man he plays basketball with. I want to introduce you to him slowly."

"Okay, me overstand."

147

The t'ing inside me trousers didn't want to understand; it just wanted satisfying, but I knew how she felt. I wouldn't want Charmaine seeing Marcia shacking up with some bwoy that wasn't her father. We drew apart and I put on my duffel coat. Yvette walked me to the door.

"Good luck tomorrow."

"Yeah, me ready."

"Phone me."

As I was about to leave, I asked:

"Why unnu nah come fe de game Sat'day? Me sort some tickets fe you and Justin."

"We'll see. I'll think about it."

She gave me a kiss on the cheek and I hurried, knowing that I would have to walk the mile or so home. These night buses are like the Loch Ness Monster; people talk 'bout dem all the time, but you never see one.

As I was heading down Soho Road, a red car I never recognised flashed its lights. I stopped and squinted, trying to make out who was behind the wheel. I walked up to the parked car and bent down to look in the window. It was Veronica, the blasted dole woman. She press a button to wind down the window.

"Where you off to?" she asked. That was probably the most pleasant t'ing she ever said to me.

"Me a go me yard."

"I'll give you a lift if you want."

I wasn't about to refuse; outside was below zero. She leaned over and pulled up the catch and I jumped in. The car was warm and smelt nice. I was about to give her directions when she cut me off.

"It's okay, I know where you live," she smiled.

The feisty raas was already taking liberty. I asked her when the dole people were going to increase my money to its proper rate because for reason they were still docking my cheque.

Man needed corn, me 'ave red letter from the gas and electricity at home to pay and 'ave to keep borrow money from me old lady. Veronica give me some official talk and changed the subject.

She started to talk about her sister coming over from Toronto tomorrow with her three yout' and asked me about places to take them. I told her to bring them to the game—the more the better. She dropped me off outside my yard. I thanked her and she just sat there like she waiting for something while I made my way to my front door.

Eventually she sped off into the dark. I don't know if she wanted me to invite her in for a drink or somet'ing...but with my yard feeling like an igloo and being totally out of food supplies, I decided against it.

Anyway, that's what woman expect, a man to make a pass at them, and when you do them get vex, talking 'bout them only offer you a lift as a friendly gesture.

But if you go on like you don't fancy them, them still get uptight— wondering if somet'ing wrong with dem, or if you's a batty bwoy. You can't bloodclaat win wid dem. I probably should 'ave took her upstairs and start somet'ing, but with her living above Yvette it would be well out of order.

When I woke in the morning my heart was pumping with fear. I just wished the day would hurry up and end.

I have never been so nervous before an interview. I just used to say *if I get it then I get it, if I don't then I don't, no blasted skin off my nose.* But this time I wanted to do well for Yvette's sake. I wanted to have some money in my pocket to take her out. She had to go to watch Shabba with one of her woman friend because I never had the corn; but I didn't tell her that though. She was vex but there was nothing I could do. Anyhow, the job of chef de partie was paying ten grand a year—more than I've ever earned.

I turned on the shower waiting for the water to get hot and couldn't believe it when it never. I rushed back into the bedroom and put my hand on the radiator. T'ing was cold like a fridge. I tried the light switch. Dead. Every blasted electric socket was dead. Bloodclaat electricity people cut me off.

I had to bath in freezing cold water and dress in an ice box bedroom.

Blast, I never wanted to but I had to check my old lady to borrow a few shekels to pay these blasted money grabbers.

I had on my one and only suit, that was now slightly tight around the shoulders and my backside. But when I wore it with my criss white Italian shirt and my different shades of blue tie, it mek me look sharp.

I know it was cold outside but I couldn't wear my old duffel coat—that wouldn't go—so I have to make do with just the jacket.

I left my flat at nine o'clock on the dot to reach this hotel in Hagley Road, just outside the city centre. Though the cold wind was tearing through my chest I felt good as I walked the street. All eyes was 'pon me and my suit. I see some women eyeing me up who wouldn't even look on me if I was in my jeans and duffel coat.

One fit-looking gyal nearly bruck her neck looking back at me. If I wasn't in a hurry I would go back and chat to her, but time was tight. The bus was late again and it was nine-thirty by the time I reached the city.

I eventually got to the hotel at ten to ten. It was like a castle in Robin Hood times, but had a good rep. I went up to the receptionist and told her my name and who I was here to see.

"Oh, yes." She looked down a list of names and ticked off mine. "Would you take a seat, Mr Codrington, we're running slightly behind schedule."

I sat in the reception area, which was full of antique-looking furniture. I was twiddling my thumbs when the receptionist came and asked if I wanted a cup of tea. I didn't. I was trembling so much that most of it would have probably ended up on the carpet. It was ten-fifteen when a blue-eyed blonde lady, who I presumed was the secretary, came and led me up to the first floor interview room.

It wasn't what I expected. The room was small with no windows. A greasy-looking white man sat behind an old Sherlock Holmes-type wooden desk with a piece of green leather stuck to the top of it.

"Mr Harker, this is Marcus Codrington," said the secretary.

He looked up above his half-cut glasses. "Ahh, Mr Codrington. Take a seat."

I know first impressions are important, and mine of him weren't good. I could tell by the way he looked at me he wasn't too keen on a black man. And looking at his Benny Hill features I could see why most of his staff were young, female and blonde.

"This is a good application," he said, breaking the silence as he read over the forms Yvette helped me fill in.

"Tell me, why do you want this job, Mr Codrington?"

This was one of the questions Yvette went through with me last night. Though I was well nervous, everyt'ing came out almost as practiced. I was feeling good.

"Mr Codrington, I'll be frank with you. For various reasons there are no coloured people working here. How would you cope with that if I were to give you this job?" He said it as if he was God judging me at the pearly gates.

Questions like that get a man well vex. I felt like shouting *the only reason why there is no blacks here is 'cause you don't want to employ them. You telling me you can't find a black cook or receptionist in the whole of*

Birmingham? But again I remembered Yvette's words.

"I would cope by doing the job to the best of my ability and hope that I would be judged on my merits and not my colour," I said confidently and in perfect English—even though it was probably the opposite of what he thought I would say.

He nodded, then went through some more routine questions before he stood up and shook my hand.

"You'll hear from me within a couple of days."

"Cha, mom, me know say 'im did ah hang 'round yuh fe somet'ing. Yuh know you nah sight dat corn again?"

The old lady had just told me that she had lent her pardner money to the old man.

"Him say him goin' give me it back next week," she replied. The brown head-tie that covered her short plaited hair showed the same wear and tear as her face.

"And where 'im goin' get it from?" I asked. "And furthermore, 'ow much yuh gi' 'im?"

"Look, Marcus, it's my money to do what I want wid it," the old lady replied after a pause. "Him say some men already kick up 'im leg."

"Dem shoulda kill 'im."

I was well vex—not 'cause I too wanted borrow money off the old lady, but 'cause the old man feel he could take liberties now that Bigga was out of the way.

"Marcus! Don't chat 'bout yuh fadder like dat. He still help bring yuh into this world."

I looked at the flowered wallpaper on the dining room wall. T'ing been there since I was a yout'. Then my eyes rose to the large framed picture of a white, blue-eyed Jesus standing over his white disciples.

All I could do was sigh.

"Me soon come," I told the old lady as I rushed from the house.

I charged straight down the road to the woman who organised the pardner. When she told me it was nine hundred buff I flipped and went looking for the old man.

I walked the whole length of Soho Road, looking in every blasted bookie shop. Although it was cold I was sweating from all the running. As I was about to call off the search I sight the old man coming out of an off licence. He had a bottle of Wray and Nephew rum in his hand and a smile on his face. I waited for him to reach the corner then hook him up by his neck. When I search through his pockets, I find

151

eight hundred and fifty pounds.

I took it.

The man never raise a struggle or even argue. Wha' 'im fe say? I just left him standing on the street corner.

When I reach back by the old lady she was vex. But it never bother me 'cause I knew if I never get it back she would never see it again. If the old man really did owe man then they going have to lick up his ass. Simple as that.

After that I couldn't take corn off the old lady, even to pay the bill. When I checked the time, it was two-thirty. Bloodclaat. I was suppose to meet Theo at one.

I borrowed a fiver off the old lady and took a taxi to Hill Street.

It was ten to three when I arrived at Goldberg and Samson. As I came through the revolving doors, two workmen were putting up a sign saying Goldberg, Samson and Pal. *One day I might see Andre's name up there*. I walked up to the desk. There was a burly security guard sitting at a table. When he sight me he got up and marched up to the front desk like he was getting ready for trouble—even though I was dressed so sharp.

"Help you, sir?"

I again put on my English accent to take the piss out of him.

"Yes, you may. I'm here to see Theo Rutherford, a solicitor with Goldberg."

"Is that so?"

"Long time I haven't been in an office building like this. Yuh know when yuh go down for twenty years, things change."

"Twenty years?"

"Yeah, fe murder y'know."

"I see, sir."

He took a step back as his expression changed.

"Okay, sir, I'll just ring right up and tell him you're here."

I pretended to look around the building while he was on the phone to Theo. The fool was asking if he should escort me up to the sixth floor.

"But we don't want murderers walking around the building, Mr Rutherford," he whispered.

His expression then changed from fright to anger. He slammed the phone down and stood up. Chest out. Back to the John Wayne stance.

"Very funny, you..."

He cut off in mid-sentence but I could guess what the rest was.

"Sign here. He'll be waiting for you. Sixth floor."

I smiled and walked towards the lifts. A lift arrived, and Andre stepped out; he had a surgical collar around his neck. He looked at me and just walked on, well vex. Bloodclaat. I thought I did somet'ing.

"Yaow Andre, wha'ppen?" I shouted.

He just waved his hand and continued in the opposite direction. I was late as hell so I never bother to run him down. Maybe he was getting cold feet about me being in his building—bad for his reputation or somet'ing. Cha. Catch him later at training.

In the lift I tried to get my head around the problem at hand. In a strange way I was looking forward to seeing Marcia again, even under the present circumstances.

Theo's ugly face was there to greet me as the doors opened on floor six.

"What time do you call this, Marcus?"

He almost had steam coming out of his earhole.

"Me had somet'ing fe tek care of."

"God damn you, Marcus. This is the most important meeting of your life and you're two hours late."

Theo hurried across the expensive-looking blue carpet to his office.

"Do you care? And what's this about you being a murderer. You sure there isn't something you're not telling me?"

He looked worried as we approached the door to his office.

"Cha, man, don't fret. Is jus' a joke me did ah run wid de security guard."

"Those kind of jokes are not funny. We've got a serious job on our hands."

"Cool nuh, no one dead," I said, holding up my hands apologetically.

He gave me a stare that said he didn't see the funny side.

"At least you're dressed for the occasion."

As a solicitor, Theo was good, bloody good; but as a man he was a bag full of crap. We entered his big stush office. There was a thin white man in a blue suit, sitting on a brown leather sofa to one side of the room.

"Marcus, this is Jeremy Howard, Marcia's solicitor. Mr Howard, this is Marcus Codrington."

"Good to see you, Mr Codrington. We thought you were lost," he

153

said with a smile.

He got up and we shook hands, but after that first comment he lucky I never slap him across him head. I sat down in front of Theo's desk. Mr Howard moved from the sofa to a chair beside me.

Theo sat in a big brown leather revolving chair.

"Don't worry, Marcus, we haven't discussed anything of importance in your absence."

Made me feel important that they was waiting for me—never have anyone waiting for me. Suddenly it hit me there was someone missing.

"So is not only me get lost, whe' Marcia deh?"

"Marcia informed Mr Howard this morning that she had no wish to be at the meeting," said Theo, twiddling a pencil.

"But if she's not here 'ow can t'ings be sorted?"

"Look, Marcus...sorry, may I call you Marcus?" Howard asked; I nodded.

"My client has told me what she wants and I have advised her on the best route to take. So we can clear everything up today."

He pushed his glasses back up the bridge of his nose.

"And wha' she wan', Mr Howard—or me can call you Jeremy?" I asked, looking at him menacingly.

"Sorry?"

He looked bemused.

Theo shot me a look, then chipped in.

"My client means, what are the conditions laid down by Miss Stokes?"

Howard took a folded paper out of his inside breast pocket and opened it.

"Well now, let me see...basically in view of Marcus' abusive nature, my client doesn't want her daughter or herself subjected to acts of physical violence."

"But me never lay a finger 'pon me pickney!" I shouted.

"Mr Codrington, my client is in fear of you and as her legal representative I would say it's best you stay away. Forever!"

"Dat's me bloodclaat flesh 'n' blood—"

"Marcus, please." Theo cut me off in mid-sentence. "Look, Mr Howard, we asked you here to discuss my client obtaining reasonable access to his daughter. What you've put forward is totally unacceptable."

"I'm sorry, but the interests of the victims must take precedence here," he said, again pushing his glasses up his nose.

"Who's a victim? *Me* is de blasted victim!"

Howard refused to look me in the eye.

"This is precisely the sort of behaviour my client is in fear of."

"Marcus, please," Theo pleaded. "Mister Howard, since the incident when my client was provoked into causing minimal damage to your client's property, and subsequently arrested, he has not been in trouble."

"Firstly, I take issue with you on Marcus being provoked. On the contrary, the damage to my client's property was a wilful act which was definitely unprovoked. He broke a court injunction by being there in the first place, and it was only through my client's goodwill that the charges were dropped. "Secondly," he said, folding the piece of paper and putting it back into his pocket, "your client has been in trouble again."

"What do you mean?" Theo asked.

"Let me refresh your memory. On New Year's Day your client broke the jaw of one Alfonzo Riley at a celebration party thrown by a mutual friend."

This blasted debate was going on above my head. I tried to get it back on track.

"Listen ere, Missa Howard. Yuh know seh Mister Riley is one of de biggest rahtid drug dealer and pimp inna dis town?"

He butted in.

"It's not Mister Riley's character that's in question here. It's yours, Mister Codrington. And I wish you would refrain from using such distasteful language."

"Shut de raas up and listen!" I shouted.

Theo tried to intervene; I held my hand up to tell him also not to say a word. This was my time.

"Yuh see, Missa Howard, I didn't wan' my yout' growin' up 'round dat nastiness and I t'ink I did de 'hole of de city a bumbaclaat favour when I t'ump 'im. And yuh know somethin', I'd do it again if I sight 'im wid Marcia or my pickney. Y'overstand?"

"Furthermore—" Theo put in nervously, "—no charges were ever filed by this Alfonzo Riley."

"Despite what you say, gentlemen, I've not seen or heard anything today that will convince my client that her safety and that of her daughter are not under threat. I mean, he's already behaving like a wild animal."

I had had enough of this little fart. I got up and grabbed him by his lapels and pulled him out of his seat. His glasses immediately fell

155

to the floor.

Theo dived across his desk to part us. As he rushed at the two of us, something crunched under his feet.

"Listen ere, yuh slimy raas," I told Howard. "Yuh go tell Marcia dat me wan fe see my yout' and not a blasted court in de world gwan stop me from doin' dat. Yuh 'ear me?"

I released him.

"Good God!"

He bent down and picked up what was left of his glasses; they must have been in about a thousand pieces.

"I'll see you both in court," he squinted at us, then felt for the door knob and hurried out of the room. When the door closed Theo bent to pick up the remains of the broken glass off the floor.

"You know something, Marcus," he said, looking up at me. "You are one fucking idiot. I'll be getting another suit in the morning. I don't think you're going to rest until you get locked up. In fact a spell inside might do you the power of good."

"Wha' de raas yuh know? Yuh know how it feel when yuh cyan' even see yuh yout'?"

"No I don't, Marcus, but it's not me that is going to end up in prison."

"Cha," I grumbled. "I'm ask fe it."

"No, Marcus, he was goading you as any barrister would if you were in the dock. And you know what? You fell for it like a sucka. When are you black men going to learn that fighting the enemy with emotions and violence is futile? You've got to start using this..."

He pointed to his head.

"I don't know why I waste my time. Look, I've got to see another client in five minutes. Give me a call on Monday morning."

I went straight home and, without changing, sat down on the settee in complete darkness. The place was freezing. I had my hands in my suit trouser pocket but it never mek a difference. Nothing was shielding me from the cold. I thought about Charmaine and the possibility that because of my stupidity today I might never see her again.

The phone rang four separate times, but I just ignored it. I must have sat there three hours before I changed into my jogging suit and went to training at the university.

It was the first time I had ever been late for training; when I reach the changing rooms it never feel right. Everybody was there except for Winston, as usual, Andre, Calvin and Coach. I placed my bag on the bench without saying a word to anyone.

"Yaow, Terminator," Sicknote shouted from behind me. "You miss it, man."

"Miss wha'?"

"Calvin and Andre, loike," Benji chipped in.

"Wha'ppen to dem?"

"Came to blows, loike,"

"Fightin' like two woman," Lemi expanded, stuffing his face with a Snickers bar.

"Look like Calvin was troubling Andre pride and joy."

"Wha' 'im gyal?" I smiled, mainly 'cause I couldn't believe Calvin would do such a t'ing.

"Serious t'ing," Roots added, his locks almost touching the floor as he bent down to tie his laces. Levi agreed.

"Especially after all him say about me and my woman dem..."

"Man always try and play smooth and is him going off wid 'im best spar woman." Selwyn was ready with a pencil and paper in hand.

"Any geezer want to take odds on neither one of them playing tomorrow?"

When I got home I went straight and rang Yvette, but her answering machine was on, which meant she was already in bed.

I didn't leave a message.

I sat down in my bedroom—which at least had the streetlight shining through from outside.

I didn't sleep well. My head was either on Charmaine or the game. At times I didn't know which was more important. Morning came slowly. I tried to cheat it by getting out of bed at five-thirty, but although my body felt it was mid-morning there was no sign of daybreak outside.

Next thing I remember I was woken by the bell. I got up and staggered to the door. I looked through the spy hole and saw two black men in suit and tie. I knew they were Jehovah Witnesses—their haircuts gave them away. I picked up the two letters that had dropped through the box and went and sat back down. They rang the bell again. I felt like going and cussing them, but as I looked down at one of the letters I could see it was a reply from the interview.

My heart began to beat hard. I didn't want to open it. I tried to hold it up to the daylight, but I couldn't read it. So I decided to open it a piece at a time believing I would spot the word 'sorry' soon enough. Eventually, I just got brave and ripped it open. When I read it, I looked up towards heaven and smiled.

"Bloodclaat, me get it!" I said, quietly.

My reaction to getting the job was too laid back. I expected to jump 'round the room, but all I could t'ink bout was that I was a man again. I could hold my head high. My dignity was restored now I had corn in my pocket. Electric can stay off for now, but you not going to test me like that again.

At nine o'clock I phoned Yvette to tell her the good news. She was happier than me. She promised to celebrate after coming to the game tonight, and when she said she'll take Justin to her old lady afterwards, I knew we'd be celebrating with more than just a glass or two of champagne.

Before the game, the atmosphere in the changing room was tense.

Yes, the championship rested on this game—but to me it had more importance. I wanted revenge on dem tricksters for beating us so bad in Manchester. I was mad, vex and angry all rolled into one.

Coach walked round the whole team and spoke to everyone individually. I was fourth along the bench between Winston and Levi. Coach squeezed in the narrow space between us. I never really wanted to hear no last minute talk, I knew what I had to do and I just wanted to go out there and sort out them bwoy. But coach was going to talk whether I wanted to listen or not.

"Marcus, y'know yuh is a bettah player dan wha' dem limit yuh to in de last game. Go out there an' stamp yuh authority 'pon dem. Don't gi' dem time fe settle.

"Dem a go look to shut down yuh game like dem did up North. But dis time we a go 'ave 'nuff movement around the key. Joni and Calvin goin' do 'nuff pick 'n' roll stuff fe draw dem man away givin' yuh de one-on-one match up.

"Den is down to you. Me know seh yuh a go kick some ass t'day but remember...do it in a *controlled* way."

"Yeah Coach, me know. Me ready."

Andre didn't turn up for the match, but Coach understood he wasn't in the right frame of mind. Calvin was as cool as ever, going on like nothing happened.

The Warriors' theme tune was blazing and everyone clapped hands and shouted as we walked single file onto the court. Cheshire were there already, warming up. As we stood in a line straddling the centre court we raised our fists in our usual black power salute before starting our warm-up.

There were about five hundred people sitting around the court. As I went up for a lay-up I saw Yvette and Justin sitting directly behind the basket. I raised my fist quickly, then got my mind focussed on the game again. Dr Music Master was hitting all the latest rap tunes as we psyched ourselves up. As he slammed down Ice Cube's latest,the crowd were stamped their feet to the beat. The Uh Huh girls were dancing and jumpin' around the place. The House of Pain was ready.

They were ready to see a slaughter and I was ready to give it to dem.

I looked at the far end of the court and Cheshire looked well 'fraid. That's how we wanted them. Their yankee guard, John Price, was trying to encourage them but their faces looked like they had never seen so many monkeys out of their cages. The noise, everyt'ing, was touching their souls. They knew they weren't going to get out of here without a good waxing.

The start of the game couldn't come quick enough. When the referees called the starting five onto the pitch all the talking had to stop—it was time for deeds. Time for action.

The American won the tip-off over Joni, but the ball bounced off the back of another player and landed at my feet. I picked it up and Jah know, there was just one thing on my mind.

The basket.

I dribbled the remainder of the court. A defender came across to try and slap the ball out of my hands as I took off from just inside the free throw line, but it didn't matter as I jammed the ball through the hoop. For about three seconds, I held onto the ring dangling above the ground, looking directly at Yvette and Justin, my face tight with emotion.

Like everyone in the place they were on their feet with their hands in the air, screaming praise.

The referee immediately called a technical foul on me for holding onto the ring. I knew that obtaining a foul inside the first minute of the game was dumb and meant I had to stay outta trouble for the entire half at least. But I had made the statement I wanted. It got the crowd buzzing and more crucially it got the team well psyched.

Though Cheshire fought hard we never looked back from the first minute. I was unstoppable. Every shot I took seem to go through the hoop. Their big centre tried to hustle me by using his elbows as I went up for rebounds, and though I looked to the ref for protection he wasn't bothered, saying: "It's a man's game."

I responded the only way I knew how. Winston came dribbling down the centre of the court, pulled a move on their American guard and went up for a two-point jumper. He was slightly off and as the ball rebounded off the rim, I rose between their centre and Joni to reach the ball at its highest point before slamming it through the hoop. The force of my forward momentum sent their centre tumbling to the ground and as I stood over him I shouted:

"Call de undertaker. Me jus' bury a bwoy!"

The crowd saw me standing over him. With all the noise there was no way they could have heard what I said, but my stance was enough for the majority of them to stamp their feet and raise their fists in the Warriors' black power salute.

The referee didn't like it and called me to one side to give me a chat about my conduct. Man even threaten to throw me out the game if I do it again. But even he wasn't going to stop me beating up on these bwoys.

At half time we were ahead at 47-40. To clinch the championship we had to win by ten clear points. I had already scored eighteen points, and as we sat in the changing rooms Coach was bubbling.

"Marcus, if de score wasn't so I would tell yuh to free up the ball more, but me nah do dat 'cause yuh hot today, bwoy!

"Whatever yuh do, people, I beg yuh gi the ball to Marcus. Let 'im do de rest. It's run and shoot time."

He handed out orange cubes as refreshment to the team.

"Coach man, yer can't send all yer delivery through one post box. Man, I'm open for da J and I ain't seein' da rock," Winston shouted.

"Me know wha' yuh a say, Winston. But Marcus is de go-to guy fe dis game here and dat's it!" Coach replied.

"Damn, what da fuck am I here for? Shit, might as well be on da bench."

"Look, brotha man—" Calvin joined in, "—it can be arranged if that's what you want."

"Fuck you, asshole," Winston exploded, throwing his orange cubes to the floor. "Muthafuckas like you ought ta git busted for touchin' yer own road dog's bitch, man."

Calvin stayed calm and totally ignored Winston's dig at him.

"Look, brothas, we got the game won if we stick as one and play the game Coach wants. It's got us this far. So, men, let's go."

Everyone shouted *yaow* and left the changing room, clapping their hands as we went back out on to the court. This is where we wanted Cheshire—down by over five at half time and now the chance to run dem ragged with the run and shoot offence.

From the second half tip-off everything worked like a dream. A two-man combination of Winston, Adam and Benji closed down Cheshire's main threat, Price, and on the boards Calvin, myself and even Joni, and then replacements Levi and Lemuel were ruling the airwaves.

We turned up the pressure a notch and played basketball, British streetstyle. Winston with his dribbling set up a chance for Calvin, then for Joni. Adam then cut a move that I've never seen him attempt, or even thought he was capable of.

With two opponents converging on him he bounced the ball behind his back—taking one out of the play—and in the same movement bounced the ball through his legs leaving the other cold. As the lane opened up in front of him, he went in for an easy two point lay-up.

This was more a team effort, and in a way Winston got what he wanted, but I continued to score regularly and when they double-teamed me with two men it always meant that there was a Warrior open to sink a bucket.

By the end—when the final buzzer sounded to put Cheshire out of misery—we felt like the Harlem Globetrotters, here purely to entertain.

I looked over to the scoreboard: 101-83. I was mobbed by fans running onto the court. For the first time we had clinched the National League Division title. Everyone was rolling about on the floor. Benji and Lemi took the barrel of water from the side of the court and poured it over Coach while he was talking to Calvin. He was wet right through but he could only laugh. Even Winston had a smile on his face as he discussed somet'ing with Mr Lindsey, who, I noticed, had a cheque book in his hands.

Handsworth was going to mash up this night here.

Mr Lindsey then went on the mike to thank the fans and say there was a party at the Star Club.

I looked around the court. Cheshire had already run off the pitch to the safety of their changing room. I was walking off court when I felt someone tugging at my shorts, looked down and saw Justin. Rahtid. I had completely forgotten that Yvette and him were here. I picked him up and turned to look for his mother. She was standing directly behind me.

I held Justin in one arm and put the other around her. "Me tell yuh we a go do it," I said.

"You certainly did," she replied.

We both laughed. We were heading through the doors leading to the changing room when I saw Veronica with another woman, a younger gyal and two yout' man.

"Veronica, what you doing here, girl?" Yvette said as she went to greet her neighbour.

As they embraced I looked at the woman standing beside Veronica. She met my gaze. To rahtid, the face was familiar. I just couldn't put a name to it. The younger gyal started pulling at her cashmere coat.

"Samantha, behave yourself," she said.

Bloodclaat! The t'ing click.

"Nadine?" I said, uncertainly.

"Hello Marcus..."

I hadn't seen her in fourteen years and she had lost 'nuff weight. She also had a slight accent. Yvette and Veronica stopped talking.

"You know each other?" Yvette asked.

Veronica butted in.

"This is my sister Nadine and this is Marcus' daughter Sam, and her two sons from her present husband."

"Daughter?" Yvette said, in a state of shock. She looked at me. I didn't know where to turn. I had never mentioned it to her. She mighta thought, what kind of man lose two of 'im pickney?

"Come, Justin."

Yvette pulled him out of my hands and disappeared into the crowd. I was still frozen to the spot. I couldn't move a rahtid muscle. All the excitement of the game slowly drained from my body.

11
Reckless Dreams

Joseph had iced himself. *Damn!*

After the homie was released from hospital shit began briefly to look up for him. Then, bam! Fool didn't take his medication; thought he was cured.

Started to hallucinate, see all this shit a sound homie couldn't see. Used to go downtown, strip butt naked and dance like a Chippendale on the sidewalk. Five-O arrested his ass many times and Janet would turn up like Madame Teresa to bail his loony ass out.

Man, I told her the homie was way gone. But she wanted to play stubborn. Thought shit was goin' to return to normal, but they were as normal as they would ever be.

Hell no, I'm not sorry he finally did the right thing. His life was hell and my sis was goin' cerebral worryin' about what game he was goin' to pull next. Shit wasn't good for Uriah, either. I felt for my sis, but I didn't share the view that Joseph was goin' to get better.

Muthafuckas like that only get worse. Period.

Shit bore fruit one day last week. Joseph had enough of breathin' live air. Homie went out on to the balcony of Janet's flat, climbed over the fence and jumped. Knucklehead thought he was Superman. Thought he'd fly back to Krypton, but wham! Ended up on the sidewalk. Doc said his face was so fucked up his own mother didn't recognise him.

Janet blames herself. She had popped out to take Uriah to the doctor. Young blood had a high temperature, but she didn't check to see if Joseph had taken his gear first.

For him, not takin' his shit was like the only game he knew he could play and win, but when the ref blew that final whistle it was Joseph who was the overtime loser.

Out of respect for Janet I was carryin' the coffin from the hearse to the burial ground with Joseph's two brothers, his dad and two long-time homiez of his. As we approached the spot, I could see the white robe of the waiting vicar; he stood out like a beacon amid the black and grey sea of mourners around him.

Even the sun—shining for the first time in February—couldn't brighten the sorrow on the faces of the people gathered.

The vicar directed us to park the coffin across three long strips of cloth beside the grave. Janet was in tears, facing me, and Mum had her arms around her. What I presumed was Joseph's family stood immediately next to Mum, who was holding Uriah's hand.

I felt for the young blood. Growin' up without dad ain't easy. Homie should know, I didn't even see mine apart from some photos Mama used to show us when she wasn't dissin' the man wholesale. Made up my mind right then to try and provide the little homie with the role model I never had. My shit's not that safe, but I was down enough. Knew what a man has to know.

The vicar read a passage from the Good Book, his hair flicking in the mild breeze. We sang a hymn that I remembered from Sunday school—another thing Mama forced on me when I was a pee wee. Since there wasn't a hymn book nearby I had to hum the tune because the lyrics escaped me.

The vicar then instructed us to lower the coffin into the grave. We grabbed one end of the strips each, lifted the coffin and held it over the grave. Then we lowered it by gradually releasing the strips.

The vicar read another prayer but all I can remember is him saying ashes to ashes, dust to dust and some of the mourners throwing flowers on top of the coffin. I picked up one of the four shovels and began to fill in the six-foot hole. Janet put her hand out for the shovel. I gave it to her and the tears flooded down her cheeks as she shovelled earth into the hole.

When the grave was covered, the vicar said something confidential to Janet and Joseph's family. Other people then came and offered their two-faced handshakes. People who dissed him full-time when he was makin' the bucks now shed crocodile tears and offered half-hearted condolences before dispersing.

It was only then that I realised Cheryl was present. She was standing behind Janet all the time, but I didn't recognise her 'cause she had a veil over her face. As she walked past me in the direction of the parked cars she just said:

"Hi."

That was it.

Damn, I hadn't been with Cheryl in over a month, and even the vicar could have seen I wanted a piece of her butt to supplement my extra-curricular activity. But the baby was disprespectin' me full time. When I occasionally cornered her at Janet's crib, I'd be rappin' hard, tryin' my best lines, but she'd give me the big zero. Stared at me like the last five years didn't mean shit. I know it takes a female time

164

to get stuff like Zorro's shit outta their system, but Cheryl was goin' into triple overtime.

Janet always pleaded with me to sort the shit out. As my sister and Cheryl's best friend, I could understand why she didn't want to make a call on any illegal shit between us. I've tried Cheryl's digits, and put my emotion up front with her, but she cuts the line dead soon as she hears my rap.

Can't understand why the baby wants to play negative tactics, but I know I'm like a homie without his high-top kicks when she's not around.

As I turned to walk back to the car Janet came up to me holding Uriah's hand.

"Winston, can you come around this evening?"

I nodded.

"Have you spoken to Cheryl?" she asked, using a hanky to dab the tears from her eyes.

"Said a few words."

"Winston, you've got to talk to her."

"She da man. Homie's played my ace, but she's dealin' nothin' but jokers."

"I'll have another word with her when we get back to Nechells. We have to go over by Joseph's dad's house for a quiet drink, then I'll go by Mum's."

"So how yer hangin'?"

"I don't know, Winston."

She looked at me as if her mind had suddenly gone blank.

"In a strange way it feels like a relief, but deep down I feel that it could have been prevented. If only someone...anyone...had helped him to cope earlier. I think we left it too late."

She began to cry. I put my arm around her and she rested her head on my chest for a while. Then she collected herself, turned and walked to the waiting car. Shit was feelin' for her. She had been on a long losin' streak and homie knew it was eatin' at her. She didn't need Cheryl and my problems on top of that now that she was a widow.

I had a quick word with Mum before I left. The ice between us was beginning to thaw, but I knew she still didn't like most of my moves.

I suppose all mums want to live their homiez' lives for them. Prob with mine is that she doesn't know which stop to get off at. And that shit still didn't hang right with me. I wasn't in the mood to go by Joseph's parents' house, so I just jumped in my wheels and headed back to my crib.

It seemed a touch disrespectful to be shakin' my wheels with Dr Dre and Snoop after a burial—but one of my bitches had just financed my new megawatt system and I had to test its range. I know my shit was bulletproof again 'cause the sidewalk homiez would turn and stare from a hundred yards away. I was the man in the 'hood again.

As I got in, Mrs O'Farrell came out of her room to greet me.

"Ah, Winston. Another of your lady friends came to see you." I could tell that she had already been on the liquor.

"Leave any ID?" I asked, knowin' Mrs O'Farrell had synced up with my vibe.

"No—but it was the one with long blonde hair," she replied, going back into her room.

"Damn...Cindy."

I jogged up the stairs to my shack. As I put the key in the lock, the door down the hall from mine opened and the weird-looking punk who lived there came out. Shit's funny, but in the eight months or so that I've hung out here I can count the number of times I've seen this dude on one hand.

Punk looked nervous, like he was tryin' to hide something behind his back. He grunted something, but I just blanked him and walked into my apartment.

The crib was warm, but in a mess. Since Cheryl ejected my ass from her court, homie found it difficult to motivate myself to become a house nigger. I took off my clothes and lay face down on the bed with just my briefs on.

Joseph's mug kept invading my space like a bad dream. A homie's life isn't worth a dime. Man was building a phat career, livin' large, then the bell rings and damn, your number's up, game over. Brought home to me that whatever was goin' to happen to me I couldn't predict, but I knew I had to get mine and get it soon before my shit was up too.

I picked up the letter on the side table. It was from Tiffany Goldberg, doggin' me for not writing back to her in the States and also givin' me an open invitation to work out with her pop's CBA team in April.

Bitch reckons she's given her ol' man a progress report with an A-plus grade. Man can't wait to see a homie perform. Fact that they don't know shit about the quality of ball this side of the pond was to my advantage. I was livin' off my Delaware rep and the bitch's infatuation—but that's all I needed to get me back to the States.

It's the break I've been waitin' for.

After I light up the CBA, then it's a natural progression to the NBA. Homie would be able to sign blank cheques, have a phat crib in the burbs, Ferrari, take care of sis, any shit I wanted.

All would be mine for the takin'.

Agent was fillin' my head with weak-ass jive that I was too old or too short to be an NBA rookie. Tried to hype up interest from some Polish outfit but, shit, if he couldn't get me an NBA contract he had no right representin' me. Why settle for instant coffee when you can have capuccino? I ought to fire his ass. How can he put an age limit on what a homie can achieve? Man don't even know me. Man, I just turn twenty-five last month. Still had a handle on the rock and my all-round game was original shit.

Okay, shit dipped a bit against Cheshire two days ago, but Marcus was on a personal bombin' mission, playin' solo. Man got us the points, and a championship win in England still sits well on my resume.

Come play-offs Marcus ain't goin' to see the rock. Homie will move up a gear, show the homiez that I'm ten steps ahead of them. No prob. *Winston 'Macca' Mckenzie, welcome to the CBA.*

The bell rang, but Mrs O'Farrell took an unusually long time to get to the door. It rang three times. Old fool must be pissed outta her brains. Eventually, I heard her talkin' to someone and stiletto heels heading up the stairs and towards my door.

Whoever it was knocked softly. I got up off the bed pulled on a pair of jeans and my Converse tee-shirt and opened the door.

"Cindy...how yer doin'?"

I wished I hadn't opened.

"Don't sound *too* enthusiastic about seeing me..."

"Damn, don't take it to heart. Jus' things on my mind."

I held the door open and she walked into my tip.

"Well, whatever was on your mind, it certainly wasn't cleaning this place up. Look at it! Some of these things were here last week."

"Yer soundin' like a bitch, get off my case," I said, sitting on the settee. "Anyway, whadda y'want?"

She came and sat beside me and placed her right hand between my thighs.

"You know what I want."

I met Cindy about a month ago. Homie's wheels almost made a pork chop of her little boy. When I got out of the car to see if he was still breathin', bitch did a mad one, went berserk, started throwin' fists and feet everywhere— even though it was her son who bolted out into the road. Homie thought I was in World War Three.

But after she chilled, we got talkin' terms and though she nests with her husband and two other kids she checks in once, sometimes twice a week—while her husband's at work—to be serviced.

Cindy was on top of me lavishing big, wet smoochers all over my face. I had to close my eyes to stop her long blonde hair blinding me. Shit wasn't in the mood and I think she caught my drift.

"Look, I didn't come all the way from Sutton for nothing, Winston. What's the matter with you today?"

She stood up and took her bomber jacket off.

"Cindy, I'm not ready for dis shit. A homie was just buried," I told her, but she couldn't give a damn. She wanted to get a piece of my ass right now and I'd need to offer her a pneumatic drill as compensation for her not ridin' me today.

"So, Winston's not feelin' randy, huh?"

Bitch bent over and rubbed the sides of my face with her hands. Then she stood up and pulled her sweat shirt over her head, humming a teasing song like in one of those low-life titty bars. She slowly pulled down the zip on her jeans, and eased them down her legs like if she was starrin' in some cheap movie.

Homie's temperature rose from Buffalo-cold to Miami-hot in the space of seconds.

Cindy stood like a pink mannequin in front of me. Her shit was a bit on the skinny side but with a booty bitches would die for; firm and curved in all the right places. She stood there wigglin' her hips in just a bra and knickers, with the thinnest of straps. Shit didn't take much muscle for her to release the bra and though the law of gravity was beginning to take its toll, her breasts were still nice for a honey movin' into mid-life.

Then she made history of the strings keepin' her knickers to her gyratin' hips. She walked up and sat facing me with her knees between my legs. She held her tits and started to rub them in my mug.

Homie was eatin' outta her bowl.

She forced me down on the settee, undid my jeans and pulled them and my briefs down to my knees. She sat on top on me purring like a cat as she forced me into her.

Woman was pumpin' away like she was drillin' for oil when the phone rang.

I didn't pay any attention, 'cause not even Red Adair coulda put these flames out. The phone rang five times, then the answer machine picked up.

"Winston, Cheryl..."

I jumped up, sending Cindy tumbling to the floor. My manhood was still wet with love juices. I tried to pull my jeans up to give me a longer stride pattern as I raced to the answering machine. When I got there Cheryl was about to hang up.

"Cheryl!" I said. I was just in time.

"Oh, I thought you were still at Joseph's family's house," she said.

"Blew it out, man. Jus' come outta da shower," I said, tryin' to get my breath back.

"Winston, I'm going home for a few weeks but I want to speak to you before I go."

"Whassup, babe?" I said, feeling content simply that her fingers had at last found the way to punchin' out my digits.

"Look...I'm about five minutes walk from you—I'll come and tell you."

I said 'word' without thinkin' that Cindy was still here. I put the phone down, pulled up my trousers and marched back over to the settee like a head coach with a new game plan. Cindy was lying there butt naked smokin' the blunt I'd rolled last night.

"Yer gotta hit da streets, babe."

"What? I haven't finished with you yet. Come here."

She grabbed my hands and pulled me on top of her like an all-in wrestler.

I fought my way free and stood up, then went around the room picking up all her clothes and throwing them at her.

"Get yer shit on and move yer cream-ass butt outta here fast!" I yelled.

She could see this was no Woody Allen movie. As she put her clothes on I looked out of the window trying to spot Cheryl coming along the street.

I looked at Cindy; she was almost dressed, except for her shoes. She slipped them on and headed for the door, then stopped.

"You know something, Winston? You weren't that fuckin' good."

She slammed the door on the way out.

Bitch was upset now, but I knew she'd be knockin' same time, same place next week.

I watched as Cindy went through the front gate.

About half a minute later, Cheryl appeared from the opposite

169

direction. Homie rushed to try and clear up, but you can't do a day's job in a minute. I sprayed the room with Pot Pourri air freshener.

The door bell rang and I opened my door to Cheryl. She had on a bright red coat with black trimmings and collar and a black beret. She looked well fly. She walked in and stood still. I could see she had a beef about the state of the crib.

"I see nothin' changes, Winston."

"Man was about ta give it da once over," I replied, feeling I'd already got off on the wrong foot.

"Anyway, that's not what I've come for."

She unbuttoned her coat, placed it on the back of the settee and sat down.

"Can I git yer somethin'? A drink or..."

"No Winston, I'm fine."

She had a 'strictly business' look on her pretty, almond face.

"So how yer been hangin', babes?" I asked, trying to break the cold-ass atmosphere that was building up.

"Fine."

Shit. We have to get away from these one-word answers. We started to talk about the funeral, but Cheryl soon let me know she hadn't come to discuss the finer points of the vicar's speech.

"How long are yer on vacation in Bristol?" I asked.

"I've taken a month off. I don't know how long I'll be spending in Bristol."

"A month off! Why?"

"I need time to think. I need to get away."

"What's on da agenda that's gonna take a month to sort?"

"Things," she replied. Then, out of the blue she asked:

"Winston, what do you want out of life?"

Shit. It was another of those deep philosophical numbers. Questions that she sprang on a homie every now and again. Questions that demanded an answer.

Homie didn't know whether to play it the Luther Vandross—cool and smooth, with some false truths—or go for the Ice T, direct, no-bull line. In the end homie fell between the two.

"Shit, dat's a powerful one, Chez."

I hesitated.

"I dunno really. I suppose I would like to make the NBA, but..."

"I mean, what about gettin' a proper job instead of sitting around all day and training every other evening?"

Shit, here we go again.

"Chez, I've got a regular job. I'm a pro b-ball player," I said, knowing she was gonna hit base with some negatives.

"When are you going to grow up, Winston? How long can you play basketball, another two or three years? What then, huh? I suppose you'll try and become a coach, bumming around the country looking for any team that wants to hire a black man with three years experience of playin' in America?"

"Shit, ain't goin' be like dat, Cheryl. I've got plans."

I went over to the table by the bed and picked up the invitation from Tiffany.

"Look, I've been invited to try out for the semi-pro league in America."

"Winston, stop kidding yourself!" she shouted.

"What's the matter with you? If you were good enough to make it you would have done it when you were out in the States. For God's sake, you're twenty-five now."

I sat next to her.

"Chez, I was never given da license to show my true skills at college. But if I make da semi-pro league, then homie's a jump shot away from da NBA."

"Winston, all I'm hearing are 'ifs'. It's time you took the blinkers off. Start preparing yourself. Go to college, get the qualifications you missed out on and try and make somethin' of yourself."

"Cheryl, b-ball is what I'm down wit'. Ask me to sink a ten foot jumper and I'll hit da money everytime. I don't know shit 'bout being a mechanic, electrician or any other nine-to-five jobs. Dat shit ain't for me. I'm da man on da blacktop."

"But you can *learn*, Winston."

"Damn, Cheryl. Homie gotta take da shot at da pros or my shit ain't gonna be worth a dime. *Damn!* I don't want to wake up when I'm fifty sayin' 'if only'. Da ops is kickin' me in da face and I wanna take dat shit head-on. Y'knowha'msayin?"

"Winston, you could wake up at fifty knowing that you have achieved nothing. Then where will you be?"

"Well, baby, I appreciate yer concern, but it's my call."

"So it is. I'll see you around."

She got up to go, her face as red as her coat. Homie didn't try to put the brakes on her. Damn shit wasn't worth pursuing. Couldn't believe that Cheryl came down here just to discuss my career prospects.

Just like Mama, disrespectin' my ability. *Shit, when is a sista goin to*

*stand behind a brotha? Give him some support instead of buryin' a homie's
ambition with negative vibes?*

One thing she did make clear was that my mind was made up. I
was going back to America to try out for the CBA in a couple of
months time.

I slipped an NBA tape in the video. It was Chicago versus
Portland in the first of the seven-match World Championships. I had
already watched it many times but damn, you could never get
enough of Jordan's moves. My mobile rang as Jordan was goin' for
another gravity-defyin' slam dunk. I paused the video to answer it.

"Hector, whassup nigga?"

I let the action play again. Hector started giving me some rap on
how Five-O raided his homie's crib last night and threw him in a
meat wagon. I knew it was probably a load of bullshit. He said something about lying low 'cause he would be next on Five-O's hit list of
drug kingpins.

I didn't want to confuse his spaced-out mind even more. I told
him I'd hook up with him tomorrow before I signed off.

No sooner had I called time on Hector's bull than the phone rang
again. Shit, seemed like I needed a personal assistant.

"*What?*" I shouted, to let the caller know they were disturbing a
private party of one.

"Guess who?"

It was a female voice, but I was in no mood for stupid-ass games.

"Look, whoever it is you better come correct or I'm cuttin' yer
dead."

"Don't you remember me, Winston?"

"Bitch, yer history, bye..."

"Okay, Winston its me, Helen..."

Shit. I haven't heard from this bitch in six weeks. I thought she got
tired of my black ass.

"What can I do for yer, Helen?"

Stupid question.

"I've got some good news."

I took a deep breath and waited.

"My father's firm's relocating to Birmingham and I'm coming to
live there. Isn't that great?"

Homie exhaled like a typhoon.

Shit, all I needed was this nymphomaniac living in the same city
as me. Damn, couldn't he relocate to damn Germany or Japan like
other firms. *Who the hell comes to Birmingham?*

172

"Winston, you've gone silent."

"Shit's come as a surprise. Straight up. Birmingham is a fly kinda city. More waterways than Venice," I said, takin' the piss. "Whassup wit yer lover?"

"He's my husband now," she replied. "We brought the wedding forward and I'm just back from honeymoon in Barbados. I've got a sun-tan just like yours."

She giggled. Shit sounded like something Frank Bruno's missus would say to him...or maybe the other way around.

The line developed a hitch, began hearin' a hissin' sound. I couldn't make shit out—except when she said something about nothing stopping us having a bit on the side now—but before I could answer the line went dead. I switched off the phone to make sure she couldn't call back.

Damn, with her, Cindy, the other one-night stands and Cheryl all in the same city, I thought it was time to do a Lord Lucan.

I finished viewing the game before deciding it was time to go and check out sis.

I forgot six o'clock was pressure hour in the 'hood. Cars, buses, taxis everywhere. Only time Birmingham played at being a big city for real. Took me almost an hour to drive a distance that normally takes a quarter. Still, I had Cypress Hill to comfort me.

Damn—had to park my wheels in a legit downtown place. Little mothers not goin' to get a second chance to re-design my interior.

I took the ten-minute walk from the NCP to Nechells passin' through the grounds of Aston University. Got my visions going back to Delaware.

As I did a black beauty crossed my eyeline. Shit looked stuck-up, bourgie, middle-class hippie with all those books in her hand and dressed like her clothes came off-the-peg from Oxfam—but I can tell the body was ready under the rags. Homie gave her the stare as she came closer.

"Whassup, babee?" I said as she walked past me.

Bitch didn't say a word. Disrespected me like I was a piece of dog shit on the sidewalk.

"Hey, bitch, I'm talkin to yer."

She walked on without lookin' back.

"Jis 'cause yer have knowledge in yer hands, think yer don't need a homie? Hey bitch, dem white dudes yer hangin wit' can't give yer what I can. Bitch."

Shit, that's why black women are a pain in the membrane. Take

173

one look at a homie and start sendin' wrong signals. Bitches all brought up by their muthas to dis the black man. Believin' he ain't no higher than the dirt they walk on.

Fuck them.

White girls takin' fine care of my ass anyway. Black women—including Cheryl—can go and swim in the deep end with hundred pound dumb-bells welded to their ankles.

I continued from the edge of downtown to the shit of Nechells. Even the streetlights became dimmer when I crossed the dividing line.

I turned into Janet's project. Little homiez were on patrol again. Shit had to confront them about my wheels. I walked up to them. Muthas didn't even flinch. At that age I would've sprinted for a hideout.

"Where's yuh wheels?" one in a Raiders Starter jacket asked, before I could open my mouth.

"Yer li'l muthafuckas messed wit' me," I replied as I grabbed the smallest of them by his Redskins coat.

"Gonna pay back all dat shit or I'm gonna bury yer one by one."

"What shit y'talkin' 'bout, man," said the homie who looked like a war veteran. I squeezed the neck of the homie I was holding.

"Let loose, man. I ain't done nothin'..."

"Pay up or return da goods, man, no other option."

"We ain't done nothin'," said another voice.

Then I felt a heavy hand on my shoulder. I looked around and there was this man-mountain standin' there like Dump Truck, the sumo.

"I'm the block caretaker. What seems to be the problem?" he said, in a voice that could make the ground shake.

"Li'l homiez broke my car, messed up my interior and robbed my system."

He took his fat white hand off my shoulder. "Is that true?" he asked them.

"Homie's foolin'. We ain't done nothin'," one replied.

"The guys say they didn't do it. I believe them. So on your way, son."

Homie wasn't about to argue so I disappeared. As I did I could hear them laughin'.

When I arrived at Janet's she was looking more together than this morning.

"Whassup, sis?" I said, following her into the dining room.

174

"I'm coming to terms with it. I don't know what's better, coping with him being in hospital or trying to get to grips with the fact that I'll never see him again..."

There was a black bag on the floor, half-filled with Joseph's stuff. Janet saw me looking at it.

"I'm just getting rid of his clothes," she explained. "By the time Uriah grows up they'll be long out of fashion."

We both laughed. I sat down beside her on the old-time settee.

"Where's young blood, anyway?"

"Mom's looking after him for the week to give me time to clear up the place. Anyway, what's up with you?"

She looked more cheerful.

"Shit still da same. Homie on a difficult run."

"What about you and Cheryl ?"

"Like I said, she ain't comin' correct."

I looked down at the floor. "Paid me a visit after da funeral. Did nothin' but diss me."

"It takes two to tango. She told me her side when she came here after leaving you."

"Shit. Does she tell yer everythin'?"

"No, only the things that worry her. Cheryl's my closest friend, and I don't like seeing her like this, but you're my twin brother. Y'know it makes things difficult."

"I know sis, believe me. So what did she have to say for herself?"

"Nothin' really. Just said she's catching the five-something train to Bristol and that she'd ring me when she gets back."

"Dat's all?"

I thought she would have left a word for me. Janet's face dropped.

"Whassup, sis?"

"Winston, I can't tell you. I promised."

"Tell me what?"

She sighed.

"Look, you really should hear it from her."

"Hear what?"

I was becoming impatient with my sister.

"Look, Winston, I don't think you're treating Cheryl right," she said quickly.

"She told me about the Zorro incident, and some white girl."

"Janet...I played a couple of extra games," I said, searching for an explanation. "Shit was a mistake but no one got killed."

"Oh, so it's a couple of times. I only heard about the once."

175

"Bitches offered it up for free. Shit didn't turn it down, y'knowha'msayin'?"

"Winston, y'know I don't like you talking like that. We're not bitches and whores."

"Sorry, sis. But you know how things go wit' da homiez."

"I know how things go with some other me, but not with my brother. I mean...a *white* girl—haven't you got any standards?"

"So because I'm your twin brother I'm supposed to be different—is that it? Janet, stop goin' on like Mama."

"I don't want to argue with you, Winston, especially today. But that girl lived for you. She stayed faithful while you were off playin' ball in America. I know because I was with her twenty-four, seven. 'Nuff men ran her down and she always said she was spoken for.

"Now she's looking for you to face up to your responsibilities and you want to go and play ball again in America."

"What goddamn responsibilities?"

Janet looked at me with an attitude I hadn't seen since we were teenagers.

"For God's sake, Winston. The girl's carrying your baby!"

Shit didn't know whether to pass out or follow Joseph over the balcony. Homie sat back in the chair totally psyched.

"Straight up? Yer not trippin'?"

"Course! I went to the hospital with her a month ago for the test."

"A month ago? And you didn't tell me?"

"Cheryl insisted I didn't. She wanted to see how you really felt about her. She didn't want you loving her up just for the sake of the baby."

"Shit should've told me."

"Well, the cat's out of the bag now."

"What time's her train?"

"Five-thirty-something, I think."

I looked down at my watch. Damn, it was almost eight o'clock.

"I'm headin' south."

"You do that. And please treat her gently."

"Got any dollars on yer?" I said.

"Winston, please."

"I'll git my Warriors paycheck tomorrow. I'll pay yer back, straight up. I need some gas."

"Take this, and remember it's my last ten pounds."

"Word, sis." I jumped up and headed for the front door.

The little punks were still on guard in the car park. As I ran past

176

them half a house-brick almost detached my head from my shoulders. I stopped, looked back 'and the muthafuckas just stood there like they were at a tea party. Damn, had no time to jack their asses up...I continued to sprint to my car.

The freeway was wide open and at times I touched a hundred-and-ten, flashing my beams at anythin' slowin' my ass down. Homie was lucky no Five-O was in the area.

I thought *damn, I've heard it all today but this is the livin' bomb. I'm not ready for this daddy shit.*

Damn enjoyin' the ghetto single life too much. Thought Cheryl was down with the programme. This felt like a bitch trap design to put the clamp on my freelancing.

My luck was over just past the Gloucester turn-off; I hit a tailback, all three lanes were moving like snails.

It had taken me just forty ticks to get this far, but by the time the traffic freed I had spent almost two hours on the motorway. I came off at junction sixteen then headed down to the St Paul's, just outside the city centre. Territory had a reputation like Handsworth. Homiez were livin' the thug life to survive. Muthas torched it, just like my own 'hood. But their gangsta shit was still down on my set.

Damn lucky—I knew the direction 'cause I used to drop Cheryl home each Friday evening when I was back for the summer vacation last year.

As I was cruisin' down the back streets of St Paul's my mobile rang.

"Whassup?" I shouted.

"Winston, where are you? I've been trying to ring you back since we got cut off this afternoon."

Helen. Damn! Wasn't in the mood to talk to her.

"Helen, there's somethin' wrong wit' da line, shit keeps cuttin out."

"Anyway, where are you? I want to see you."

If I billed everyone who wanted a time-out with Winston McKenzie today, I would be as rich as the biggest gangsta rapper.

"Gotta full schedule, tonite's not possible. I'm busy."

"Busy doing what?"

"That's my fuckin' business! Anyway, the line's gettin' faint."

The line was as clear as mineral water, but I had to get rid of this bitch. I switched it off before she could reply.

It was almost eleven-thirty when I parked in front of Cheryl's crib. The street was so deserted you could've heard a baby fart. I got out of the car and walked up to the house. All the lights in the house were off.

Didn't want to ring the large brass bell, so I gently knocked the letterbox. I waited what seemed like five minutes but no-one came. I knocked again, slightly louder. The passage light came on.

"Who is it?"

Thank God it was Cheryl's voice.

"It's me, babes."

She open the door and stood there in her nightgown.

"Sorry for wakin' yer, Chez, but we gotta talk."

She showed me into the living room.

"I expected you earlier. Janet told me you left at eight..."

"There was a massive jam by Gloucester."

I took the seat she offered in a room the size of a b-ball court. Ancient ornaments occupied the shelves above an old fireplace and a picture of the Pope stared down as if he had a personal message for them.

"I know Janet told you. I didn't want her to, but I guess you had to know sometime."

"Wasn't it worth givin' da father a breath of da good news?"

There was a short silence, then I heard footsteps upstairs.

"Is who dat, Cheryl?" a Trinidadian voice shouted from above.

"It's okay, Dad," she said, getting up and going to the doorway.

"It's only Winston. I forgot my cash-card in Birmingham and he brought it down for me. Go on back to bed."

"Aahh, tell 'im t'anks."

Cheryl came back into the room and sat down.

"They wise to da situation?"

"If you mean, do they know? No, they don't."

That was a relief. I don't think Pops would have been too pleased at me gettin' busy with his only daughter out of five homiez. Shit would also make it easier for her to have an abortion without the old timer bringing the whole of Rome into the equation. Cheryl stared at me silently.

"Well?" I said.

"Well what, Winston?"

"Damn, you havin' it?" I said, feelin' agitated.

"Of course I'm having it. What kinda question is that to ask. I'm a confirmed Catholic."

It was a bit late to be preachin' religion. "Don't I have a say in this?" I asked.

"Winston, I tried to include you when I came round earlier today. And as far as I'm concerned you made your decision then."

"Damn, Chez. I not ready for dis baby shit. Man, you've got yer career to look out for. So have I."

"You're not ready for this, Winston? Well, how many times did you use protection?"

"Shit, I thought you were down wit' da programme."

"Why you always relyin' on me to safeguard your ass?"

"Damn, dat's da way it is. Period."

"It's not the way it is—'cause I'm pregnant and I'm having it."

"How can you play me dat way, Chez?"

"Look Winston, I didn't plan this, but it's happened, okay? And I'm having this baby. If you want to be part of it you've got to be fully committed to me and the child, or you can start walking right now."

The more I thought about it the more I felt trapped. She had a homie by the neck and was goin' for the jugular.

"Shit smells like blackmail, Cheryl..."

It was the only response I could come up with.

"Is that how you see it, Winston? If your sister hadn't told you, you wouldn't even have *known*.

"You're so caught up in your own little dream world where only you, basketball and smoking weed are important. I didn't want to tell you, let alone blackmail you. Give me a break, you asshole!"

"Ssshh, Cheryl, cool dat shit out! Wanna wake da whole of St Paul's?"

"Don't tell me what to do. Look, I think you'd better leave. It's obvious you have no intention of being part of this."

She got up, her face red as beetroot, and marched towards the door.

"Go on. Get out!"

I walked towards her.

"Cheryl, I'm sorry, shit came out wrong."

She chilled a little and moved away from the door. She looked directly into the mirror, frustrated, and blew out a gust of air before bending down and at last igniting the gas fire. I came up behind her like the hero in one of those damn love stories and put my arms around her waist. Homie felt like Rhett Butler. Didn't feel like a young blood growin' inside.

Shit, for the first time ever I hoped Cheryl was playin' me, but the tears fillin' her eyes were the real deal.

"I'm sorry, Cheryl. I didn't mean it to sound the way it came out."

Damn, was still confused but agreed to abide by the conditions she laid down.

By the end of the evening I had also agreed to give up my dream of playin' b-ball in the CBA, stop smokin' blunts, and give up my personal crib and move into her place in Moseley.

Shit, what else could a homie do? If I hadn't, the CSA would be on my ass for upkeep.

Cheryl would be on it for desertion.

Mama would be on it just to diss.

And Janet would probably just want to kick me up it.

Man, homie had no choice but to play along with the scheme. Shit's like robbin' the poor to feed the stupid, and Cheryl was stupid for messin' with the programme and gettin' pregnant. And damn fool for havin' it.

She knows I'm not the fatherly type but still she goes and jacks me up like this. Worse, I don't even get a vote in becomin' a father. If I was equally responsible for this shit, how comes I have no rights when it comes to decidin' if the baby's born or not?

It's a fuckin' scam.

Cheryl said she would tell her parents in the morning and she didn't want me around when she broke the news. I didn't need much persuading. Damn, could sense more than a sermon from her parents.

I borrowed a Shakespeare off Cheryl and drove straight back to Birmingham.

The journey back was quicker. I spent most of the time thinking that I had surrendered my whole shit to Cheryl.

It was three by the time I turned the corner into my street. I could see Helen's Mercedes parked, and could make out the back of her head. The bitch must have been sitting there all night!

I did a three-point turn and drove off in the opposite direction—up to the frontline, to get a draw. Cheryl had not yet got my ass on a full-time contract.

Hadn't been up in the heart of Handsworth for some time 'cause I was tryin' to steer clear of the hell-holes where I was likely to find Zorro wormin' his nastiness. Brotha still broke me out in a cold sweat.

I double parked by the Star Club. The place was rammed with high quality motors—BMWs, Saabs, Mercs, the lot.

Damn, if this ghetto's poor then I'm Michael Jordan.

I could feel the reggae bassline from the club jackin' up my wheels a hundred feet away.

The babes goin' in were in fine form, booties that lasted all week, but shit, all a homie wanted was to spark a blunt, go home to my crib and sleep off the shock of Cheryl.

I looked across the road and noticed Hector cuttin' a deal with two white punks. That idiot must be the only drug dealer in Handsworth that deals out in the open.

I got out of the car and walked over to them. The white boys became nervous and started pulling away.

"I know de breddah," Hector shouted after them, but it didn't seem to matter—they were almost sprinting down the street. Hector tried to call them back, but they were long gone.

"Wha y' a do man?"

He flung his hands in the air.

"Y' jus' mess up a perfect bloodclaat deal!"

"Chill, Inspecta, calm yer shit down."

"Look. look, y' jus' cos' me forty rahtid notes, wha' y' gon' do 'bout it?"

I laughed when he tried to put on a dead serious face. Hector couldn't look serious even if he wanted.

"Hector, if yer shit's dat good, homie ain't got shit to worry 'bout...there'll be others."

"Wha' y' want anyway?"

"Jus' hangin'."

Hector got to talking about how he spots his punters. But in the hour I was standing with him the only person he sold shit to was me. He put it down to being a bad night for business—and to me for making people afraid to deal with him because I looked too much like an undercover Five-O.

The cold was biting and as I got ready to go I told Hector, out of the blue, that I'm going to be a father.

"So y' stop firin' blanks now," he laughed. "Who de baby fe anyway?"

"Cheryl, yer sorry-ass bum."

"Lord God, y' in trouble, star!" he said shaking his head.

"Me know dat girl wasn't gonna stop til' she trap you, t' rahtid. Bad news, believe me."

"Why yer trippin', man?" I asked. "I'm movin' into her crib."

"Naa man, don't do dat—"

Hector shook his head again.

"—she a go control y' business. Yuh goin' ave fe sack all a dem white girl now. See me? None of my six baby mother live in none of my yards. Dem see me when dem see me, and if dem don't like it dem know where fe go."

Truth is, Hector must have had kids by some artificial shit or adopted them, 'cause he's never had a whole bitch in his twenty-six year existence, let alone six kids. But I wasn't in the mood to turn his shit on its head.

"Look, homie, high fives for da low-down but I'm outta here."

"Me been tryin fe get you fe do dat for the last one-and-a-'alf hours. Y' bad fe bizness, man."

Hector helped me into my car, shutting the door for me like a commissionaire at a top London hotel. I reached into the pocket of my track bottoms.

"Hector, come 'ere homie."

"Wha' y' want now?" he said, kissin' his teeth as he came back to the window.

"Grip dis for yer troubles," I said, flicking him a pound coin.

"Wha' dis? Man, fuck off. You t'ink me a lickle bwoy? Y'see me? Me only deal inna de big bucks." He threw the coin down in the street and marched towards the Star Club.

I drove home wondering if there was something in what Hector had said about sacrificing myself to Cheryl.

When I reached the corner of my street I slowed my wheels right down to check if Helen's car was still there. When I was sure it wasn't, I pulled up outside my crib, got out and went in thinking only about my bed.

Then, in the passageway, I met the white dude from upstairs comin' outta Mrs O'Farrell's room in a string vest and boxer shorts.

He was tryin' to hide something behind his back. Homie looked closely and saw it was a vibrator—then he pushed past me anxiously and hurtled up the stairs faster than Colin Jackson.

Damn, all this time I thought Mrs O'Farrell was frigid and the old girl been havin' more fun than a homie.

Shit brought a smile back to my face.

12

Welcome To Dodge City

Calvin slumped down on his settee, his body well fatigued.

It was eight o'clock in the morning and he hadn't even drawn a Z yet. He came home straight from the doors and began last-minute work on Black Pound Day.

The whole thing was one of Lorna's brainwaves, and it looked to be a winner.

That day the community would be encouraged to spend their money in black-owned shops, and in turn the owners would deposit five percent of the day's profits to the Youth Conference Fund.

Skipper the barber was in on it, Mr B, the bakery man, the man who owned the electrical shop and the owners of the small food shops on Lozells Road.

Only one African shop-owner—one of Skipper's rival barbers—had said he wasn't interested. But Calvin knew the slave mentality still ran deep in the community.

Calvin couldn't think straight—if he had he would have been well pleased with the organisation of the day. He had distributed leaflets about it to every home in the Handsworth area, and put posters up around the Soho Road area, before they were mysteriously torn down or pasted over.

The local non-African traders had criticised the plan, even had a meeting and put in a protest to the city council; they said it was racist, but Calvin wouldn't back down. After all, even though he had initiated it, he wasn't twisting the arm of any African person to enter the stores and support the 'cause.

The council couldn't do a thing to stop it, 'cause it didn't involve the use of their precious funds, and the Youth Conference Committee were adamant that no public handouts were to be accepted.

When the other traders saw the strength of the force they were dealing with they wanted to throw their hat in and donate ten per cent of their takings on the day to the fund—but Calvin wanted it to remain a black thing. Wanted to show what his African people could achieve.

He was encouraged by the co-operation and the almost united front shown by the business community. He knew most were motivated by the potential increase in their revenue, but that didn't matter.

They had agreed to take part and now, today, the consumers had to do their part. For a day they had to give up shopping at their usual places and do something constructive.

Calvin was anxious. The Youth Conference needed funding, and he couldn't afford the community not to support him.

Without a successful day, funds would be drastically reduced. The event might even have to be put off until next year. He had managed to create great enthusiasm amongst all the X Centre posse—except for Kwesi who, as usual, didn't like the idea. Failure would be a major setback. His fingers, toes, even his low-cut hairs were crossed hoping for a big day.

The phone rang and Calvin slowly dragged his aching body across to it.

"Hello."

"Hi darlin'. Some good news."

"Give it to me slowly, Lorna. I don't think my brain has engaged itself yet."

"Listen, I phoned LA earlier this morning and the guests are set," she said gleefully.

"Well done sista!" Calvin shouted.

He wanted to dance around the room, only his body wouldn't let him.

"Who's comin'?"

"They're faxing me their names and a brief biog of the four. But they're all nineteen, they come from South Central and are all reformed gangbangers. Listen to this. Two were sent to the juvenile centre at thirteen, for murder; one for a drive-by shooting where a six-year-old girl was maimed on her way to school; and one for assisting in the amputation of a rival's legs.

"Gosh, Calvin, are we doing the right thing in bringing them?"

"I understand the reservations, sista, but these brothas portray the brutal reality. It'll scare the heck out of these phoney gangsters over here, show them point blank what their petty little turf wars can develop into—and hopefully force them to change their lifestyle and attitude."

"Yeah, I know...but they sound so vicious."

"Sista, they're reformed characters now. They preach about doing the right thing, setting up black businesses in the ghetto instead of creating war zones. They give talks in schools about staying away from gangs.

"Their stories are the most powerful and legitimate testimonies we're going to get. Shake the whole community down."

"You're right. I was wearing my liberal student hat, being pessimistic. Anyway, how's Black Pound Day going up there?"

"Kicks off at nine. We have X Centre members at every location to keep a check on the amounts raised, and we're hoping the community comes out to support it."

"I still can't believe you didn't get Maurice Lindsey in on it."

"I have other plans for him," Calvin explained. "Thing I learnt about Lindsey is that he likes to see himself as the father of black business in the area. Can you imagine when he hears about Black Pound Day and knows all the other African businessmen took part and he wasn't invited? He'll do anything to get involved."

"But he must know about it. All the posters are up."

"Sista, believe me, Lindsey drives from Solihull to Handsworth and back every day and notices nothing. Brotha doesn't even know who's playing at his own club."

"I hope you're right. Anyway, I've got to dash."

"Okay, give me a call a little later. I should have things sorted by the end of the day. Go in peace, sista."

"Bye darlin'."

Calvin's body felt like it had been spun in a washing machine. He shuffled to the kitchen. On the way he stopped and looked in the hall mirror at the huge bags under his eyes. He kissed his teeth at the thought of what organising this conference was doing to his health. But, in the end, if it got one young brotha to wise up it would be worth it.

Calvin fixed himself a cup of black coffee. Caffeine was the only thing that could keep him awake now. And awake was definitely what he needed to be. He had to be at the X Centre by eleven, so there was little point in dozing off; he'd only feel much worse when he got up again.

He went back to the living room and sat down at the desk. His dickie bow was lying on a pile of leaflets, with Monday 12th April standing out in bold type.

He had chosen Easter Monday—day after the play-off finals at Wembley—to host the Conference.

He'd had two thousand leaflets printed and every morning he would go and deliver some to the schools in the area. Some teachers didn't want him handing them out because there wasn't a gang or violence problem in their school—but Calvin only wished they would open their eyes to what was happening in the area.

Two days ago another young kid from his block of flats had been stabbed by a rival. The police said it was drug-related, but Calvin heard it was over a girl. But whatever it was, it took a different mentality to stab another person.

It was ten-thirty when Calvin eventually left his flat. He'd dragged himself into the shower before changing into his grey jogging suit. His ankle-length leather coat made him look like something out of a blaxploitation movie, only he wore a dachiqui. He did a quick spin and clicked his fingers as he recalled the *'Shaft'* theme music.

The lifts were out of order—nearly every day some vandal would mess the lifts up—so he went through the fire doors and started to jog down the thirty-odd flights of stairs, watching as the treetops came closer with every step. He could hear voices below. As he got to the fourth floor he saw a gang of young brothas standing by the fire exit, all dressed alike—jeans half way down their backsides with baggy sweatshirts hanging out of them, and baseball caps. As Calvin approached them he recognised one as Ganja Kid. He reached into his pocket, pulled out a handful of leaflets and gave the six brothas one each.

"I got one already," said Ganja Kid aggressively.

"So you'll have two reasons to come," said Calvin.

Ganja Kid kissed his teeth.

"What the fuck for? This ain't sayin' diddly to me. What the fuck is a youth conference gonna do for me?"

He screwed up the leaflet and threw it away.

The others laughed and three of them followed suit, throwing their leaflets at Calvin's feet.

Calvin stared at them in dismay. These guys had little respect for anything. If they could do this in front of a six-foot-six, thirteen stone African brotha, how the hell would they treat their mothers? He felt like sorting them out physically, one by one, but kept his cool.

He didn't want to inflame the situation and he still wanted to see them at the conference.

Calvin tried to project his anger in a positive way.

"Look, little brothas, those things cost money. If you don't want to come, that's fine, but don't disrespect me. Pick them up."

They looked at each other, then at Ganja Kid, hoping he would solve their dilemma.

"I said, pick them up!"

This time Calvin's voice was louder, and his expression more serious. Ganja Kid looked perturbed.

"Look, man, why don't you jus' go on your way? We're not goin', so that's the only place for 'em."

"So, you're not going to pick them up?"

He could see Ganja Kid was feeling for his back pocket. Maybe if the pocket wasn't so far down his leg he'd have found what he was looking for.

"Don't even think 'bout it, little brotha. I'll string you up before you even get your hand out."

Calvin looked down at the teenager like he was ready to go fist to fist with him. Ganja Kid hesitated, then bent down slowly, picked up the leaflet and pushed it in his front trouser pocket. The others followed suit.

"That's better, brothas. Now, why aren't you in school?"

Ganja Kid kissed his teeth again when the rest looked to him to respond.

"We don't need school," he said. "It's never done anythin' for us."

"How do you expect to obtain jobs and better yourselves if you don't go to school?" Calvin didn't like sounding like a teacher, but he was concerned about the young brothas' welfare.

"Look, I'm earning. I don't need no fuckin' school. Dat is fe bwoy."

"At your age?" Calvin played naive. He knew what they were up to, but wanted confirmation from their own lips.

"Earning doing what?"

"That's my business," Ganja Kid snarled.

"You're pushin', aren't you?"

"Hey, mister, you're outta order. I don't know you from Adam and you come down here asking all these fuckin' questions and accusing us. You an informer or what?" Ganja Kid took a step towards the exit door. "Well inform on dis."

He pulled a wad of ten and twenty pound notes from his pocket.

"Goin' to school didn't teach me how to mek dis. Come gang, let's trod."

They disappeared through the exit.

Calvin stood silent for a moment before continuing down the stairs. He believed that if he could get through to Ganja Kid, then the rest would follow.

But how could he get through to young brothas who earn in one day what he earns in a month, and tell them to throw away that lifestyle?

After all, Calvin thought, they're products of the individualistic, capitalist society they live in. In a sick sort of way Maggie Thatcher should be proud of them. Here were some of the young entrepreneurs she was so keen to produce.

Calvin decided to make it a priority to get Ganja Kid and the others to come to the conference.

When Calvin got to the X Centre, Abdullah Rashid was there to welcome him. In his Moslem garb, he looked regal. His heavily-bearded face, black skullcap and upright posture made greeting him an occasion in itself.

"Salaam, brotha," he said as they touched fists. "How's the conference?"

"We're on track, brotha," Calvin replied. "We've just confirmed the four young brothas from LA that will be comin'. We've just got to find accommodation for them."

"That's good news, brotha," Abdullah replied.

"Listen, I hate to remind you, but don't forget the centre can only afford two thousand pounds—and that's for everything, including the use of the phones.

"The repairs after the fire cost us a small fortune, and the insurers are still trying to get out of paying for it. They believe it was an inside job; said we did it ourselves to claim a big pay-off."

"I hear you, brotha." Calvin knew he would need at least two grand more to realise his plans as they now stood, even without counting the telephone bill—which would be huge.

"I'm glad they didn't burn out the safe."

"Don't worry, brotha, your secret is still secure," Abdullah smiled.

Calvin left him and made his way to the back of the building. The white walls of the narrow corridor were decorated with oil paintings of great black heroes and heroines of the past and present.

Shaka Zulu, Harriet Tubman, Marcus Garvey, Kwame Nkrumah, Malcolm X, Martin Luther King and Nelson Mandela were all there. The lingering smell of burnt wood still hung about the building and reminded Calvin that just as some brothas were working with him on his vision for the community, just as many—if not more—were working against him.

He went into the office that had virtually become his home for the past two months and sat at his desk.

There were two other desks in there, but sometimes as many as eight people working at the same time.

He rubbed his face vigorously before picking up the letters in front of him. One was the agreement for the rent of the school hall, and two others were quotes from security firms tendering for the contract to police the event. Calvin had tried to get his own men, but decided that if one set-up could take care of things that would ease some of the organisers' workload.

As he flicked through some of the other papers on the desk, Deborah Obeng—the publicity manager for the conference— came in. Her parents were from the Caribbean but she changed her surname by deed poll to represent her true origins.

She was dressed, as always, in rich African attire.

"Hi, brotha, don't you ever go home?" she said, smiling.

"It doesn't seem like it, sista. How are you, Debs?"

"I'm fine," she said, sitting down at the desk opposite him.

"You do know Kwesi missed the printers yesterday?"

"He didn't, did he?" Calvin replied in shock.

She nodded.

"Damn, that means the posters won't be ready until a week today at the earliest. Is the brotha seriously with us on this?" Calvin saw this as a major setback.

"He says he was on the phone tryin' to organise a talk in a school to inform the kids about the conference and forgot the time," Deborah explained. "Can't they do our order as a special favour?"

"Naa, sista, they're chock-a-block until next week. Last night was the only free time they had. I needed those posters out at the weekend. I've got people on stand-by to paste them up all around the city. Damn you, Kwesi."

"What about another company?" Deborah said, tryin' to ease the situation.

"I want to keep it a black thing and they're the only black printers I know in Birmingham. Do a good job, too."

They resigned themselves to getting the posters a week late, then chatted for another ten to fifteen minutes. Calvin was drawing up the guest list when the phone rang. Deborah was on the other line so he answered it.

"Hello, X Centre Youth Conference Committee."

"You sound so official, darlin'."

It was Lorna.

"I've just got a message from the group in LA. It looks as if there'll be one more comin' with them in an advisory capacity."

"Advisory capacity? The brothas are takin' the mick. Do they know our budget? Tell them no. We're over-budget already."

"Darlin', calm down. Look, we only have to find half of the air fare and accommodation; they'll find the rest—and, another thing, I don't think the others will be too happy if we turn down this request."

"I understand, sista, but we can't pay for every Tom, Dick and Harry. It will end up costing us a fortune."

"How much are we over-budget?"

"Black Pound Day will have to bring in over two grand to keep us in the black, sista."

"I'll ask Dad if he can raise some in Coventry by holding a dance or domino competition."

"Work on it, sis. We're goin' to need every penny."

"Things are never as bad as they seem," Lorna said, soothingly. "I'll speak to you later."

When Calvin put the phone down he felt a lot better than when he'd picked it up.

"Problems?" Deborah asked.

"Nothin' we can't handle."

Calvin wanted to check how well Black Pound Day was going— but he had some pressing business to attend to first.

"C-C-Calvin, Calvin, listen. There's no money inna de night club business. W-w-why when every black person inna Birmingham wan' money dem come to me like me a de rahtid Bank of England, eh?"

"Look, the youth conference I'm organising could run over my two-and-a-half grand."

"J-J-Jesus Christ, me nah wan' hear no more!" Mr Lindsey covered his eyes with his hands and rocked back in his chair.

"We're hoping to find a grand, or possibly a grand-and-a-half our-selves, but we need a donation of a grand to help towards the accom-modation. That's where you come in, brotha."

Mr Lindsey pointed to the door.

"And *dat* is where yuh go out, b-b-brotha. I know what you doin' is a good t'ing, especially wid dem teefin' lickle buggers 'round here, but I don't 'ave dat kind of ready money."

"Brotha, you always talk a good game about doing things for the community," Calvin said, flattering Mr Lindsey.

"So is wha' y'ah say, I don't do nut'n fe me people?"

Lindsey pushed his neck backwards and forwards like a giraffe while adjusting the knot of his tie.

"I'll have you know I'm well respected as a philanderer in this community. Well respected."

"Philanthropist, brotha."

"Dat's wha' me say," Lindsey insisted.

"Anyway, this would give you the opportunity to have a wider reputation. Especially since you missed out on Black Pound Day."

"De wha'?"

"Black Pound Day. Every other African businessman in Handsworth is takin' part."

"So h-h-how come nobody tell me 'bout dis? Me is de best known businessman inna Birmingham."

" 'Cause we have bigger and better plans for the best known black businessman in Birmingham."

"Wha' dat?"

"Main line event sponsor. Jus' think, brotha. All the young brothas out there would be callin' your name in the same breath as Ian Wright, John Barnes and Michael Jordan."

"Michael Jordan, who 'im?"

"Never mind, brotha. But think 'bout it. Media exposure to the whole of the Midlands, probably Britain and possibly the world. Banners, leaflet—the full works."

Lindsey began to smile. Calvin could see the brute got a kick out of anything that would enhance his reputation in the area.

"Okay, okay, yuh convince me," Lindsey said, reaching into his pocket for his cheque book. "I'll tell yuh what I goin' do. I'll give yuh two hundred-'n'-fifty."

"Brotha, that will leave us well short."

"L-l-look, two hundred-'n'-fifty is all yuh gettin. Give praise. Who should I mek de cheque out to?"

"The X Centre," Calvin replied, not yet ready to give up the fight.

"Brotha, since you're only giving us two hundred and fifty—"

Lindsey looked up when Calvin said 'only'.

"—we're bringing four former gang members and an adviser over from South Central LA, and we need somewhere to put them up for four days. How about you making up the shortfall on the cheque by letting them use your house?"

"No, no—no way!"

Lindsey stood up and waved his hands like a madman.

"I'm *not* havin' dem mad-ass gangstas wid dem Uzis in my yard.

191

I already have dat waste of space from Bosnia still in there. Me house only 'ave six bedroom and two of me seven kids already sharin'. Look, tek de cheque and run before me change me mind and rip it up."

Calvin knew Lindsey only had two kids, but he didn't push it. He just took the cheque and left before Lindsey did change his mind.

He was about to put the keys into the door of his BMW when there was a tap on his shoulder. He turned to see two rough-looking raggamuffins, both over six foot tall and wearing dark shades. They backed him up against his car.

"Listen man. We don't like de kinda work yuh a do inna de community," one said.

Calvin played ignorant.

"Brotha, what work's that?"

"Dis drug march. Now yuh wan' poison de yout' mind wid stupid conference. We don't like it and is we run t'ings inna dis community, so all we a tell you is fe back off 'cause next time the centre burn you a go be in it."

They walked off across the street to a black BMW with tinted windows. Calvin instantly recognised it as Zorro's. The car sped away, tyres screeching.

Calvin stood firm for while. He now knew who torched the youth centre and who was ripping down the posters, but he couldn't go to the police.

That would be the worst thing he could do. Informers don't go down well in Handsworth and the whole youth conference would be in jeopardy if word got around that the workers organising it were a bunch of police boys. He decided he'd have to beef up security.

There was no way he could call it off because of a threat from Zorro and his raggas.

The youth conference office was full when he got back. Kwesi was sitting at Calvin's desk, but Calvin waved him to stay there. Amara was busy on the phone and Debbie, Luke and Tunde were deep in discussion. Calvin decided not to mention the threat, but told them they needed to increase the funds for security, because they could expect trouble.

"Oh, Calvin..." Debbie stood up.

"BPRL have finished the promotional jingle but they're asking a hundred quid for doing it."

"What? The brothas are out of line," Calvin said, trying to remain

192

calm. "They were supposed to be doin' it for free."

"They said they'd give you free air time, but they had to pay for some special equipment to make it effective."

"Is that a reasonable price?" Calvin asked, taking a seat.

"I'll tell you tomorrow when I've heard it."

"Okay, sista, but don't let them give you any bull. I know how those brothas are down there."

"The hall we booked has been cancelled," Kwesi interrupted, his deep-set eyes boring into Calvin's chest.

"Oh, I don't *believe* this. Why?" Calvin shouted.

"Apparently, they got an anonymous phone call sayin' that if they don't cancel it they're going to wake up and find the place burnt down."

"Zorro," Calvin whispered.

"What was that?"

"Nothing, brotha."

Calvin had to think fast.

"Check brotha Abdullah about the possibility of holding it here. I know it's smaller, but at least we can control it better."

"Do you think that's wise, considering what happened with the petrol bomb?"

Kwesi's gloomy expression almost pushed Calvin to reconsider.

"You got a better idea?" he challenged, knowing the negative was to be expected from Kwesi.

Kwesi held his hands up in a gesture of surrender.

"You're in charge, brotha," he said, trying to lighten the mood.

"Yes, I am," Calvin retorted. "Any more problems before we move on?"

"Just a minor one," Luke said apologetically. "I heard on the grapevine that Tory councillors are moving to ban the ex-gang members from entering the country."

"How come they know already?" Calvin asked. " We only got confirmation this morning...anyway, on what grounds?" "Somethin' about not being conducive to good race relations—and they have criminal records," Luke replied.

"What are the black Labour councillors saying?" Debbie asked.

"You know how they stay. Won't touch a black issue with a barge pole."

"Get one of the three on the line." Calvin demanded, now totally pissed off.

"Damn. If we elect them they've got to be accountable to us or we'll get them out of there."

He spent the next five hours trying to piece everything together. He talked individually with each committee member, and luckily they were only marginally behind schedule. Abdullah said there wouldn't be a problem using the centre, but changing the venue meant printing and distributing new leaflets.

Calvin also spoke to two black councillors about the threat to ban the guest speakers. They refused to help at first, saying they couldn't be seen to be supporting gangsters. But when Calvin told them he planned to mobilise the community against them, they soon promised to help fight the ban.

It was eight o'clock before he left the X Centre. It was mild for February.

Calvin was back to working five nights a week when he added The Jam, a rave-type club in Tipton, to his schedule. He hated going up there—the place was full of white kids drugged up on ecstasy—but he needed the money to pay the bills, especially since he was dipping into his own pocket to fund extras for the conference that weren't budgeted for.

He didn't have to be there until ten, so on the way he took a detour and visited his parents whom he had neglected with his workload.

They lived at the bottom end of Handsworth, about two miles from the front line. His mum rushed out and greeted him with a hug when she saw the car pull up. She had never jumped on him like that before in his life.

"Is where, y' beden?" she said in her rugged Bajan accent. "I beden tryin' to ring y'all day."

"Sorry, Mom, I spent most of the time at the X Centre. What's up?"

"Our lawyer rang us today and say dee tenants are out and we can move in when we ready!"

She was almost skipping with joy. Calvin hugged her tightly, then asked:

"Where's Pops?"

"Heee jus' dis minute step trew dee door. He gone for a drink wid yuh uncle Ceecil."

Calvin went into the dining room. Geraldine and Sofia, two of his three sisters, were already there, and were as excited as Mum.

"So when are you going?" Calvin asked.

"Weee don't know exactly yet but within dee next couple of months. Yuh fadder goin' see 'bout it tomorrow."

Calvin spent the rest of the time listening to his mum planning what she had to do before they left. She was talking so fast that she was almost singing.

Calvin thought it was about time that they had a little good news. It was no fun for them sitting in this half-empty house in the moody British weather, when they had their own place in the sunny Caribbean.

Calvin left his mum and sisters at around eight-thirty to go home and change for work. He was about to drive away when he saw the big figure of Marcus walking with a pretty-looking young sista. Calvin wound down his window.

"Brotha Terminator, what's happenin'?"

"Me cool," Marcus replied, crossing the street.

"Dis is Samantha, me daughter," he announced proudly. Calvin couldn't hide his surprise.

"Me know wha' yuh a t'ink, but is a long story and me nah 'ave time fe go inna it now."

"Okay, brotha. Listen, I need a favour. I'm looking for good security for the conference and your name is high on the list."

"Y'know, sa, me nah love dat kinda work. You inna de business, y' cyan' find nobody else?"

"Brotha, I need people who know who's who around here, who nobody's goin' to take steps with," Calvin explained, without actually mentioning Zorro's name.

Marcus put his hand protectively around the young sista and drew her closer to allow a car to pass.

"Me know some man who use to be security at dem blues long time ago set up a security bizness. I t'ink dem name Front Line...yeah, Front Line Security."

"Reliable?" Calvin asked.

"Put it dis way, nobody nah get past dem. Dem tuff. Check dem and mention me. Might get y'self a discount."

"Okay, brotha."

"So 'ow is de Birdman, unnu mek up yet?"

"Brotha phoned to apologise, but he's under a lot of pressure at the moment. I can understand."

"So wha 'appen, y' did trouble 'im wife?" Marcus asked, smiling.

"Brotha man, all I was doin was helpin' out a sista I've known for ages. She was in difficulties and the brotha got things mixed up, but things are sorted."

"Dat cool den, cause we need 'nuff unity inna de play-off. 'Ave fe

195

stop all dis in-fightin' or we nah get nowhere."

Marcus took a step away from the car.

"That's very true, brotha."

"Alright, later."

"Go in peace, brotha...and young sista."

Mum's excitement had had an effect on Calvin. He sped all the way home singing 'O-o-o-h, I'm goin' to Barbados'.

But his enthusiasm was soon doused as he drove up the street leading to his block. From the bottom of the road it looked like strikes of electric blue sheet lightning illuminating the sky. He got closer and saw an ambulance and masses of policemen.

He pulled up as close to the police cordon as he could, got out and walked nearer to the block. There were people standing around and others hanging out of their windows watching.

"What's goin' on, brotha?" Calvin asked an African brotha.

"Me nah know, sa. I t'ink someone get shot."

"Shot?"

Calvin couldn't believe his ears. In his block? What's Birmingham coming to? For a minute he stood speechless watching the commotion, then he tried to walk through the police barricade.

"Sorry, sir, you can't cross."

A policeman put his hand across Calvin's chest to stop him.

"But I live here."

"No-one's allowed to go any further, sir."

"So what's happened?"

"A young kid has been shot and the gunman is still loose in the building," the cop replied.

"Is the kid seriously hurt?"

"That's all I know, sir." He motioned to the growing crowd. "Now, can you all move back?"

Calvin stood outside the block for half an hour. Six policemen surrounding a short black figure marched out of the flats. They had guns in their side holsters. One was holding a black kid by the shoulder; it was one of the young brothas Calvin had seen on the stairs that morning.

His heart sank.

Two paramedics ran into the flats with a stretcher and came out five minutes later carrying a body. They rushed to the ambulance, one carrying a supply of blood over the victim's head.

Calvin edged closer to get a better look. It was Ganja Kid. His mum got into the ambulance with him, almost doubled over in tears, then they shut the door and sped off, sirens screaming. A few minutes later the policemen took down the barricades.

Calvin walked slowly into the building.

He felt total despair.

Only this morning he was talking to those young brothas. Now, one had been shot and it looked like another was facing a long stretch inside.

When he got home, he walked straight through to the living room and sat at his desk by the window that overlooked the city.

Stars appeared in the dark sky, twinkled, then disappeared. A bit like life, Calvin thought. He didn't feel like going to work. He rang The Jam and gave them an excuse about a bad back, then sat gazing into the night.

Was he kidding himself with this youth conference? Would it make any difference? Calvin felt like jacking the whole thing in, until he thought about all the hard work people had put in; the amount of encouragement that Lorna, especially, had given him.

He couldn't stop now.

It had gone too far.

He wondered how Ganja Kid was, and realised how little he knew about him. He didn't know which floor he lived on, or his real name.

His thoughts were disturbed by a knock on the door. He got up and answered. It was one of the little brothas that he'd seen on the stairs that morning—his hands forced deep into his pockets and his head hung low. He'd been crying. Calvin invited him in.

The boy remained standing, shifting his weight from one leg to the other. He wanted to say something, but was having trouble getting the words out.

"Ahm...I...ah..."

His breath was coming too fast.

Calvin realised he was in shock.

"Take your time, brotha, just take your time."

The boy took a deep breath.

"I...I need to get out of this gang," he blurted finally.

Calvin looked at him. He looked like the scared, confused child that he was.

"What's your name, brotha?"

"Chris. Chris Thompson."

He looked up for the first time. Calvin nodded.

"My spars call me Chedda," he continued.

"How old are you, Chedda?"

"Fourteen," he replied, wiping his eyes.

"Where're your parents?"

"Mum's at work. I don't know where my dad is—haven't seen him for almost five years."

"So who's home with you?"

"Just me."

"What time does your mum get home?"

"About seven in the morning. She works nights. "

Calvin sighed and put his chin on his chest. He didn't know what to tell him.

"What happened down there tonight?"

Chedda remained silent. His eyes said he didn't want to tell for fear of being labelled an informer.

"Chedda...if you won't talk to me how can I help you? Don't worry, the gang can't harm you here."

He understood the fear and pressure the youngster would be feeling after what had just happened. The first rule of gang culture was loyalty—*you don't inform on the brothas.*

Chedda looked up at Calvin and began to speak.

"Ganja Kid was messin' with Boxer, y'know, slappin' him about 'cause he didn't sell what he was supposed to and Boxer jus' had enough. Went and got his dad's gun and shot Ganja Kid in the back."

Tears welled in his eyes.

"We never thought he would do it. Thought he was just foolin'. Honest."

"Are you involved in it?" Calvin asked.

"Not the shooting," he said quickly. "I carry drugs for the dealers sometimes...I never knew this would happen. We jus' wanted to make some money. Now all this...I can't...I just want out. Can you help me?"

Hard as he fought them, the tears rolled down his cheek.

"They ain't gonna like it if I leave. I dunno what will happen. If you're not in a gang, you're nobody...a target."

Calvin pulled up a chair for him, and for the next forty-five minutes Chedda told him what had been going on in the block.

It was worse than Calvin had thought. He promised Chedda he'd try and get all the gang members to come to the conference in the hope that it might make a difference. Calvin felt so hopeless that he couldn't offer more than the youth conference. But it was the best he had at this stage.

Chedda eventually left about twelve. Calvin made himself a cup of coffee and sat for about two hours trying to come up with a solution to the youth's problems. He came up against a dead end; there were no easy solutions. He was just getting ready for bed when he heard a knock on the door. He thought it might be Chedda again.

"Heather!"

He looked down at his watch.

"What time do you call this, sista?"

"I just needed someone to talk to...if it's too late I'll call again..."

"No, no, come on in." He showed her in.

"I just finished working on some plans for the youth conference."

Heather took off her coat and slumped in the middle of the sofa. Calvin sat next to her. "Can I get you a drink or something?"

"No, I must have drunk about forty cups of tea already tonight. If I keep asking to use your toilet you'll know why..." she smiled.

"So what's up, sista?"

She shrugged.

"I just needed someone to talk to. Jermaine is still in hospital."

"*Damn!* I forgot. How is he?"

"The doctors say he'll pull through, but I feel so helpless seeing him lying there when I can't do anything for him."

The pain was visible in her face.

"Sista, I'm sorry I haven't been down, but I didn't think it was wise with Andre in that mood."

She dismissed his apology with a wave of her hand.

"He's there now, for what it's worth," she said bitingly.

"Come on, sista, you don't mean that!"

"Yes, I do."

She paused, then looked at him.

"I heard you had a fight over me?"

"I wouldn't say it was over you, sista. Brotha thought that, 'cause I was taking the kids to school in the morning, I must have woken in your bed," he said, almost apologetically.

"He thought you were *sleeping* with me?"

"Disgraced me in front of the whole team," Calvin replied.

"The bastard. You know why that little red bastard's doing this?"

"No. But I know I don't want to be in the middle of this dispute any more."

"I'm divorcing his ass on the grounds of adultery. He's been caught out, so he's trying to pin something on me, the low-down rat.

199

Thinks he's Mr Smart but I've got his ass sussed."

"Sista, you know Andre didn't have no affair," Calvin said.

"Oh, really? He's probably shacking up with his white piece now."

"A white girl?" Calvin exclaimed in surprise. "No, not Andre. Never."

"Yes, a white girl. And yes, Andre."

"Sista, I think you've got it wrong. I know the brotha and he's not seeing anyone, especially not a white girl."

"Calvin, you two might be best friends, but I was sleeping with him for seven years. I know him in ways you couldn't even imagine. Anyway, the white bitch confessed on the phone to me."

Heather seemed positive about it.

"As God is my witness," she continued. "His secretary, Tracy. Remember you told me he had kisses all over his face and his shirt was ripped? Now you know what he was doing. It was going on for six months before that."

"But Sista, I told you that was a Christmas party prank. Y'know, when spirits get high—"

Calvin didn't believe Andre was capable of being unfaithful. But then again, he'd never thought Andre would burst into the changing room and try to behead him either!

There was a silence in the room. He looked at Heather. She seemed to be in another world.

"Calvin..." she said, after a while. Her tone was less angry now, and more mellow.

"Sista?"

She ran her hand up the inside of his thigh.

"Easy, Heather. This is a no-go," he said taking her hand off his thigh.

"That's not what you said when we used to go out. You couldn't wait to get my knickers off," she said, grinning slyly.

"Heather, don't be silly. We were fifteen then."

She got up and stood in front of him, and lifted her black woollen jumper over her head. She had no bra on.

"Well I'm not fifteen anymore. I'm a real woman."

She bent down and pressed her breasts into his face; he felt his resistance weakening. She knelt in front of him and started kissing him softly all over his face. He held her arms to pull her away, but at the feel of her naked flesh, he succumbed, running his hands over her.

They fell off the settee onto the floor and made love.

It was over relatively quickly. Calvin just sat motionless, watching Heather get dressed. She looked pleased with herself. She gave him a kiss on the cheek then said goodbye. When he heard the door close it felt like someone had slammed a jail door on an innocent man.

He had betrayed Lorna, Andre and himself.

And after all the indignance he'd felt when Andre accused him. Maybe Andre should have knocked his head off after all. He felt used—but he couldn't lay all the blame on Heather. He was guilty too. He hadn't kept control of himself. The temptation was great, but he should have resisted.

Lorna's face flashed before him now. How was he going to tell her he had been so weak?

13

Moment Of Truth

"Look, Marcus, we haven't got a problem. Just go in there, tell the truth and it's going to be all right. You've got a fine team in your corner. Just keep calm."

I nodded my head in agreement, not really believing a word Theo said.

Why should I go on like a lamb when I feel like a lion inside?

Because after what happened with Marcia's solicitor, two months ago, I was not in a position to demand an alternative.

Theo was pacing up and down behind his desk, gripping a pencil. Despite his confident words, it was the first time I'd seen him look so ruffled. Y'know, real bloodclaat 'fraid. Just made me more nervous than ever. He must have been through thousands of cases, but today the man looked like a rookie.

"And another thing, Marcus. Give clear answers, none of this patois shit. You're not Jamaican, so stop trying to speak like one. You can't expect the jury to believe what they can't understand."

The pencil he was holding snapped in two. He threw the pieces on his desk and then sat down in his revolving chair.

"This case is going to make me...I mean, us. We can't afford any slip-ups."

He opened my case file, then looked at me.

"You were fast asleep on that October night when you were woken by a tremendous noise coming from your front door. You got up to investigate, but before you could reach the front door it was smashed off its hinges.

"You were confronted by a mass of men waving what you thought were pickaxe handles. You didn't know how many because you didn't have time to count them.

"Before you could say a word they were on you like a pack of animals hitting, punching and kicking. You had to defend yourself so you fought back. That's what happened, isn't it, Marcus?"

"Somet'ing like dat."

"With that attitude, Marcus, you'll definitely go down," Theo said, slamming the file closed.

"Cool na, wha' yuh say is wha'ppen den."

I looked at my watch. It was almost quarter to one. I stood up. "Me haffe go back a work."

"Okay. Look, Marcus, stay cool and try not to worry about it. I've got it sorted. After this is over we'll sort out proper access to your daughter. But for now leave it to me." The words sounded fine, but they came from a man who was shaking like he'd just seen a duppie. We shook hands and he said he'd see me in court on Wednesday morning.

I left his office. When the lift arrived it was full of white executive types who looked at me like I had a contagious disease.

It's amazing how spacious a cramped lift suddenly becomes when a black man gets in.

I made my way down Hill Street to catch the bus back to Hagley Road, with my mind firmly on how this barrister was going to shape up on Wednesday.

When we met him late last week at the court to swear in the jury, he didn't seem all that confident but he did get his way when he objected to the lack of black people on the jury. By the time they were sworn in there was a black man, a black woman and one Asian man.

I arrived back at work bang on time at one-thirty. The head chef had me working on preparing vegetables for a dinner party this evening. It was boring as hell but at least the job paid real corn.

As I peeled and chopped brussels sprouts and threw them in a pan of hot water, the head chef approached me.

"Marcus, can you work a split tomorrow? Steve's had to go off ill and won't be in."

"Look Paul, me cyan really do it," I said, trying to look apologetic.

His round face went from pink to bright red. "Marcus, there isn't anybody else available."

"Look, man, me 'ave t'ings plan fe tomorrow..."

"Can't you cancel them?"

"Cancel, ta backscover?" I stopped chopping the sprouts and flung the knife down on the table.

"No, me cyan' cancel."

He could see I was vex.

"Okay; I'm not happy about this—" he said "—but if you can't do it, you can't do it." Then he marched off.

I could see he never like me standing firm. Look like he's used to dealing with the kitchen staff however he rahtid want to. If it wasn't for the final game of the season at the weekend I would probably oblige, but we have a new game plan for Cheshire on Sunday and I needed to practice it, so Paul just have to sattah.

The case was occupying my head top. I was beginning to t'ink more positively. It was like I knew I was going to be acquitted...anyway, I had to t'ink like that, it was the only way I could keep going.

It was a long day at work and I'm sure Paul made it so 'cause I refused to work the splits tomorrow. I was supposed to leave at four-thirty, after starting at seven, but I didn't get out of the place until quarter to six. There was always something else to do; peel this, clean that, put that away. Paul made sure I had everything spotless before I was allowed to step.

I got home roughly an hour after I left the hotel. There were no letters on the doormat. The place was colder than it was outside. I had turned off the central heating because I spent the night at Yvette's. I switched the heating on and kept my duffel coat on while I waited for the place to warm up.

I went into the kitchen and looked in the cupboards, then the fridge. There wasn't much in there you could call food. I decided to make do with a can of banana Nurishment for now and grab a Chinese later.

It was Charmaine's third birthday tomorrow. I already bought her a card, some little Nike trainers and a tracksuit. Wrap them and everyt'ing. It was still burning me that I couldn't see her. The old lady was so vex yesterday when I tell her Charmaine not coming around. She never miss a relative birthday. Never. She ask why me and Marcia can't get back together. But if she knew the real reason I suppose she'd understand how Marcia feel 'bout me.

I switched on the television. Not a blasted t'ing to watch again. Rahtid detector van was in the area last week a try fe capture people who nah pay dem licence fee—but is dem should get arrest, fe tekking people money under false pretence.

I reached for the remote to the stereo I bought with my first paycheque and switched the tuner on to BPRL. I caught the back end of a phone-in programme about the state of black relationships. The presenter on the radio show was some idiot called DJ Ernie the Executioner, who took pride in cutting callers off if they didn't fall into line with his point of view.

Come to think of it, he cut off almost every caller before they could breathe 'cause his point of view changed like a high wind in Jamdown.

"Ernie," a male caller began, "there's only one person to blame for the break-up of the black family, and that's the woman. All they want man for is money—and if you ain't got it they don't want to know."

"Hey, bro, simple solution. Go find yourself a better paying job," Ernie chuckled, before chopping the call with jingle biggin' up his skills as a phone-in host.

"Rudebwoy from Aston, wha' yuh wanna say to Ernie?"

"Yesss, Ernie. Yuh see 'oman? Is pure white bwoy dem a look now. Go out 'pon de street of Birmingham an' all yuh see is black gyal wid white bwoy."

"Hey, man—"

"Let me finish na! Look, de 'oman dem jus' believe de badness white people say 'bout black man—"

"Sorry bro, not relevant."

Ernie hit the button again.

"Who's next? Colette from Handsworth."

"Hi Ernie. I just wanna say I think those two men are misogynists."

"Miss who?"

She sighed.

"I mean they hate women. See, today's black woman is free and independent so she can make up her own mind who she goes out with—black or white, it's her choice. Black men have to realise that we black women ain't standing for their nonsense when there's alternatives."

"Hey, so wha'? Yuh movin' with a white bwoy?" Ernie asked.

"I don't think that's nobody's business but my own," she answered.

Ernie cut her off for disrespecting him.

"Yo Hyacinth from Balsall Heath, what yuh sayin', black man are no good?"

"Exactly, Ernie. Dem plant dem seed here, there and every-damn-where and don't wan' look after the yout' when dem born. Y'see me? Me 'ave three baby father and not one a dem is any good. Dem just jump 'pon me a night time, ready to—"

"Hey, hey, hey! Dis is a family programme."

"Sorry, but de black man dem too wotless. Why dem cyan' face up to dem responsibility?"

The gyal was vexing me. How come she have three baby father? She mus' be equally to blame. I was ready to phone Ernie up to put the gyal right when another woman with a sexy voice from posh

205

Edgbaston did the job for me.

"There are good and bad brothas out there as well as good and bad sistas. This whole debate is not doing the black community any good. My husband is a good man who supports and looks after our two children."

"Jus' 'cause you content don't mean everybody else happy," Ernie replied, with his ignorant self.

"Oh stop being so sanctimonious—"

The airwaves suddenly went fuzzy. I could hear nothing but a hissing sound. I tried to adjust the frequency, but still nothing. Then I realised it must be another DTI raid. After that show I hope they lock up Ernie the blasted Executioner for fraud.

As I turned off the radio the bell rang. I got up and answered it. Yvette and Justin walked straight in. I was surprised 'cause she normally phones before she come 'round. I guess now she knew I was fully hers and couldn't be up to anything she didn't know about.

"How was the meeting this morning?" she asked, after we'd settled in the living room.

"I t'ink Theo did a bit nervous. Well, very nervous, but 'im say we can win."

I still wasn't convinced.

"Oh, that's good," Yvette said, taking Justin's coat off.

"Wha'ppen, yout' man?" I said, bending down and picking Justin up.

"I'm okay, Uncle Marcus. Can we play basketball?"

"Not now, Justin," Yvette interrupted. She took him out of my hands and placed him on the settee, then handed him a book. "You've got ten pages of *Delroy's Adventure* to read."

I could tell by the name it was a black yout' book. Yvette always wanted to instill black pride in Justin. I wished my old lady did that for me when I was a yout'. Once Justin was settled we both went into the kitchen.

"Sorry me cyan' offer you or de yout' somet'ing—fridge empty y'nah."

"That's alright. Justin's already eaten and I started my diet today."

She proceeded to tell me about how great this diet was. It allowed her to eat what she wanted, so long as she didn't mix her carbohydrates with proteins or something like that.

To tell the truth I was nodding but not really listening. I think she was trying to get my mind off the case, but she could tell I wasn't paying attention to what she was saying.

"Marcus."

I jumped, and realised that she was waving her hands in front of my face. It was like I was in a trance.

"Look, I'm sorry about the way I was with Samantha and Nadine. I never really apologised," she said.

"Me overstand. Me know it did tuff fe you."

"No, I was wrong. I shouldn't have responded that way."

"Don't worry, dem gon back a Canada and is probably another fourteen years before I sight dem again. Anyway, Samantha don't feel like fe me own. Me was like a stranger fe she. I don't know wha' she like fe eat or drink. I didn't even know what music or movie she like.

"Sam have her own family, an American footballer as her father. Jus' make me doubly serious 'bout seein' Charmaine before t'ings get too late."

"Your Mum misses her, though?"

"De old lady? Yeah, man. She did tek Sam everywhere, yuh know? Bruck she heart when dem lef'."

"It must be hard for her?"

"Yuh know."

"You seem distant today. You're worried about the case, aren't you."

"I wouldn't be human if I wasn't worried. But we jus' 'ave fe wait and see 'ow t'ings go."

Yvette came up to me and hugged me around the waist and laid her head on my chest. I pushed my hands under the back of her long red jumper and held on to the two halves of her backside. I don't know if it's possible that you could feel the effects of a diet within a day but her backside felt firmer than it did when I was touchin' it up in bed last night.

She looked up at me and I kissed her. "Marcus," she murmured. "Whatever happens on Wednesday, I'll wait for you."

It was good to hear, but if I got sent down I wouldn't expect her to wait for me. Justin came into the kitchen and we released each other quickly. But he was no fool; he looked slightly embarrassed.

"Someone's at the door," he said quickly, then rushed back to the sofa and picked up his book.

When I opened the door I almost dead. It was Marcia holding Charmaine in her hands. As usual, I never know what to say. We jus' look on each other without speaking for a good thirty seconds.

"Aren't you going to invite us in?"

I moved sideways and she stepped into the passage. When I closed the door she turned and handed Charmaine to me. I put her face right next to mine. I could feel the emotions welling up inside me, but big man nah fe cry mek people see? I held her at arms length and looked at her beautiful face. She started to wriggle like she wanted to get away. It had been so long that I didn't think she remembered what her dad looked like.

"Happy birthday, beautiful," I said, kissing her on her lips. She began to fight even harder to get back to her mother.

"You remembered?" Marcia said.

" 'Ow yuh mean? Me t'ink 'bout nothin' else today."

Marcia closed her eyes as if to apologise for the tribulations she put me through.

"She 'ave fe yuh eyes," I said, handing Charmaine back.

"But she's got your lungs, believe me," she smiled.

We went into the dining area. Yvette was now sitting next to Justin on the settee helping him with his reading. She stood up when we came into the room. She looked more surprised than I did.

"Hello, Marcia," she said. I detected a touch of bitchiness in her voice.

"Hi, Yvette," Marcia replied, surprised to see her.

The atmosphere was already tense. I didn't know what to say. Marcia broke the silence. "How you doing anyway, Marcus?"

"Not too bad yuh know. Me 'ave de court case 'pon Wednesday."

"I know. That's why I brought Charmaine around to see you."

She put Charmaine on the floor to stand.

"It's taken you this long to let the man see his child," Yvette jumped mouth-first into the conversation.

"You should be ashamed of yourself, coming in here the day the man could go to prison, like you care about his feelings."

"Yvette, butt out. This has nothing to do with you."

"Oh yes it has," Yvette said, walking up to her. "I'm the one that has to sit and suffer with him when he's worrying about how his little girl is. Day in, day out he talks about little else. So don't tell me it has nothing to do with me."

"Don't you think Charmaine and I suffered? I wanted her to see her father," Marcia argued.

"So what stopped you? You managed to find him today—or is it because you feel guilty that he might go down because of you?"

"Y'know something? Women like you make me sick. You meet a man yesterday and suddenly you're an expert on his past. Look, I've

208

known Marcus a lot longer than you, so don't you tell me I'm to blame for anything."

I didn't know where to put myself. I suppose it's every man's fantasy to have two women fighting over him; only they weren't fighting over me. This was more like a personal turf war over who had more right to be in my yard.

"Women, quiet nah, de yout' dem inna de room. It nah good for dem to see dem modder fightin' so."

Yvette went and sat back down beside Justin.

"Look, Marcus, we better go. I shouldn't have come anyway," Marcia said.

I tried to talk her out of it but I guess it was for the best, since there was no way we could discuss things with Yvette sitting there. I gave Charmaine a big kiss and handed her the present before leading them to the door.

Before she left Marcia said:

"You can come and see Charmaine whenever you want, Marcus. You don't need to worry anymore."

"Dat cool," I said, feeling nothin' but relief.

"Despite what she's saying, I didn't want this to happen."

"Me overstand," I said.

She gave me a faint smile, then left.

When I came back into the living room Yvette was still seated. I went straight into the kitchen and she followed me.

"I'm sorry, Marcus. I'm normally tellin' you to keep your cool, but I just couldn't take the way she marched in here like she hadn't a problem in the world."

"Me know," I replied looking in the fridge, though I knew there was nothing inside.

"In a way yuh say de t'ings me did want fe say, but me did so happy fe see me yout' again, me never feel de anger me 'ave towards Marcia."

"I'm sorry...I should have let you have some time with your daughter before Wednesday."

"Nah, me never wan' yuh fe do dat."

I walked towards her and held her. "Marcia's not a part a me life no more, so why should you leave? All me ever wan' from she was fe see me yout'. Dat's it."

She again laid her head on my chest but this time she started to cry.

"Marcus, I don't want to lose you."

"Yuh nah lose me," I replied quickly. I never know wha' fe say when women start cry. "You watch. T'ings a go work demselves out."

Although Justin had school in the morning, Yvette let him sleep on the settee while we talked before driving home at ten o'clock. When they left it was just me and my thoughts. I thought about Marcia, wondering if she really felt guilty about what had happened. Because in reality she had nothing to feel guilty about, except calling the Babylon when I kicked her glass door in. But I guess she had no choice. It was the beastbwoy who then abused dem power, and I can't really hold her responsible for that.

My thoughts drifted as I headed off to bed for what might be my second last night in this bedroom for some years.

There was a huge traffic queue on Broad Street leading to Hagley Road when I was on my way into work next morning. Somebody said something about an accident in the bypass, but when the bus went past there I never see nothing.

When I got in I went straight to the changing quarters and put on my chef's clothes. My blue and white check trousers was well creased 'cause I never hang them up properly. But I never worry, 'cause I wasn't working in no big-time kitchen. As I was buttoning up my white jacket Paul came up to me.

"You're late," he shouted.

I turned and looked at him.

"Me would've been 'pon time if there wasn't a traffic jam," I replied, wondering why is today 'im start pull up man for lateness.

"Well, you should catch an earlier bus then, shouldn't you?."

He was starting to vex me. "Me catch the one me always catch."

I fixed my chef hat straight in the mirror. I could see him behind me getting mad.

"So, wha'ppen Paul? Me less dan five minute late."

"You're on the veg today and I want all the potatoes, brussels sprouts and carrots diced by lunch time," he said.

I knew this was a physical impossibility, but I never say nothin', 'cause later today I wan' ask him about time off to attend the case.

Paul knew I hated the veg—well, every chef hated chopping veg, but I almost always got the station. It come as a joke amongst the kitchen staff, only I wasn't laughing and none of them dare say anything out of line to my face. They know I wasn't a man for them to chux it with.

I set about the veg in quick-quick time. By lunchtime I had the potatoes and sprouts finished and was half way through the carrots. Paul came round checking. When he passed my station he inspected what I had already done without a word. By one o'clock, I had everything finished.

After lunch I decided the time was right to ask Paul for time off. He was sitting in his two-by-two office at the back of the kitchen and with him being about eighteen stone of blubber it was a tight squeeze.

As I approached he looked up from his copy of *The Sun*. His mouth was full with what looked like a cream bun, and he had an enormous mug of tea in front of him.

"What do you want, Marcus?" He put the newspaper down and took a sip of his tea. I could see he had it open at page three. He was probably wanking over Linda Lusardi.

"Chef, me a look some time off?" I said.

The man spit out his tea like he was choking. "You must be joking," he said, wiping his fat face. "I mean, you come in here late this morning, and you were insubordinate yesterday...anyway, we're busy for the rest of this month and I need all the help I can get."

"Look me'll work de split t'day, if yuh wan'."

"No, I don't want, actually," he said with a false smile. "Steve's not as ill as we first thought, so he'll be in around five."

Cha. This fatty bum-bum was taking steps, but to sort him out now would be a mistake. I kept my cool but for good measure I asked for the time off again.

"Read my lips, Marcus. N-O spells no."

I left his office and went back to chopping the extra veg that he had put on the table when I was at lunch.

For the rest of the day I wondered how the hell was I going to get time off work. I had to be in court tomorrow unless I was going to do a runner. Then the old lady would lose the five thousand surety she had put up. So that wasn't an option.

In the end I decided that I just wouldn't turn up for work. I'd phone in sick until the trial was over, and if I was acquitted I'd return to work with a slight sore throat. If I was sent down, they wouldn't need to know where the hell I was because I wouldn't be back.

The old lady was hand beating and pulling at the dough as if she wanted to kill it. "After wha' yuh father do to me, I cyan' believe yuh would turn 'round and beat Marcia."

The old lady was near to tears.

"Mom, it never go so. Yuh a mek de t'ing look worse dan it is."

The old lady eyeballed me as she rolled the dough into dumplings.

"Well dat's wha' Marcia tell me when I go see 'er."

"Yuh went to Wolver'ampton. When?"

"Charmaine birthday. I had fe see 'e'. Give 'er a present. An' Marcia tell me everyt'ing. I cyan' believe a son of mine grow up to lick woman. I don't believe it."

"It nah 'appen again," I promised, not knowing what else to say.

"Hmm. A so yuh fadder used to say."

"But yuh gave 'im another chance, innit"

"I did, but you ought to know better. I had to plead wid Marcia fe bring de chile dung by you."

"Thanks, Mum."

I gave her a hug. The old lady shook her head.

"I don't know what I do to deserve this."

"It's my fault, de mess me inna. All my own makin'."

I released her and she went back to her dumplings.

"I've been prayin' for you, Marcus," she said.

"Me a go need it," I replied.

"Leave it in God's hands."

"Yuh comin' tomorrow?" I asked, knowing it would be hard for her to see her second son in the dock after already witnessing Bigga being sent down.

"Yes, Marcus. I'll be there."

I was pleasantly surprised.

"Me nah go down like Bigga," I said, knowing what she was thinking. I couldn't go to prison and leave her on her own. Jah know.

"I 'ope so, son...I 'ope so."

She dropped six pieces of dough into a pan of hot oil. Brought me back to the times when me and Bigga were yout', the old lady used to make fry dumplin' every Wednesday without fail. Bigga used to love them. Man used to eat ten in one rahtid go.

Now all 'im eat is spuds and porridge. I haven't seen or heard from Bigga since he was moved from Greens to some borders place. Yvette and me had always planned to go and visit, but wid me having to work every other Sat'day or Sunday morning it didn't leave much time to venture out of the city. Anyway, Bigga never even write to tell us or the old lady how he's bearing up.

"Yuh 'ear from Sam," the old lady asked. I noticed her face was showing the strain of a life that had well and truly done her bad.

"Nah, not yet, but when dis court t'ing over me a go bring Charmaine 'round to see yuh every week."

"What a sweet-looking girl, eh?" The old lady took her eyes off the dumplings for the first time and looked at me.

I felt good that at least I had brought a little somet'ing to the old lady's heart. I gave her a big hug. Before I left, she insisted I wait while she wrapped six dumplings and three jerk chicken legs in foil and placed them in a carrier bag for me.

I put them in my sports bag and rushed to the university for training.

Boom, boom, boom.

The ball hitting the wooden floor sounded like a rock on concrete.

My mind wasn't on the training. I kept hearing 'I promise to tell the truth, the whole truth and nothing but the truth. So help me God.'

This court t'ing was messing 'bout with my head. The team wasn't talking 'bout it, which made it much worse. Not even a little joke from Benji or a feisty remark from Levi. They musta thought it best to keep my mind off the t'ing. Dat was cool.

But when Coach started to run through drills using Levi and big Lemuel, then I screwed. It was like he had already sentenced me.

Usually, I stay on and practice the drills and my back-ups come in occasionally to make sure they knew the scheme come game day. But this evening it was the other way round, with me feelin' like the blasted reserve.

The other starters in the team could tell I was well vex.

Calvin called to Coach and they had a private word while the rest of us went through some shooting drills. I could see Coach getting worked up and Calvin trying to calm him down.

"Okay, lets scrimmage," Coach said when they rejoined the group. "Startin' five at de top end."

Everyone looked at each other. Calvin moved, then Joni, quickly followed by Adam. Winston made his way slowly to the top end clicking his fingers and singing some rap tune. I looked over at Coach.

"Well, wha' y'ah wait fa Marcus? You inna de startin' five."

T'ing was a rahtid relief. For a minute I thought Coach was going to skank me by letting me play with the bench players.

When we got into the game it was well physical. T'ing felt worse than when we play the animals from Wolverhampton. Even with the final only five days away, it was like nobody cared if they got injured.

213

Sweetbwoy Levi shot a three pointer over me. I retaliated by slam dunking over him, shouting: "Inna ya face, bwoy" as I landed on the hard wood.

Levi returned down court to score an easy lay up for two after I messed up my defensive assignment. He was now one up on me and shaping to Coach each time he scored. It was going to his head that Coach was bigging him up by choosing him ahead of me in training.

Adam came down the court with the ball, passed it to Winston just outside the key. Winston then faked his shot, moved inside the key, went up for a shot, but withheld the ball and dumped it off to me coming up from behind. I rose over Levi again and stuffed the ball through the hoop. When I landed I looked at Levi and shook my head as if to say *beat that, shaper.*

Winston touched my hand as we went back, to acknowledge the dunk.

"This is personal, brotha man!" Calvin yelled from the opposite side of the court. I looked at him and laughed.

The session went on way past our proper time, but Coach was enjoying my duel with Levi, so he made the badminton players wait to use the court.

Anyway, I think the badminton people got more enjoyment out of watching us play basketball than they got out of playing their own game.

At the end of the session Coach called me to one side of the hall, which now stunk heavy of man; hard, tough sweat.

"Look Marcus, me know say yuh never like when me pull yuh out, but me 'ave me reasons," he said, quietly.

"Yeah, me know. Yuh t'ink me guilty and yuh nah see me fe de nex ten years."

I was jesting with him.

"No, no is not dat," Coach said. "Look, if me t'ink yuh was guilty I'd be de first fe say so, but me been 'round a long time. Me know 'ow justice work fe black man inna dis place 'ere. I t'ink it right dat me should try out Levi and Pat, jus' in case."

"Me overstand, don't worry yuhself Coach."

"Nice game, brotha man," Calvin said when I walked into the changing room.

I shrugged.

"Well, y'know..."

"Serious t'ing. I hope yuh play dem lawyers dat tuff tomorrow," Roots said from behind the showers.

There was a loud laugh around the room. That pleased me 'cause it was nice to see t'ings were the same even if I was inna the dock the next day.

There was more noise in the changing room than I'd heard for some time. Everybody was talking shit. Adam was taking the piss out of Winston for settling down with his gyal.

"How long, Winston? How long before you get hungry for the white pussy?"

The men around them were killing themselves with laughter.

"Good luck tomorrow."

I turned 'round and nearly knocked over Andre standing behind me, his face red from the training.

"Yeah man...me ready."

We touched fists.

It was nice to see Andre back with the team, but he was even more distant now than before. He was talking to Calvin again, but they weren't as close as they had been. And while everybody else was a joking 'bout, Andre dressed in silence.

Levi came over to me and we slap hands. "Next time I gonna get you," he said, smiling. Man look like one of them top male models, to rahtid.

"De only place yuh goin' school me is on Fantasy Island, t'rahtid. As de Jackson bwoy say, yuh keep dreamin'."

I went off to the showers. When I came out most of the team had gone.

Joni Krantovic stood by the mirror decorating himself. Man and man was whispering that he was checking one of the 'Uh Huh' gyal and had moved out of Mr Lindsey's yard. But you still couldn't get two straight words of English outta 'im. When you asked him a question he just looked in your face like a long stick of blasted white misery.

I don't know if he's going to be allowed to stay in the country after the game on Sunday, so he's probably looking to shack up permanently with the 'Uh Huh' gyal to avoid deportation.

But 'im white, so dem people probably goin' let him stay.

I changed quickly and hurried to the bus stop to get to Yvette's yard before it was too late. I arrived at about eleven-fifteen. She was already in her night clothes when she opened the door.

"I thought you decided to be alone tonight. I kept ringing but there was no answer," she said as we went into the living room.

Then she saw my training bag.

"I might have guessed. Nothing, but nothing, interrupts you and basketball. So, did you eat this evening?"

I suddenly remembered the chicken and dumplings the old lady had given me. I took them out out the bag and Yvette warmed them in the microwave, and three minutes later I was samplin' some good home cooking.

Yvette watched me eat but didn't once ask for a bite, which was a miracle. I musta been mixing my starches and proteins. All me know is dem taste good together. She sat in front of the gas fire looking worried.

"So is wha'ppen? Yuh nah speak to me?" I asked.

She smiled, but I could tell it took effort.

"It's just that after you leave here tonight I don't know how long it will be before I see you again. Marcus, I'm scared."

I put the plate down on the floor and went down and sat beside her, putting my greasy hands around her.

"Yuh nah haffe worry. Yuh a go see me widdin twenty-four hours. Yuh 'ave me guarantee 'pon dat."

"Marcus, stop fooling. This is serious."

"Yvette, me cyan' get too serious, me haffe stay sane."

She gave me a kiss on the cheek and I hugged her tight. The two of us sat down until two in the morning talking about everything that had happened to us since we met six months ago. We laughed, she cried, we kissed, she ate, just like we had always done. When I left, she promised to be at the court house early. I walked the lonely half hour trek to my yard with nothing on my mind but the outcome of the trial tomorrow.

14

Sweet Reality

The early morning sun shone like a spotlight on Mickey Mouse's head, making the carpet in Jermaine's bedroom look like a stage. Andre was standing in the shadows, helping Jermaine pull on his school jumper. Jermaine looked at Andre as if he had a burning question to ask.

"Come on, son, pull your trousers up properly," Andre said, casting his eye around the bedroom.

The place had changed since he'd moved out. The room had been entirely redecorated. Super Mario Brothers adorned the walls and the grey carpet had motifs of the kiddies' favourite Disney characters woven into it. Donald Duck, Goofy, Mickey Mouse and Minnie were all there.

"Dad."

"Yes, Jermaine?" Andre sat him on the bed.

"Marvin's got a new Super Mario game."

"So what, son?" Andre replied, waiting for the sucker punch. He knew this tactic well, he'd used it often enough on his own father.

"Can you buy me one, dad?"

Right on cue.

"Jermaine, you can't have everything your friends have."

He decided to play a hard-nosed game. He watched Jermaine's face dissolve into sulks. "But he never lets me play with it," he protested.

Andre guessed that his best friend Marvin guarded Mario as closely as he had cherished his marbles at that age.

"Well, if he doesn't want you to play with it, that's up to him. He must have his reasons."

"But Dad, it's not fair," Jermaine moaned, as Andre put his socks on. Jermaine was old enough to dress himself, but the accident had made Andre realise how precious moments like these were. To spend time dressing his son was now a privilege.

For three days Jermaine had not been able to move. Andre had relived the anguish of his father's last days. When Jermaine pulled through, he thanked God. Now he just wanted to spend every possible minute with his kids—every *second* counted. He wanted to give them all the love and anything else they wanted. Except a new Super Mario game.

"Tell you what. If Mummy says yes, I'll get you one. Deal?"

Jermaine looked unsure of whether this was a good deal or not, so he didn't answer. But as soon as Andre lifted him off the bed, he shot off like a bullet to relay the small print of the pact they had just made to Heather.

Heather's attitude towards Andre had changed since the accident. The hours they spent together by Jermaine's bedside had put a new perspective on their relationship. If they couldn't live together in peace, at least they could live apart in harmony.

The children's welfare was the main thing, and Andre realised that their parents' constant fights were having a detrimental effect on them. As far as he was concerned, selfishness went out of the window and understanding and co-operation were born.

He also believed that Heather was trying, for the first time, to meet him half-way. He wouldn't say they didn't still have major differences, but now these were discussed in a more conciliatory way than the stand-up confrontations of old.

Andre got to thinking this was the secret to handling women. When they start to rant and rave, agree with them. Apologise for being out of order. They'll appreciate it. Some would look on it as diminishing male sovereignty, but Andre was past caring what others thought. It worked for him. At least he and Heather were being civil, talking like human beings instead of fighting like animals.

Their new entente cordiale extended to Heather phoning him when she needed help with the kids. Before, she had only phoned when all else failed. Now he got first refusal.

Last night, as he got in from training, Heather had buzzed him to take the kids to school and nursery, because she had to get to work early. She apologised for leaving it so late, but even calling when she did gave Andre time to organise himself.

He could get up an hour earlier, make the trip to Heather's, take care of the kids and still be in time for work.

Heather had realised that Andre's alleged affair with Tracy was a figment of the girl's imagination. She also now knew she couldn't get a divorce in two days. The divorce was something Andre wanted to talk to her about, but he had to choose the right moment. A false move might easily destroy the trust they were rebuilding.

Jermaine came running back into the room, his initial exuberance dampened by Heather's refusal. A moment later Heather came in and shouted:

"Stop your snivelling."

She then watched Andre as he tried to get Jermaine to comb what little hair he had on his head, and avoid the scar tissue on his forehead.

Heather was wearing a black suit and navy blue blouse; she had lost some of the weight she had put on earlier in the year. She claimed she was working out to some exercise freak on one of the early morning programmes. Andre had never known her take any interest in exercise, but the kids confirmed it so it must be true.

She stood in the middle of Mickey Mouse's face and watched Andre struggle to get Jermaine to follow his stroke from the back of his head to the front.

She laughed.

"Men! Look at the two of you! You're both hopeless," she said, taking the comb from Andre's hands.

"This is how you do it, Jermaine."

Andre stood back and let the expert work. Andre noticed she still wore the watch he had given her for her twenty-fifth birthday.

"Right, I've got to get going," she said, tossing the comb on the dresser.

"What time do you have to be in?" asked Andre.

"Eight-thirty."

She started back down the stairs.

"I've made their lunches. Could you just pack them in their containers? Make sure you give them the right ones, they'll only argue if you don't."

Heather was working full-time now. Andre wasn't happy about this—he believed Heather should be at home caring for the kids—but he accepted it. They were at critical stages of their development and needed to know there was someone there whose sole purpose was to look after their needs. In Andre's view that responsibility lay with their mother—but he was wise enough to keep silent, since he couldn't claim to be performing his fatherly duties to the letter.

When he and Jermaine went downstairs, Josephine was already wearing her black hooded coat. It was all bunched up at the front because she'd buttoned it up wrong. She looked so proud of herself that Andre felt bad about having to take it back off so she could have breakfast.

"I'll see you later," Heather said, planting a kiss first on Josephine's forehead, then on Jermaine's. Andre wondered if he'd get one, but detente didn't extend to kissing just yet. Not even a peck. She just smiled at him and left.

After giving the kids their breakfast, Andre sat down and read the paper. He was surprised she still had it delivered, as only he ever read it. Old habits die hard, he thought.

"Dad, why don't you come and live with us again?" Jermaine asked when he'd finished his breakfast. Andre wiped the Ready Brek from around his mouth and pulled the boy gently towards him.

"Do you miss Daddy?"

Jermaine nodded.

"Most of the kids at school don't have a daddy and I want to keep mine."

Andre smiled.

"Everyone has a daddy, it's just that you haven't seen the ones of the children at school."

"Marvin says his mum said he hasn't got a dad..."

"Jermaine, just remember, no matter what anyone says, *you* have a daddy who loves you whether he lives here or not, okay?"

Jermaine smiled then ran off to pester Josephine. Andre got up and phoned for a cab. His Rover had failed to start again this morning, even though it had just been repaired after the accident. He must be keeping these cab firms in business these days. But he couldn't complain; Heather had finally got Josephine into the local authority nursery, so he no longer had to fork out fifty pounds a week for her to go to Mrs Madge.

Andre got into work slightly late, but with Mr Pal now upstairs in the partners' suite, it wasn't such a major crisis. He came out of the lift looking the total professional. Dark green suit, lime-coloured shirt and tie and black briefcase in hand,

He was whistling the jazz classic 'Take Five' as he strode purposefully to his department. On the way, he noticed someone in Mr Pal's old office. All he could see was that the person was wearing a skirt.

When he arrived at his desk, Andre's mood shifted abruptly at the sight of the other three.

They really were the pits; William and John were working, but Michael sat gazing into space with a coffee in his hand. He decided to get the formalities out of the way. "Morning, guys..."

They all grudgingly returned the greeting. Michael woke up from his dream.

"Guess what, Andre?"

"I give up, Michael."

He wasn't in the mood for guessing games or stunning revelations.

"They've appointed Mr Pal's successor and it's a woman."

"About time, too, its been almost two months."

"Yeah—but she's a *woman*," Michael stressed, determined to push the point. William and John raised their heads waiting for another reaction from Andre.

"A *woman!*" Michael almost shouted.

Andre supposed it was a bit of a surprise, since all of the top solicitors at Goldbergs were men. But Michael seemed to think the female of the species came from a different planet. Andre looked at him knowing he wouldn't let up until he got a response. "Well, it makes a change," he said, shrugging his shoulders.

Michael looked disappointed. John raised his big face to address Andre.

"Did you see that programme last night?"

Andre sat down at his desk and started to sort through his files.

"What programme's that, John?"

"What was it called again?" John slapped his right hand against his forehead like he was trying to bash his memory into action.

"On BBC2 around nine o'clock. Umm...*The Real*...something. What're those nice crisps called again?

"McCoys?" Andre offered.

"That's it, *The Real McCoy*. Did you see it?"

"No, I didn't. I was training."

Andre just wanted to get on with his work.

"Yeah, it was alright. Didn't understand half the jokes, mind you, but they looked funny."

Andre just chuckled. What else could he do?

"I say, what is this *Real McCoy*?" William asked.

"Black comedy programme, BBC2," Michael answered, as if you had to be living on Mars not to have heard of it.

"Quite frankly I can't see the need for all these separate programmes myself. I think programmes should be for everyone."

Andre looked up scornfully at William—then realised it was just one of those simple ass things he came out with, and not worth answering. He lowered his head again. William got the message.

"Do you think the new boss will fancy me?" Michael said, peppering the air with his vanity.

"Come on, what d'you think, eh lads?"

He brushed his hair back John Travolta-style.

"Not a prayer," John replied.

"You better put your money where your mouth is. I'm going to spin her around my little finger," Michael said, taking his wedding ring off and dropping it in his desk drawer.

"By the end of the day she'll be eating out of my hands."

Andre was finding this intolerable. He wondered how he'd put up with listening to so much bullshit for so long.

"Hey, listen," John said, calling everyone to attention. "What do you call a Sikh with a red turban, eh?"

Andre inhaled deeply.

"Frankly, I haven't a clue," William replied.

"A match stick!" John answered with a sickening laugh.

Michael showed his appreciation by laughing heartily. Andre swore that the next racist joke John bleated, he'd lay him flat on his back.

At that moment Tracy walked into the room. Her skirt looked even shorter than usual, if that was possible. William's glasses almost steamed up, John's tongue hung out and Michael lay back in his Romeo pose. She seemed a little upset.

"Mrs Kennedy would like to see you individually in her office. Michael at ten forty-five, then Andre, William and John in that order at fifteen-minute intervals," she informed them before leaving accompanied by a wolf whistle from Michael.

It was only then that it dawned on Andre that Mrs Kennedy had the job Theo had been certain he would get. Blast, Andre thought, Theo must be cursing. He immediately phoned down to Theo's office, only to be told that he would be in court all day.

Of course—it was the first day of Marcus' trial. He hoped the evidence he had passed on to Theo about the inconsistencies in the police version of the incident would get the case thrown out.

Andre hated seeing a friend behind bars—but he had more selfish reasons for wanting Marcus to be acquitted.

The Warriors needed him for the final on Sunday.

There was no doubt in his mind that Marcus could make the difference between the sides. The forty points he'd scored against Cheshire in the second game of the regular season was the best performance he'd seen by a British player in any of the English leagues. From the first dunk he was on fire—and to lose him for the final would be a disaster.

Eleven-fifteen came around quickly. Andre set off for Mrs Kennedy's office as Michael arrived back.

"What a bitch!" Michael said, shaking his head with a look of total disgust. She obviously hadn't mistaken him for Rudolf Valentino.

"Why so sore, Michael? Did she eat the skin off your hands or something?" he chuckled.

When Andre knocked on the door of the office, a soft but authoritative voice said:

"Come in."

He could feel his adrenaline pumping. The office still had the ambience of Pal's interrogations—the only change in the room since Pal's departure was a new photo-frame on the desk.

Mrs Kennedy looked up and smiled.

"Which one are you?" she asked.

"Andre Beckford," he mumbled. He hadn't been this nervous in front of a woman since his headmistress summoned him to her room for pushing in the dinner queue.

"Take a seat, Andre."

She took off her gold-rimmed glasses and set them carefully on the desk.

"I didn't see you in the office when I came in this morning."

Blast. Trust him to be late today of all days.

"Er, yes, I had to take my children to school. I was slightly delayed."

His legs were trembling.

"I know the problem. I have three of my own," she replied. Andre almost died. Did she really just sympathise with him?

"Married?" she asked.

"Well, ah, yes..."

Andre didn't know what to answer. He couldn't tell her he was in the middle of a divorce and didn't have a stable home life—like a stereotypical black man.

"I wish I could get my husband to take the kids to school in the morning. If he did, we wouldn't need a nanny. But I won't bore you you with my personal problems," she said, smiling again.

She wasn't particularly good-looking, but there was something about her that was attractive. She had shoulder-length brunette hair, slightly buck teeth and a light suntan. She opened a file on her desk, which he supposed was his personnel dossier.

"Well, Andre, I've looked over your record and apart from some

223

trite remarks from one of your seniors, I must say I'm very impressed. You certainly have what it takes to be a top-drawer legal executive and a good solicitor in the future. Just make sure you don't slacken."

Andre couldn't believe what he was hearing. Pal had never said anything like that to him.

"What are your long-term plans as regards the company?" she asked, pressing her hands together on top of her desk.

Again, he didn't know what he should say, but he decided to come clean.

"Well, I was thinking about leaving when I complete my studies."

She looked concerned.

"Why is that?"

Andre became tongue-tied, he wasn't sure how much further to go down the truth trail.

"I would rather hear the truth than some cock and bull story," she said, as if reading his mind.

That startled him.

"Ahh...Mr Pal and I didn't exactly see eye-to-eye," he said, fidgeting in his seat. "In fact, we didn't get on at all."

She nodded.

"Yes, I gathered. His reports on you were the only negatives in your file. Well, I've had some run-ins with Mr Pal myself, so I know what you're talking about. But it would be a shame to lose you, especially since the company has invested so much time and money in you."

"I haven't made up my mind to leave yet," he added quickly.

"That's fine. Hopefully we'll be able to do something to persuade you to stay."

She put her glasses back on.

"Tell me. What's it like as a black man working in the office?"

Andre was taken aback by the openness of her question. It was something that Pal had never discussed with him. Pal seemed to think that any problems you encountered as a black person in a white office were a figment of your imagination. But Andre decided not to spill his guts to Mrs Kennedy.

He liked what he saw and heard, but he had to suss her out some more. He settled for a diplomatic response.

"It's like any other place where there are a few black people, but I suppose it's okay."

She nodded.

"That's something else I want to change around here. Soon I hope to employ more minority and female staff in senior positions. So if you know any suitable people at any level, let me know. Mind you, I don't want just anyone—I'm looking for qualified people who can do a damn good job for me and the firm."

Andre nodded.

"Do you have any questions?" she asked.

"No."

He'd already heard enough.

"Well then, here's to hard work and dedication."

She offered Andre her hand. As he got up to shake it, he caught a glimpse of an old black man in the photograph on her desk—stood incongrously in the centre of an intimate white family gathering. Andre wondered who he was. The gardener maybe? Mrs Kennedy saw him looking and put him out of his misery. She picked up the picture and introduced her family, pointing lastly to the old black man.

"This is my grandfather," she smiled. "It's a shock to many people, since you can't tell I have African blood in me. But yes, my late grandad was from Ghana. And I'm proud of it."

She was right—you couldn't tell.

When he got back to his desk, Michael was still complaining about how badly he had been treated by Mrs Kennedy.

"Do you know, she criticised my analysis of cases. Who the hell does she think she is? Bitch!"

He was throwing papers around on his desk. "How d'you find her, Andre? Did she give you the same kind of grilling?"

"No, on the contrary," he gloated. "She was extremely civil to me."

"No, on the contrary," Michael mimicked. "Well fucking bully for you."

Satisfied that he had helped wreck Michael's morning, Andre turned his attention to his workload.

He found a note on his desk.

'Wifey-poos called. Will call back.'

Andre raced out of the lift towards the revolving doors, hurrying to get to the library for a couple of hours' study.

As he pushed through, Theo rushed in the other side. Andre pushed the doors a full three-hundred-and-sixty degrees to end up back inside the building.

"How did the trial go?" he asked, eagerly.

"Not good. The police came well prepared. Still, it's early days," Theo said—but his expression suggested that the case was going well.

Andre was confused.

If this was how he looked when a case went badly, how smug did he look when he was winning?

"How's Marcus bearing up?"

"To be honest, I don't know. I didn't have that much time to talk to him today. But he better be in shape tomorrow, 'cause he's in the dock."

In the dock.

The words sounded ominous. Andre had never before imagined himself on that side of the courtroom—and now he realised, for the first time, what hell Marcus must have been going through in the run-up to the case.

Theo interrupted Andre's thoughts, changing the subject abruptly.

"So...have you met your new boss yet?"

"Yes I have. She's alright."

Theo looked surprised.

"The bastards fucked me up good and proper on that one. Look, do you have time for a quick drink?"

Andre looked at his watch. "Well, okay, a really quick one."

They roared off in Theo's red Porsche. Andre could see Theo really enjoyed the glances he got from other drivers and passers-by. He slowed at every crossing, even when there was no need to. Each and every black woman they passed looked twice when she saw these two well-dressed black men sitting in a motor that obviously cost over twenty-five grand.

Theo looked across at Andre and smiled, changing up to fifth gear on a brief open stretch.

"You could be driving one of these soon if you play your cards right," he casually informed Andre.

Andre enjoyed playing the millionaire, even if it was only for the five minutes it took them to get to the wine bar.

It was virtually empty when they got there, and they sat on the tall stools which circled the bar. Theo ordered a double gin and tonic, but Andre made do with a pineapple and lemonade. There was no way he could study with alcohol in his system.

"I'm leaving Goldbergs," Theo blurted once their drinks had

226

arrived.

"But I thought you had plans at the company?"

Andre knew that Mrs Kennedy's appointment was a major setback for Theo.

Theo sipped his G and T.

"No, I have to get moving. As a professional black man you have to do your own thing. No-one's going to do it for you."

Andre couldn't believe this was the same Theo who, two months ago, was singing the praises of corporate Britain. He'd changed his tune now he'd found out the corporate world didn't want him. Deserted him. Left him in the lurch, like Andre knew it would.

"I'm setting up a couple of practices in Birmingham. I'll have one in the city somewhere and one in Handsworth," Theo said.

So Andre was right. He mentally gave himself a pat on the back, as he opened his ears to Theo's plans. Only one thing disturbed him.

"Why Handsworth?"

"Kudos. Good for the image if you're seen to be helping the community. Putting something back, they call it."

The tone of the discussion was beginning to worry Andre. Theo was looking more and more sinister to him now.

"But first I've got to make my name. Earn a reputation that'll bring the clients flocking to the practice. Got to build up that profile, get people to believe in me. I've got the finance. Rachel and I made a killing selling our two homes in London and we bought at a steal in Solihull, so we've got a bit to invest. Look, the point I'm making is that the future is bright. Do you want to be part of it?"

Andre hesitated.

"Come and work for me, Andre."

Theo sank the last drop of his drink. Andre thought carefully. If Theo had come with that proposition two months ago, he would have jumped higher than Carl Lewis to accept it. But there was too much about Theo that disturbed him.

His whole attitude stank.

It reminded him of what he'd always promised never to become, no matter how successful he was. But he didn't want to dismiss the offer out of hand. Like all good professionals, he wanted to test the water on both sides of the pond.

"Look, Theo, I'll have to think about it."

Theo shrugged.

"Your prerogative, but don't take too long, there'll be others begging for the same opportunity."

He ordered another G and T. Andre changed the subject to Marcus.

"How did the stuff my source managed to dig up on the police go down?"

"Didn't use it." Theo said flippantly.

Andre drew back, astonished.

"You didn't? Why?"

"Strategy, Andre, strategy."

"I thought it proved the police doctored their initial statements when they conflicted."

"Yes it did, but—"

"Theo, you're withholding evidence that could get this case thrown out of a kangaroo court, let alone the Crown Court."

"Andre, I've got to make this work properly. If I'm going to build a reputation in this city, I've got to start somewhere and this case is as good as any."

"What do you mean?"

Theo drew closer and lowered his voice to almost a whisper.

"I'll introduce the evidence at a later trial—the Appeal Court or even the House of Lords. That's what I'm looking at, a real biggie."

"House of Lords!"

Andre shrieked.

"Are you saying you're going to deliberately lose the case?"

Theo smiled.

"It's the perfect opportunity. Drum up publicity by making a song and dance about how British justice screwed up again. Then introduce this new evidence at a later date. Get an appeal hearing. Case gets overturned and I become a celebrity—the new kid on the block!"

Andre was horrified.

"Meanwhile Marcus rots in jail for something he didn't do."

"Oh come on, Andre. Don't make it sound so bad. He'll pick up a tidy sum in compensation."

"*Compensation?* What about his freedom? You'd really stitch up a brotha?"

"Brotha? Listen, Andre, black and white doesn't come into it. You can't get bogged down with all that. Looking after number one is paramount. Anyway, why are you so concerned about a raggamuffin like Marcus Codrington? He'll end up in jail sooner or later—there's nothing you or I can do about that. It's just that on his way, he'll give our practice the start it needs. Think of it as an investment."

"Our practice?" Andre asked, incredulous. "Count me out of this one, brotha!"

"Andre, if the black thing is worrying you, forget it. Face facts. You're already a sellout as far as the majority of blacks are concerned. Look at you in your fancy suit and tie. You don't know a thing about the streets. You're not one of them, no matter how hard you try. You've moved from the streets into the suites my friend, and you'd better learn the rules of the game, or you'll find yourself under the sole of some executive's boot."

"I don't play by the same rules as you."

Theo downed his second drink with one gulp and sat back and looked at Andre. "You can't solve the problems of the world, Andre. So you'd just better take care of number one by any means necessary, as *Brotha* Malcolm said."

"I'd prefer to know I can walk the street with dignity as a black man. Or look a brotha in the eye without having to wince because my underhanded, opportunist dealings got him sent down. You're no better than the police who did Marcus over. Thanks for the drink." Andre slid off the stool and headed for the door.

"You're living in a dream world Andre. When you get a little older you'll see," Theo shouted, as he hurried out.

Andre forgot about the library and walked briskly back to the office. He couldn't let Theo get away with fitting Marcus up. He caught Mrs Kennedy as she was about to leave. He invented a hypothetical case with fictitious characters to extract her advice on what to do. She was adamant it would be unethical for a solicitor to get involved with a colleague's case behind his back. Worse, it would likely put the interfering solicitor's career in jeopardy. He reluctantly came to realise there was little he could do for Marcus.

Andre stuck his hand out as yet another black cab with its available light on whizzed past him in the pouring rain, as if it were the invisible man standing on the curb waving his Guardian newspaper. He was soaked. He decided there and then not to go back to his lonely flat but to pay Heather and the kids another visit. Maybe he should phone to let her know he was coming but that would mean traipsing around the city centre searching for a phone that worked. And in this weather, that was not an option, unless he wanted to be in bed with pneumonia the next day.

He watched the rain bounce off the tarmac and rush down the gutter, but the monsoon conditions couldn't take his mind off Marcus and his plight. Was he trying to absolve himself from blame by believing there was nothing he could do? Was Theo right that only the tough and ruthless survived in this world? Maybe, just maybe, Andre thought, he had sold out.

A car pulled up beside him. It was Calvin's BMW. He leaned across the passenger seat and opened the door for him. Although he felt awkward, Andre gratefully accepted. He and Calvin were back on speaking terms since his apology for the changing room incident, but things were not the same. At training, their conversations were fleeting and on game day, businesslike. The old boyish togetherness had gone.

"Hi, Calvin," Andre said, with the formality he reserved for the three in the office.

"Good to see you, brotha man," Calvin replied, as he pulled away.

Andre slapped his outstretched hand and smiled. There was a deafening silence for a while, both were unsure of what to say. Then Andre broke the ice. "Don't see you in town often."

"Yeah, just been to a meeting at the town hall." Calvin calmly replied. "They voted by one not to put the blocks on the Americans coming over. I tell you brotha, politicians are the most deceitful people you can deal with. Even the black ones who promised support did the Judas. All of them abstained. Why are we so afraid of ourselves? Brotha man, we only got ourselves to blame when things like this happen. Four blacks in the house and every one an Uncle Tom. Sometimes you have to thank God for these white liberals. I never thought I'd hear myself say that."

Despite his frustration, Calvin maintained his cool exterior. He didn't give Andre time to comment. "One Tory councillor even said we're inciting riots. Can you believe that? They try to ban 'Boyz 'n the 'Hood' from cinemas in Birmingham. Try to move the Carnival from Handsworth Park to suburbia. Cut funds to black self-help groups...brotha, we got to get out on the streets and demonstrate and if those black councillors won't join the fight, we should use the ballot to turf them out of office."

Andre didn't answer, though Calvin provided a much needed break from thinking about Marcus. He decided not to mention it to Calvin because he would only blow it out of proportion and get a picket of his radicals to demonstrate at the court. Maybe that was what it needed, a bit of radical action, but not the Russian-style revolution Calvin had in mind for the town hall.

Calvin took his hand off the wheel and fiddled around on the back seat for a plastic bag. When he found it, he pulled a handful of leaflets out of the bag. "Seen these, brotha?" he asked, handing them to Andre.

"Yeah, I've seen a couple posted up in Handsworth."

"We've got 'em pinned up all over the city. This thing is going to be big."

Andre looked at the leaflets, reading that former members of the Bloods and Crips LA gangs would be guest speakers at the conference.

"So when are the Tinseltown posse coming in?" Andre asked,

"I'm picking them up from Heathrow on Friday morning...Good Friday."

"You must have a hefty hotel bill."

"No, we've persuaded Brotha Lindsey to put them up."

Andre's expression changed to one of surprise.

Calvin chuckled. "Brotha man, I did a deal to hold an end of conference party at The Star club and we've already sold a hundred and fifty tickets. Well, not sold. The conference committee and the X Centre put their hands in their pockets and bought the tickets and we're going to give them away free. The Star club gets the money and whatever they make on the door, plus the bar.

"Sounds like you'll lose out big time."

"Yeah, but that's the kind of deal you have to make with sharks like Lindsey. Anyway, we saved well over a grand on hotel bills. So, where you goin', brotha?"

Andre was by now so caught up in what Calvin was saying that he didn't realise that he hadn't told him where he wanted to be dropped. He hesitated at mentioning the H word. "I'm visiting Heather."

Calvin remained quiet for a couple of seconds. "How is she? I haven't seen her for a couple of months. Been really busy."

"Things are improving. The accident really made us focus more on the important things."

"Good to hear it, brotha."

Andre looked at him. Calvin's eyes were fixed on the road. "Listen I'm sorry for accusing you of messing with Heather," he blurted.

"Brotha, we all say and do things we regret afterwards," Calvin replied.

"Look, why don't the four of us go out for a drink one night? Me, you, Heather and Lorna. We haven't done that for a long time."

Calvin looked hesitant. "I don't know, brotha. You sure you can speak for Heather? She might not want to go."

"Why not?"

"Nothing, brotha, just thought she might have other plans?"

"Like what?"

"I don't know. Suppose she's dating someone. I mean, she's not going to stay single for the rest of her life, is she?"

Andre became uneasy and defensive. But he knew Calvin was right. What right did he have to Heather? And what if she had found herself a new man! The thought alone made him tense and anxious.

Calvin pulled into Heather's road and parked outside the house.

Andre got out the car. "Coming in?" he asked.

"No, brotha, got to dash. Got to finish off some business at the X Centre, then pick up Lorna from the train station. Tell Heather I said hello."

"Okay, I'll see you at training tomorrow."

"Go in peace, brotha."

Heather answered the door wearing an orange leotard over yellow leggings, and breathing heavily. She'd obviously been working out.

"We must stop meeting like this," she smiled. "Anyone would think that we were married."

Andre was relieved that the welcome was warm. He followed her into the dining room and discovered the source of her athletic exuberance, a Jane Fonda exercise video tape was on the TV. He watched her go through her bust exercises before Heather pressed pause on the video. The room went totally quiet.

"Where are the kids?" he asked, casting his eye over Heather's ever-improving physique. Calvin's words echoed in his head. Maybe that was why she had become so body conscious all of a sudden.

"They're with Mum," Heather replied. She sat on the sofa and wiped her forehead with a towel. "They should be home soon. Are they who you came to see?"

Andre shrugged, embarrassed by her question. "Well, yes and no."

"Lets deal with the no first then," she said, smiling mischievously. "Who else have you come to see?"

"Who else is here?"

"Hmm. Why is it men can't tell woman how they feel?"

"Same reason women always nag, I suppose."

Heather threw the towel at him. "We don't always nag."

"You do. You nag because you don't understand what we go

232

through."

"We understand plenty. We understand that we can't rely on you men, because when we do, we get left in the shit. And we understand that if something needs doing, we should do it ourselves, otherwise you'll accuse us of nagging or getting on you backs."

"Y'see, that's exactly it! No woman is an island, Heather. This independence thing is what's causing the problems; like you going off to work and leaving the kids with someone else."

"And who forced us to change our attitudes? It's you men. You can't be relied on to provide. So we have to take charge of our destiny. That's why I decided to go back to work. And I don't think the kids have suffered one bit. If they have, you've got to take some responsibility for that."

"The old divide and rule tactic," Andre muttered. "Emasculate the black man, force his woman into the labour market and destroy his family relations."

"Nonsense, Andre. The only people destroying black family life are black men."

"Heather, check this out. We get it in the ear all day from the white man at work and then come home to another ear bashing from our women, who should at least have some sympathy and understanding!"

"How can we, if we don't know what your pain is? If you shut us out by not communicating with us? We're not mind readers, Andre. And you always use this white man thing as an excuse. The white man doesn't live with you. The black woman does...sometimes at least. You need to tidy your own house before you can go clean up for someone else."

"You just don't want to admit that the black man's problem stems from his powerlessness in this country."

"Andre, don't start. You're beginning to sound like Calvin. Anyway, you're talking in general terms. What about on a personal level? When was the last time you told me you loved me?"

"I haven't been around, Heather."

"See, you can't even answer that straight. It's like you think telling your wife you love her makes you less of a man, for Christ's sakes! Emotionless. You know, sometimes you used to come home and you'd be so cold, I thought you needed a couple of hours in the microwave to defrost. Even when we made love at times it was like we were strangers."

Andre was shocked. She'd always hinted at it but never put it as

233

directly as now.

"And..." she continued.

He wasn't sure he wanted her to.

"...You're too predictable, too safe. I was getting bored with our marriage. I mean, where did all the spontaneity go? Like whisking me off to restaurants, buying me flowers, finding romantic ways to celebrate our anniversary—you completely forgot this year by the way—what happened to all that, Andre? If I just wanted to be safe, have a nice house, two kids and two cars parked outside, I wouldn't have married you when you had nothing. I would have gone and found myself a nice rich guy and lived happily ever after. But no, I married you because of the passion we had, and the communication. In a nutshell, because there used to be magic between us. We've lost that over the years."

"The honeymoon doesn't last for ever, Heather. Seems like you've been watching too much television."

"Oh come off it! All I'm asking is to feel special every once in a while, to be romanced and cared for. That's all. Is that too much to ask? Well is it?"

"I suppose not."

"You suppose not? And what do you want, Andre? What do you need from a relationship ?"

"I don't really know."

"There you go again—shutting me out. There must be something you value more than anything else."

Andre fell silent for a while. Eventually he said, "I value my kids and my marriage, and..." he paused. "I love you." He looked at Heather. Tears were welling in her eyes. Andre couldn't help himself; he cried too.

She pulled him towards her, laid his head on her breast and kissed his head. "It's okay to cry, Andre, it's okay to show me your true feelings," she whispered.

Andre wrapped his arms around her. "Why are we hurting each other, Heather?"

She shook her head. "I think we're just rediscovering ourselves."

"Oh, is that what it is? Felt like pain to me."

They both laughed. Then they hugged. Andre picked the towel off the floor and dried her eyes. "I never wanted to leave you, y'know?" he said, feeling more confident now to talk. "I was pressuring myself so much, trying to prove I could be a brilliant husband, father, legal executive and ball player, all at once. Something had to give. I guess

234

I took the easy option, turned my back on my wife and kids. It was easier blaming you than telling Mr Pal, or anyone else who was on my case, to go to hell. Turned out to be the worst decision I ever made in my life."

He looked up and saw the tears rolling down Heather's face. "You know that's the first time you've ever honestly told me how you feel." She leaned over and kissed him, just a peck at first. "Thank you." Then she became more passionate. They pulled closer and held each other tightly.

"Is there anyone else in your life now, Heather?" Andre asked.

She hesitated. "What makes you ask that?"

"I don't know, something Calvin said."

"What did he say?"

"Just made me realise, I was taking you for granted, and how I'd feel if I lost you for good."

"Andre, I want us to put the last few months behind us and start afresh. You're the only man I love or ever will love."

Andre sighed with relief and buried his head in her breast. Just then, the doorbell rang. Heather dried her eyes and went to answer it.

"Daddy, Daddy!" the kids screamed as they ran into the room.

Heather's mum followed her into the room. "Wha' wrong wid you, chile?" she asked, looking suspiciously from Heather's red eyes to Andre's.

"Nothing Mum, really."

"Don't tell me nothin'. I can see you've been cryin'. Yuh t'ink me blind? Is him, innit, wha' him do?"

"I'm tellin' you, Mum, he didn't do anything."

"Why you always a cover fe him, eh?" She turned her attention to Andre. "Wha' yuh do me daughter?"

He looked at her and sighed. "I just told her something I should have told her a long time ago, Mrs Parchment."

"Mum, Andre's coming back home. We're not getting a divorce," Heather said.

Andre was first stunned, then happy the decision had been made. All he wanted in the world right now was to come home.

"Are you really coming back, Daddy?" Jermaine asked, excitedly.

"Yes. That's if you want me to."

"Yeah! Yeah!" he and Josephine screamed, jumping in his lap. Heather's mum was speechless for once in her life. Then she looked slightly embarrassed. "Well. Dat's good news. Yuh know I was against dis divorce t'ing anyway, but I couldn't stand fe see me daughter so unhappy."

Andre's jaw dropped. The old dragon was human after all.

Mrs Parchment gave the kids a kiss. "I better leave yuh alone, let yuh talk. Glad yuh sort t'ings out finally. Bye, Andre."

Andre could barely believe the turnaround. "Bye Mum." he managed to say.

She shot him a look that said, "Don't push it!" before Heather led her to the front door. She was gone for a full fifteen minutes. Andre supposed she was explaining the turn of events to her mother. When she returned, she told the kids, "Bed, you two."

There was a tremendous cry of 'aahh' from both of them before they were ushered up to their rooms. While she was upstairs Andre phoned the twenty-four hour Interflora and left an order for twenty red roses to be delivered to the house at four o'clock tomorrow. Heather was right. The romance had gone out of their marriage and it was time they did something about it.

She came back down half an hour later and started clearing away the bags the kids had dumped. "I'm sorry about Mum. She means well but she gets carried away, as you know."

He snuggled up closer to her. "It's okay, if she wasn't like that I wouldn't have any mother-in-law jokes to tell."

Heather sat next to him on the sofa."You tell jokes about my dear sweet mother," she asked, forcing him back with pinches. "You wait till I see her, I'm going to tell her."

"No, don't. Please. I like her how she is now..." he laughed. "Humble pie all round her mouth."

Heather giggled. "Oh, before I forget. Here..." She got up, pulled a set of keys out of her pocket and dropped them in his hand.

"I think you'll be needing these. Welcome home."

15

Home Alone

Cheryl had spent dollars on a large double bed to replace the single she had before I moved in. *Damn!* Had been six long weeks since I gave up a homie's rights as an open-all-hours service station to stranded hoochies who needed refuelling.

As I lay beside Cheryl it must have been four o'clock in the morning. Man couldn't even be bothered to turn my head to look at my clock-radio, the only merchandise from my humble crib that Cheryl felt was worth puttin' on display in our new shack.

Damn, wasn't nothin' ours. This was Cheryl's pad and she lost no time reminding a homie of that fact. My pots, pans, kettle and other stuff were safely hidden. Even the majority of my drapes were dumped in black binliners and thrown in the bottom of her wardrobe. Shit got me thinkin' the only thing that separated a homie from the black bag was that I could walk freely, Cheryl hadn't yet put the stop on that. I turned to look at her. She was lying on her back and I could swear the little homie inside her was visible even under the thick quilt...or was I damn imaginin' things?

Still couldn't believe I was going to be a pops. It was the thing a homie dread most. The honey now want you to act differently, start all this romantic shit, so the little homie can see mama and papa in total harmony. But the whole shit sucks. Homie could do without this. Happiness was somethin' only Cheryl was enjoyin' now. She got want she wanted; my ass beside hers on a full-time basis like the damn Huxtables. Make my stomach sick.

How the hell did I get in this deep? Why did I bang her without protection? Should have checked she was on the programme, but not even that's one hundred per cent safe.

She swears it was a mistake. But females are a devious species, more slippery than meltin' ice. Damn, could've given the programme the red card without informin' a homie. Then, bang, the next you know she's in yer face with shit about being pregnant and wantin' you to reverse your entire lifestyle to help her and all along she's scammin' you.

She had a game plan and was executin' it like Joe Montana.

I placed my hand on her stomach and gently massaged it through the quilt. She was dead to the night, probably dreamin' about wedding bells, christening parties and a nice happy family with me sittin' at the head of the table. But I had a different take on events. Less a dream, more a damn nightmare of givin' up the op to play in the States again.

In fact last week I went to collect my mail from Mrs O'Farrell. Tiffany Goldberg, my rich piece from America had sent me a signed letter from the head coach of her father's team statin' that he will be at Wembley Arena for the play-off final. He was armed with a contract and an open return ticket. All I had to do was impress. Fire the bullets and I was airborne to New York, New York for pre-season scrimmage. Homie hid the letter in my sports bag knowin' the stink comin' out of it would always prevent Cheryl from invadin' my personal space.

The CBA was a chance a homie couldn't be negative about, but I knew Cheryl wouldn't see it through the same enthusiastic eyes. Damn, life had become so complicated. What nigga worth his shit would pass up an opportunity of a free flight to the States—all expenses paid—to try out for a semi-pro b-ball team? No fuckin' takers. And here I was sleep-walkin' at some unearthly hour playin' happy families.

I must have drifted back to sleep 'cause the next thing I knew was Cheryl had opened the curtains and the bright sun nearly blinded me even though my eyes were closed. She came over to the bed and planted a kiss on the side of my face.

"Good morning, Winston," she said with a contented smile.

"Whassup, Cheryl. Homie ain't seen yer mug since last nite," I laughed, but Cheryl didn't get the joke. "What's da time?"

"Time you were out of bed."

Shit meant it was around seven-thirty. Cheryl thought I was a lazy, no-good bum if I didn't get out of bed when she did, despite the fact that she had to go to work for nine and I had the whole day to get my shit in order. Ain't no damn early riser, but to save your ass from a tongue-whuppin' each daybreak, you had to play along with the music hopin' one day the shit would get stuck.

I could hear her in the shower, listenin' to the radio with its volume on max. Shaggy was rappin' 'Carolina' and Cheryl was using her full vocal range to stay with him. That was all a homie needed at dawn. A live-in bitch wakin' you like a cockerel on a farm.

I got up and went into the kitchen. Cheryl had already had breakfast, she left some spilt milk on the top of the work surface. *Gotcha*,

238

bitch—always frontin' on my ass about cleaning up after myself and puttin' things back where a homie finds them. *Now, Miss Shake 'n' Vac, how you goin' to explain this?* Shit, wanted to frame it and bring it to her. But wasn't worth the damn effort. She'll only make up some other bull excuse, so I clean it off the table.

The phone rang. I let it ring, since no one phones here for me. After six rings she still hadn't got to it so I decided to go answer it.

"Whassup? Da butler speakin'. Lady Cheryl Harris is too damn busy to answer da damn phone. So yer got me live and direct."

"Winston, that's not funny. It could've been an important caller," Janet scolded.

"At damn eight-fifteen in da mornin'? Stop trippin', sis."

"Winston look...ah it doesn't matter. Did I wake you?"

"Yer wish, homie's rustlin' up breakfast." Shit, I almost felt proud about being up at this hour.

"Good God, Cheryl must have you well-trained. Not even Mum could get you up before nine even when you had to be at school for ten-to."

"Go on, diss me like everyone else. Take yer aim, girl, hit me wit' yer best shot," I said jokingly.

"Anyway, it's good practice for you," she replied.

"Straight up, how yer work dat out, sis?"

"You know, when the baby arrives. I mean, you are going to do your share in terms of getting up at night to feed it aren't you?"

"Hate to be da one to drop dis on yer sis, but homiez have pecs. Bitches, sorry women, have titties. That's what little homiez like to suck on. Where da shit do I fit into dat equation?

"Winston, I don't think I like you very much," Janet replied, a little perturbed.

"Psyche, sis, jus' playin' wit' cha. Course I'll be doin' my shit," I said—but I was just thinkin' how a baby cryin' all night would mess up my system.

"I'm afraid I do know you, Winston, and your habits," Janet replied sarcastically.

"Whassat s'posed to mean?"

"Nothin'. Is Cheryl around?"

"Yeah, I'll call her. Check you later."

I banged on the bathroom door but there was no answer. I opened it and a gust of steam came whooshing out like a sauna. She wasn't in there. I went into the bedroom just as she was putting her bra on. Her breasts had swollen from firm tennis balls to the size of two of my Spalding b-balls over the last two months and the even bigger lump on her stomach was now no figment of my imagination.

"Janet's on the phone."

She quickly threw her nightgown around herself and went into the living room, while I went back to the kitchen to fix breakfast.

When I was half-way through my bran flakes, Cheryl came into the kitchen lookin' well fly in a lilac business suit and white silk blouse. She planted a kiss on my cheek.

Homie never had such a regular supply of lips, but it only camouflaged reality like a cortisone injection. When the shit wears off, the pain comes back worse than before. Damn, she weren't foolin' a homie educated at the University of Ghetto Life. Could spot that fake love shit a mile off. Man, her parents are still doggin' her big-time 'bout gettin' married and I know she gonna spring that shit on me soon. Woman just fattening me up like a Christmas turkey. But homie's got it sussed. Look after little homie when it's born, yes. Marriage, nope.

"I'll be late home this evening, I'm going for a drink with Janet," Cheryl said.

"Is that right? And who's looking after youngblood?"

"Your mum is lookin' after Uriah, so there."

"Oh yeah?"

"Yeah. Anyway, when was the last time you visited her?"

"Chez, quit buggin' me."

"No Winston, I won't. When was it?"

"Damn I dunno, a month ago or so."

"It's not natural for a son not to see his mum."

"Shit feels good to me."

Cheryl shook her head.

"Look, I'm inviting her round for dinner at the weekend and we're goin' to sort this thing out."

"You da man. Ain't my look out," I replied, through a mouthful of flakes.

"What's wrong with you, Winston?"

"Ain't nut'n wrong wit' me. Jus' not in Mama's top hundred, dat's all."

"Don't be silly, she's always asking Janet about you."

"Damn, if she wanted ta know 'bout me who better to ask than me? Ain't said shit."

"Look, I've got to go, we'll discuss this later."

She bent over and gave me another kiss on the cheek.

"Like I said, you da man," I replied. "Anyway, I'll be late too. I've—"

She cut me off in mid-sentence.

"—got training, I know," she said without breakin' her stride.

By ten in the morning, I didn't know what to do with myself. I got shot of the mobile after Cheryl had a beef with the number of times it rang, so now I was wireless. And I couldn't phone anyone under cover, 'cause Cheryl learnt from her pops and had itemised bills. Bitch would phone every number that didn't sync up with her filofax.

I decided to watch an NBA tape. Cheryl didn't have Sky, which was a bitch 'cause the NBA play-offs were in full swing. And she wouldn't buy a satellite 'cause she feared I'd sit down and watch sport all day.

She had to understand that a man without his sport is a damn unhappy man, and that's how I was feelin' right now. I went into the bedroom and looked in one of the many black bags in the wardrobe and pulled out a tape. It was Orlando Magic versus New York Knicks. Like all the other games, I must have seen it about four times. If I remembered correctly it was the game when new blood Shaquille O'Neal dunked over vet Patrick Ewing 'nuff times.

I went back into the livin' room, placed the tape on top of the white VCR—damn white VCR, I'd never seen one before, but shit, Cheryl always tried to be original—then I went for a shower.

Dried off and got dressed in a pair of black Nike sweats, red Chicago Bulls tee-shirt, and my Atlanta Braves cap. Damn, everything was so straight forward could do it with no eyes. Got some refreshments from the cooler and settled down on the settee to watch the game.

Ten minutes into the action the front buzzer rang. Strange shit, it rang exactly as the ref had called a bullshit foul on Charles Oakley. Shit, whoever's outside must be into serious ball if they could see that infringement from there, I joked to myself. The bell rang again and again. I looked down at my watch. It was almost eleven. I ignored it 'cause it couldn't be for me; Cheryl made it clear that no homiez from the ghetto were to call, whether she was in or out.

The bell continued to ring. I had to get down on my hands and knees to press the pause button—because the batteries in Cheryl's remote was as dead as the person that disturbed me was going to be when I answered that door.

I got up and looked through the net curtains into the street. I could

241

see a phat, brand kickin' new seven series BMW. Homie whistled to myself before turnin' my head slowly to the right to see who was at the door.

Shit. Whadda hell she doin' here? It was Helen. I thought I got shut of that bitch when I left Mrs O'Farrell.

Damn, I slowly took a step back to avoid her seeing images inside. My damn wheels parked directly outside gave the shit away. She rang the bell again and again and each time for longer. Bitch was pushin' the right button to get a slappin'. My shit was fever pitch when her finger got stuck for a good three minutes on the bell. Shit felt like some kind of torture. Damn had enough. Had to confront the bitch.

I walked into the passage way and opened the door.

"Whadda yer want?" I shouted, giving her the evil eye.

"What a way to greet an old flame," she said, smiling. "Were you on the toilet? I was ringing *forever*."

"Shit, woman, wanna stop playin wit Five-O sirens!" I shouted again. "How da hell did yer get this location?"

"Winston, when you have money you can get anything you want...and I mean anything," she replied with a fake smile.

"How did yer get the address?" I asked her again.

"Are we going to stand out here for the rest of the morning?"

"Hey, look, yer not comin' in here," I said, holding my hand up like I was stopping traffic. "No fuckin' danger."

"Then I'll just have to wait here until your girlfriend comes back," she said, resting against the metal rail that divided Cheryl's path from the neighbours'. Shit, bitch was cruisin' for a bruisin'. Slammed the door nearly off it's hinges, went inside, pressed play on the video recorder, then got comfortable again.

After five minutes I got up and looked through the curtains. The bitch was still there. *Damn!* Got up at ten to fifteen-minute intervals for a whole hour and each time she was still there. I got fed up. I switched off both the TV and video and opened the door.

"Git yer ass in here," I demanded.

"Thank you, Winston," she replied as she breezed past.

Got a damn sinus full of some strong perfume. I knew the shit was very expensive, 'cause Helen didn't buy anything that wasn't. Before I closed the door homie played P.I. and looked around outside just to check no one saw her enter.

She was already seated when I came into the living room.

"See yer gotta new toy," I said, feeling totally pissed off.

"Oh, the car. Daddy bought it for my twenty-fifth."

Damn, you dollars-no-object pile of white trash. Hell, decided to get to the bottom line.

"Dis shit ain't correct. Yer already on overtime. So whadda yer want?"

"Stop tryin' to kid me, Winston. Your little girlfriend is not back until six."

"Yer been spyin' on me, bitch?"

I went over and grabbed her by the arm.

"Take your hands off me and don't you ever call me a bitch," she replied. "I haven't been watching you. Your pathetic mate Hector told me where you lived for twenty quid, and for another twenty he told me where your girlfriend worked, and what time she finished. I probably could've got your ex-directory phone number for another twenty. Life's cheap, Winston when you have a rich daddy. Suppose your buddy Hector can buy himself a new coat now. The one he had on stunk."

The bastard sellout. He couldn't bring his narrow ass within a mile of this place when Cheryl was here, 'cause she would've poured boiling oil over his butt. But the punk ass scrawny runt had really messed up things for me big time.

I chilled a bit.

"Look I'm sorry for bustin' on yer," I said, as Helen sat down in Cheryl's favourite chair.

"And so you should be."

"Look, Helen, Cheryl is my...my regular shit, she's havin' my homie. Yer hearin' me?" I said hesitantly.

"Yes, I know that."

"Damn. How much did yer pay Hector for da info?"

"That was a freebie," she replied looking at me seriously. "Anyway, because she's having your baby does that mean she owns you?"

"Nope," I replied—needing to prove that I was still my own man.

"Well then," she replied.

"Well then, what?"

She got up then came over and kissed me on the lips.

"If she doesn't own you then it doesn't matter what we get up to, does it?" she said, gazing into a homie's eyes.

"Whassup wit yer regular live-in dude?"

"You mean my husband? We split after a couple of weeks," she said flippantly.

"Frustrated. Came too quickly. Thought he'd get over it with practice but he spilled out before he even got close to me. Had to get rid of him. Sad, really, he was a nice guy."

Damn didn't want a diagnosis of her shit. I knew I had to get her ass outta here. I took a step back to put some space between us.

"Look, yer come ta da wrong place if yer lookin' for a stud on Duracell."

"Now why would I need a stud, Winston?"

"Hell, woman, yer know y'ain't gettin' da correct treatment."

"And can you help me with that, Doctor McKenzie?"

She was lookin' at me with this come-and-rip-my-clothes-off stare. She took a step forward to close the gap I'd just created between us. My resistance was on the slide. I hadn't had another bitch outside Cheryl for the past two months, so this free booty was temptin' the shit outta me. But I couldn't look Cheryl in the eye if I took it, so I blew Helen's shit out.

She looked shocked.

I turned away. Couldn't let her see that my homeboy was in the let's-get-busy position. Bitch would only go crazy and jump on him.

"Okay, Winston, I see the young lady has got you under her thumb, so I'll go." As she walked towards the door she turned and said:

"Can I use your lavatory?"

I couldn't believe she was giving in without a fight. Damn knew her seduction would've succeeded if she had stood a little firmer. Musta found all this domesticated shit as big a turn-off as I did.

"Turn right and it's the door facing you," I said, as my bone came off red alert.

I went and sat down in Cheryl's chair. Must have been there for about ten minutes before I started to wonder where the hell Helen had got to. Maybe she was having a hard time gettin' the crap to come out of her ass—if it's anythin' like the bullshit she raps then I'll be sittin' here twenty-four, seven.

But when the ten ticks became twenty, then twenty-five and I still hadn't heard the toilet chain, damn had to go and investigate. I knocked on the bathroom door. No answer. Called her name. No answer. Opened the door, and unless she was the first hoochie whose shit didn't stink, I realised she hadn't as much as farted in there.

"Goddamn bitch!" I shouted, and sprinted into the bedroom.

Helen's clothes were strewn across Cheryl's shagpile; her shoes, skirt, blouse and bra strategically placed to lead to the bed. Her panties were lying on Cheryl's pink satin quilt. And she was spread naked across the bed, legs wide open, running one hand through her hair, giving it that fly, sexy look, and stroking her titties with the other.

My shit got thicker and thicker, 'til it started busting through my sweats.

Then her fingers started heading south.

"I thought you'd never come," she said pouting and giving me a come-and-get-it look.

Damn. This shit was outta order. I walked over to the bed, summoned up the willpower of a damn weight-lifter goin' for a personal best and ordered her out of the bed. She could tell it was only a sissy request and just dragged me by my arms down on top of her. That was all it took. For the next forty minutes we got busy.

Shit was good, too.

Afterwards, as I lay exhausted, Helen got up and dressed. Before she left she gave me a smoocher and told me she'd see me next week. Damn couldn't—or more to the point didn't want to—turn down the offer.

I got up slowly, my black ass still movin' to the rhythm of the session, and went for a shower before coming back into the bedroom to change the sheets. Shit, for the first time during the whole episode Cheryl flashed on the membrane. Didn't want to dwell too long on the shit. If she ever found out I'd be history with her. And my sis.

I hoovered the crib. Never used the shit before, and it took me half hour just to switch it on. Homie also sprayed the whole flat to get rid of any lingering smells.

Got dressed and, although it was only two o'clock I packed my b-ball gear together to take with me cause no way was I goin' to be back till nightfall.

Decided to pay lowlife Hector a visit. On the way Dr Dre was keepin' me company, my bones vibrating on his every word. Formed a duet as I turned around Smallbrook Circus on the red tarmac road that marked the outer boundaries of central downtown. Almost caused a pile-up as I exited, 'cause a fly black sista caught my eye. Boomin' in every area. Took my hand off the wheel to let her know how she was makin' me react, and wheels turned in all directions. Nearly ran up the ass of another homie's Saab. Brakes were well-tight and saved my black ass. Can't afford to mess with my no claims shit. Got no bitches to pay for it now.

Hector lived on the seventh floor of a tower block just outside central downtown. When I arrived homie pressed the intercom buzzer four times. No reply. I knew he would be home because his phoney drugs trade is a night-time career and, like any man that works nights, the Inspector needed to recharge during the day.

Pressed it again. Shit, the security must be to stop homiez gettin' out. Can't think for one tick why they wanna prevent people gettin' into this seventeen-floor tower of misery. Pressed Hector's digits again.

"Damn muny, git yer ass up," I shouted.

Still silence. As I headed back to my wheels, a young sista pushin' a pram opened the door to leave. Homie rushed to hold it open like a respectable brotha and slipped in behind her. Lift stank of piss. Damn, how could Hector bear this twenty-four, seven?

I banged hard on his front door with my fist three or four times before I heard Hector taking the safety chain off the door. Damn, who the hell was goin' to rob him?

"Blo-o-o-odclaat, wha'ppen, star?" he said, wiping the sleep from the corner of his eyes. He stood there in a pair of red and white striped pyjamas, and, like automatic shit, the Columbo mac.

"Hey, yuh nah fe knock so hard? Fe all I know yuh could be Babylon and yuh end up gettin' shot or somet'ing."

"Stop frontin' on me, Hector, man. Y'know shit ain't goin' down' y'knowha'msayin'?" I replied, walking through his dimly-lit, undecorated passageway into the living room.

"How y'mean nut'n nah go down. Wha y'know anyway? Y' jus' a civilian," he said, following me. "Let me tell yuh, yesterday de same t'ing 'appen over Wolver'ampton to a spar of mine y'know, 'im deal big-time like me. De Babylon kick off 'im door and try arrest 'im. He jus' tek out 'im Uzi and bullaugh shot three of de Babylon dead."

"What Chicago bullshit yer tellin' me, man? I ain't heard shit on TV, radio or damn CNN, y'knowha'msayin'?"

"Cha man, de police nah tell de public when dem get shot up. Me know 'cause, as y'know, me 'ave inside information," he said, winking. "So wha' y' wan, employ me as yuh supplier again?"

"Homie, yer know I don't do da shit again."

"So wha' de rahtid y' come get me outta me bed so fuckin' early fa? Y'know say me work de nite shiff."

"How come yer freelancin' wit' a homie's new ID?"

"Wha' yuh a talk 'bout, Yankee bwoy?"

"Helen, yer punk, dat's what I'm on about."

246

"How y'mean? Yuh should be shakin' my bloodclaat hand fe doin' it. Dat Cheryl 'ave yuh backside 'round deh so like a bwoy. Yuh cyan' 'ave no friend 'round, yuh cyan' smoke, yuh cyan' watch basketball. I was doin' yuh a favour by lettin' you get a bite of de white meat while she was out earnin' de crust."

"Damn whadda shit y'know 'bout what a homie wanted or git, muthafucka?"

"Me know you cyan' resist a piece of thigh or breast," he replied, shrieking with laughter and exposin' his custard-coloured teeth and brown gum.

"Man, yer made a bank outta it in da bargain?"

"Macca, yuh haffe believe me, is a bizness t'ing, pure an' simple."

Hector looked at me direct and placed his hands on my shoulders. Homie's breath smelt like a dog pound.

"She wanted somet'ing and I could supply it. Y'know de first t'ing dem teach you at dem top bizness school inna London is when demand is greater dan supply den yuh can charge 'nuff shekels. Ask Maggie Thatcha if me right. She bloodclaat tell yuh."

Hector's free market business shit didn't extend to his crib. Damn livin' room was in a state worst than mine on a bad day at Mrs O' Farrell's. It contained just a TV and an old sofa which looked like bugs had eaten the best part of it. Damn windows were painted black with little slits to let in daylight. Fool thought it was another strategic ploy to stop undercover cops seeing him make deals. Damn, in my hood shit uses blinds. but this was Hector coming full steam with original shit.

Man was always rappin' about some hundred thousand pound pad he has out in the phat 'burbs of Solihull, but kept the address undercover in case a homie turned informer on him. Mutha couldn't have spent any time there, cause you could always find his drugged-up ass here twenty-four, seven. Man was trippin' big time. Livin' in a dream world where only his skinny little butt made any sense.

"Hey, me a read 'bout dat yout' conference dem a have at de X Centre Monday," Hector said, pulling some Rizla paper out of the breast pocket of his pyjama top.

"Yeah, da punk ass behind it hangs wit da Warriors."

"Dat true?" he said, licking the tips of the paper. " 'Cause me hear seh some gang bwoy a come over from Stateside."

"Schitt's da word, muny," I rapped.

"Well if y'know de organiser den yuh can get me a lickle squeeze, innit?"

He pulled a small plastic bag of weed out of the same pocket and carefully placed some in a neat line on one side of the Rizla.

Shit closed my eyes in despair. Homie couldn't believe the bum even slept with his gear.

"Why you wanna hook up with them?"

"Well, dem must know de runnins over there. Maybe we can set up some kinda transatlantic t'ing, 'cause dem Colombian bwoy a 'ave t'ings dem own rahtid way fe too long. So if dem gangstas can join wid a yardie like me we can mek big corn," he said, lighting the spliff. "Wha' y't'ink, yuh feel say y'can fix me up wid dem?"

Homie couldn't do nothin' else but laugh. Hector drew back deeply and then let out a big puff of smoke. Damn distinctive smell lit up my nose buds and made the back of my throat cry out for some. Hadn't smoked in almost two months, but shit was bustin' for a draw this second. Hector offered it up, his face camouflaged by the bluish smoke.

"Nope, homie," I replied, tryin' to remain true to my word to Cheryl.

"Tek de damn t'ing, man. Cheryl nah 'ere to t'row dat BSC raas 'pon yuh."

"BSC?" Damn homie had flipped.

"Y'know, dat mad cow disease or wha'ever dem call it."

I laughed. I had broken one vow already today so damn, another wouldn't matter shit. After all, I was no nun—not even a confirmed, baptised born again whatever homie. A brotha plain and simple.

Shit didn't have to live like no saint.

Homie took the spliff and drew it right back before slowly exhaling. It was so relaxing that Hector had to snatch it out of my hand before I got married to the shit.

"So wha' yuh a say? Yuh can fix me up wid de yankee bwoy den?"

"Hector, homiez have chilled, man. Tryin' ta do da right thing, helpin' da brothas out and shit. Y'knowwha'msayin'?"

"Let me tell yuh sump'n, once a drug dealer, always a bumbaclaat dealer. If I lick dem wid de lyrics dem a go wan' a cut like any other man. Don't let dem fool you, dem no diff'rent."

Hector and I rapped on for another two hours about him muscling in on the American drug cartel, and seein' what I could set up for him when I flew to the States on Monday. Homie also mentioned that Five-O had clamped Zorro for butcherin' two of his closest rivals in a Sodom gang war.

According to Hector, word on the street was that Five-O are keeping Zorro under lock and key for his own protection, since every wannabee G in Balsall Heath had put a price on his head. Whether or not Hector was playin' me damn didn't know, but shit, I hoped he was straight up this time.

Memories of what Zorro had done hung around a homie's neck like a thousand pound gold chain. Fed up with not goin' where a homie wanted in case this nutter appeared and started bustin' on my ass. Damn lock the mutha up and throw the keys in the deepest river you can find. Mutha's no good.

"We show we did de best team in de league by winnin' de championship. Now we haffe prove dat we good enuff to be promoted," Coach rapped to loud applause and words of 'yeah' at the end of a busy last session.

"Me glad fe say dat Marcus will be playin' wid us on Sunday, and at full strength no one can stop us," Coach continued.

Hall came in like a house party, crazy with cheers, high fives and back slaps. The old time badminton players comin' on court with their well-seamed whites must have thought they'd bum rushed a niggers crack den.

There was no let up in the locker room. Shit was well outta order. Marcus filled a bucket with ice cold water from the taps in the piss hole area and emptied it over the top of the showers, freezin' the dicks off Adam and Levi who were standin' together rappin'. Niggaz came out dancin' like body poppers.

Muthafuckin' Calvin was handin' out invites to his conference party. Shit didn't even let me smell one. Musta felt like the big man in the hood. Damn lanky ass. Not even fit to lace my jock strap, but still always tries to diss me. Tellin' everyone to turn up for some discussion in the afternoon. Nigga wasn't gonna see my ass even if he did hand me an invite. 'Cause shit, I'll be thirty-thousand feet over the Atlantic—destination, New York City.

We all touched fists in the centre of the locker room before anyone was allowed to leave. Shit was probably the only time in the entire season all the homiez left the university together. Calvin also mentioned there would be a surprise party for Coach in a fortnight, but homie didn't pay it any attention. Damn wasn't gonna be here.

"Make sure you're on time for the bus, brotha," Calvin shouted to me as I unlocked my wheels parked outside the gym hall.

Damn first thing the punk had said to me all night and it was a diss.

"Why da fuck yer keep buggin' me, sucka?"

Man put on that chilled kind of confident look.

"Brotha man, the team's only as strong as its weakest link."

I slammed my car door.

"So whatcha tryin' to say, punk? Dat I'm some kinda liability?"

"Brotha, don't take it to heart—"

"Don't brotha me shit. Homie's carried dis no good team on my back dis season, so fuck you!"

We were now facin' each other on opposite sides of his clapped-out BMW.

"All I'm sayin' is that if we are to win, we must show some unity. Being on time shows that commitment."

"Damn you, asshole."

Marcus came and put his heavy hand on my shoulder.

"Easy, man, easy."

"Brotha's losin' it just when we need a cool head," Calvin said, getting into his car.

"Yer slob ass punk. Someone gonna put some work in on yer ass," I shouted as I bent down to look at him through his side window. Mutha just waved his hand cool as Luke, turned the ignition and calmly rolled away.

Homie felt like puttin' a cap in his ass. Marcus put his hand around my shoulder.

"Why's he always bustin' on me, man?" I asked, lookin' for a not guilty verdict from Marcus.

"Y'know 'ow Elastic stay already. De man jus' like fe see t'ings 'appen de right way."

"Damn, if da muthafucka fronts on dis homie Sunday, his ass is history."

"Well y' nah see too much of 'im 'cause im a drive down 'pon 'im own. Somet'ing 'bout gettin' back early to start 'im conference. Anyway, y' can give me a liff?" Marcus asked, throwin' his bag over his huge shoulders.

"Homie, man gotta step," I replied, just wantin' to return to my crib, get to the bottom line with Cheryl over about me jettin' to the States and rest my blunt-filled head.

"Look, it's jus' to Handsworth, me gi' yuh petrol money," Marcus replied as I got into my wheels and wound down the window. Homie wrote himself his own invitation. Took two pound coins outta his red Converse sweats, dropped them through the car window into my hand and walked around to the passenger side. As he got in, the suspension took a heavy dive. Mutha was so big I hardly had room to operate the stick.

I started the car and headed for Handsworth.

"Whassup G, how's da case goin'?" I asked.

"De jury dem nah come wid a verdict 'til Tuesday. Dat's why me free fe play Sunday."

"So how's it lookin' for yer, homie?"

Marcus let out a huge sigh that almost misted up the whole of my windscreen.

"Well me lawyer say is touch and go, y'know? Dem gi' me some problems inna de dock today."

"Yer hang strong, man?"

"Me nah know. Dem bring up all dis history of me being violent. Some of dem me cyan' even remember. Y'know, dem try fe paint me as some kinda raggamuffin. When de real bad bwoy dem a still walk street. Anyway dem try test me to see if me'll get angry in fronta de jury, but dem nah con me. Me stay as cool as a cucumber, to rahtid," he laughed.

"Gimme five, homie."

We slapped palms.

"Talkin' 'bout bad bwoy, me hear say dem lock up Zorro," Marcus said.

"Word has it. Is the source legit?" I said eagerly.

"Yeah, man. Me hear 'nuff gunman after 'im too. Y' see it don't mek no sense playin' bad 'cause there's always someone worse dan you."

Shit sounded like Ice-T to my ears. Hector for once in his sorry life had bona fide reports.

Marcus directed me around the roads of Handsworth to his babe's crib.

"So how t'ings a go wid you and yuh gyal? Me hear say you a 'ave yout' on de way?"

"Yeah, man, shit's still messin' wit' my membrane."

"Is wha'ppen, y' never plan fe it?"

"Shit was da last thing on my agenda."

"But yuh can't go on de way y' go on wid woman and not expec' it fe 'appen. Miracle y' nah 'ave more."

"Homie thought she was down wit' da programme."

Marcus kissed his teeth as if to say *and you believe that, stupid fool.*

"But yuh a stick wid 'er though?"

"Dunno."

251

"Wha' you mean, y' dunno?"

Damn spilled my guts to Marcus about the dilemma I faced—going to America or staying with Cheryl at home.

Marcus sat back in the white leather seat.

"Well, dat's a difficult one. Yuh haffe talk to she. Show 'er seh dis is important to you, but don't mek her feel dat you leavin' 'er holdin' de yout'," he said, before directing me to pull up.

"Bitch already said she'll eject my black ass if I even think about da States."

"All woman would say dat," he replied, opening the car door. "Dem wanna feel dem a control you. Jus' let she know how yuh feel and t'ings a go work out, believe me."

Marcus jumped out of the car and I did a U-turn and drove back to Moseley. When I arrived at the shack I felt like just gettin' under the sheets, but I knew I had to confront Cheryl with the word that I'm off back to the States. Shit, I knew she would start actin' crazy; start trippin' and doggin' me about leavin' her five months pregnant. Damn, who's to say me and her goin' to be together for eternity? Shit could end Monday and my op in the States would've been blown out 'cause of some fake-ass love thang. Man can't take that chance. I'm outta here.

As I entered the front door I sensed shit wasn't normal. Homie could hear sounds from the bedroom like something was ripping. I rushed down the hall. Bitch had gone mad. Mutha was slashin' her new bed into threads with a kitchen knife. She looked up at my shocked face and started actin' crazy.

"You...bastard!"

She came running at me with the blade. I dropped my bag, believin' she was out to bust me a good one this time. She took a swing and I put up my hand to defend my head. The knife sliced through my Nike tracksuit like a chainsaw and pierced my right forearm.

Blood everywhere.

Bitch pulled her arm back to have another dig. Shit, this time I caught her by her wrist. Man, we were strugglin' with each other, her eyes filled with a hate homie had seen only once before—the night after Zorro nearly sent me to the graveyard. Now she was attemptin' the same shit.

I managed to get the knife out of her hand by twisting her wrist 'til it fell. Bitch was still outta control, she kicked me on the shin and scratched my face. After her fingernails dug into my flesh I grabbed her arm and pushed her onto the carved up bed.

Damn, had to pin her hands down and use my feet to trap her legs to stop her from playin' ball with a homie's nuts. Didn't put my full body weight on her stomach, but applied enough pressure to stop her from movin'.

"Get off me, you bastard, get off me!"

"Baby, baby, chill down man?" I pleaded, knowin' the reason for this crazy shit.

"Get out of my house. Get out of my house or I'm going to scream this fuckin' place down. Fuckin' get out."

True to her word, she started screaming at the top of her voice.

"Cheryl, cool dat shit out. Cheryl. Chez, chill out!" I shouted but it was no use. Then I slapped her across her face with enough force to try and snap her back to order not to bruise her. She continued to struggle. Shit had to hit her again.

She managed to roll me off her but she didn't have the strength to get up.

"Winston, get out of my fuckin' house now. I said now!"

All of a sudden shit became her property and I was just the damn lodger. She went to the bedroom door, picked up my bag and threw it at me. I saw her eye the knife which was still lying on the floor but I was too quick, damn managed to dive on it before she got her mad ass there first. While I was face down on the floor, bitch began to kick me like I was a damn football and screwed the pointed heel of her shoes into the back of my left hand. Pain made me scream like a bitch. Then the bitch went and fell face down on the bed, cryin'...

"Cheryl," I called as I got up off the floor.

"Just get out."

Homie knew there was nothing left. Shit had to walk. Went into the dining room. Every piece of clothin' I owned was cut to threads and thrown over the floor. Bitch had taken every item from the bedroom and sliced them better than a paper shredder. My Starter jackets, sweats, even the leather on my kicks was sliced beyond repair. Bitch had done a good number on me. I searched through the b-ball tapes. Only a few remained intact. Cheryl even put the blade through my Spalding basketball. Homie didn't know whether to feel anger or pain.

I just picked up my sports bag and left the crib as it was.

Got into my wheels. Damn had nowhere to go except to Janet. Shit, if I went to Mama she'd only start that clever shit about I told you so. Damn well knew Janet would also start trippin' but in a choice between being dissed by Mama or sis, Janet was the lesser of two evils.

Man, the pain was seizing up my body. Shit from my wounds was gettin' everywhere, on my leather seats, dashboard, even on my system as I leaned forward to let Snoop Doggy kick off some tracks.

My left hand had swelled to three times its normal size. Muthafucka couldn't even grip the steerin' wheel without cryin' out in agony. I took a glance in my mirror, man looked like some African tribal chief. Three strips were torn outta my face like a homie was sponsored by Adidas. How did the bitch find out? Homie cleaned the damn place like a Kirby. Why did she have to roll on my ass thirty-six hours before the damn game of my career. I pulled into the car park at the rear of Janet's project. Luckily the place was deserted. I struggled outta the motor and secured it before headin' for the steps.

It was twelve midnight when I arrived, but her light was still on. Sis opened the door, and almost dropped dead when she saw me.

"Oh, my God! Winston what happened? It's that Zorro, isn't it?"

"Hell no. Cheryl flipped," I said as she led me inside.

"Cheryl? Cheryl did this to you?"

"Word, sis."

"I don't understand. Why?"

"Shit dunno, Janet. *Damn!* Just went crazy."

We went into the bathroom and Janet helped me off with my clothes. She ran some warm water in the basin then began to tend the wound on my forearm with cotton wool laced with Dettol.

Stung like the livin' shit.

Wasn't that deep, but no Elastoplast was goin' to heal it. Janet dressed it with bandages and some other shit but damn couldn't lift my right arm above my navel.

The phone rang.

"Oh, that's probably Mum. She said she was going to phone," Janet said as she went to answer it with blood still drippin' from her hands.

"Shit, don't let on to Mama," I shouted.

I looked in the mirror. Cheryl had put some real work in on my mug. I began to dab it with cotton wool and minute amounts of Dettol, didn't want to burn no more holes in my face. After about twenty minutes Janet came back into the bathroom.

"If you weren't my brother I'd finish you off," she said, looking at me with a mixture of anger and disgust.

"How could you, Winston?"

Damn! Gathered it was Cheryl and not Mama on the wire, fillin' her head with bullshit. I know she gonna believe every last word...she's a woman, ain't she? Blood don't come into the equation when bitches start doggin' a homie.

"Whassup, sis?" I asked, trying to buy some ticks to make up an explanation.

"Winston, don't take me for a fool. My God! I mean, in her bed. I just don't believe it."

Damn, the bitch had given her the full, unedited shit. There was no way out. I had to come correct. I turned to face her, the pain was killin' a homie.

"I dunno what to say, man, shit jus' happened," I said, as if askin' for special dispensation from Janet.

"How the hell does something like that just happen?"

"Janet, da bitch jus' turned up, y'knowha'msayin'?"

"Use that word one more time and I'm gonna throw you out, brother or not."

"Okay, sorry, sis."

"So I suppose you're going to tell me she just let herself in, took her clothes off and fucked herself in Cheryl's bed, without you knowing?"

Damn, couldn't she see that I had lost enough blood. Shit! She wanted to bite deep, too, like damn Dracula. Wanted her full pint of the red stuff, and she wasn't lettin' up 'til she got it.

"Janet, please—"

"Don't say another word. You're a disgrace."

She left the bathroom and went into her bedroom. I gave her five minutes and came and knocked the door. She didn't answer, so I took the liberty and slowly walked in. She was laying face down across the bed, the only furniture in the room.

"How did she find out, Janet?" I asked, hopin' it wouldn't set her off again.

"You thought you were so clever didn't you, changing the sheets? A lazy sod like you? That's bound to make her go searching. But you forgot the pillow cases, Winston, you forgot to change the pillow cases..."

She eased up until she was sitting upright.

"Cheryl doesn't wear Coco Chanel—can't afford it—so it had to be another woman. Then she found some long brunette hairs on the pillow cases. Case closed. You had a white woman in her bed, when she's out working? She's carrying your *child!* Where are your morals, Winston?"

She stared at me so hard, I wanted to disappear. Then she shook her head and turned her back to me.

"S'pose Mama would say I'm just like Pops..."

I didn't even know why I mentioned him.

"What's he got to do with anything?"

"Dunno—don't yer ever wonder where he is or why he left?"

"No, never. He couldn't face up to his responsibilities either."

"Mama drove him away. Uncle Sylvester told me when I was about twelve or thirteen."

"Ha!"

Janet gave that bullshit laugh.

"And you'd believe what Uncle Sylvester said. So that's why you've been givin Mum the cold shoulder?"

"I'm jus' sayin', y'knowha'msayin'?"

She swung round to face me.

"I bet he didn't tell you he tried to hit on his brother's wife when he was asleep upstairs, or that when Mum refused, he started spreadin' all this crap about her? No, I don't suppose he told you that. Did he Winston?"

Shit couldn't believe it!

Uncle Sylvester tryin' to get some from Mama. Mutha hadn't shown up at our crib since. Ought to put a cap in his old ass.

"Winston, Mum brought you into this world. Worked three jobs a day to make ends meet when Dad ran out on her. It was hard bringing us up alone, but she did a good job. You know nothing about the crap she went through. Yes, she is a tough woman. Yes, she does lay down the law, but damn you, Winston, she did her best for us and the least you can do is show her some goddamn appreciation and stop thinkin' about yourself all the time. "Furthermore, what happened today had nothing to do with Dad, Mum or Uncle Sylvester. You had a choice to make and you made yours. Be a man and at least take responsibility for that. Now just get out of my sight. You make me sick."

Damn couldn't say a word. Just turned and walked out of the room. Emotional pain was worse than the physical shit now. I went downstairs to the dining room. I wanted to phone Cheryl but I knew it wasn't the time. I took the letter from America out of my bag and looked at it. Then I sat on the settee and closed my eyes.

Damn if there was one day I wanted to arrive in a hurry, it was the day of the final. But by the time I got to Handsworth the bus had already gone. Homie was an hour late but they could've chilled their asses and waited. Dissed me like I was some circus ball act instead of their blue chip performer.

To teach them not to mess with me I should bust on their asses. Just not show and where would the muthas get without me? But damn, that was no option, coach from States was runnin' the rule over me. Seeing if my game was fresh enough to earn those free air miles.

Took me three hours to steer through the freeway traffic to Wembley—then a punk ass nigga had me wait another twenty-five minutes while he find out if I was a legit member of the roster. Damn showed him my gear and kicks, but the nigga wanted to play the big man in the house. This was his damn door and shit wasn't goin' through it without him musclin' his Dr J seventies 'fro in on the action. Gave the fool ten dead presidents and the mutha soon forgot about his prison officer duties.

Shit I was late big time—game had already started. The States coach must have thought my ass had been cut. I hurried into the locker room, my left bicep still stiff with pain and my left hand still swollen. Damn hospital said it was fractured. Wanted to put it it in plaster for weeks. Said no damn way, man, I'm not gonna miss this op to go back to the States. Nurse just put a couple of threads in my arm and bandaged my hand. Hector got me some cortisone from somewhere, damn wasn't goin' to ask, just injected the shit. Took the pain away but now it was wearin' thin. Homie couldn't raise my right hand above my head and my left hand was wack. Damn couldn't feel the shit as I tried to flex it.

Coach must have known I was goin' to put in an appearance, 'cause he left my gear out on the bench. Got changed as quick as I could and walked out of the locker room, my dome bustin' with thoughts of my performance. The break I've been waitin' for and my body was all fucked up.

By the time I had pulled my achin' butt up through the tunnel leading to the court, play had already begun. Damn benches were on the other side of the court, had to jog around it. Shit, all eyes like they were on me. Sixteen thousand people. Full house bustin' ear drums suddenly went stone dead as I took my place on the end of the bench next to Benji.

"What time yow call this, loike?" Benji asked.

Why some mutha always gotta ask questions like that at a time like this?

"Blimey, what's wrong with yer face, loike?"

Shit, I had forgotten that my face was marked more times than a sports hall floor. Damn Cheryl. Damn bitch.

"Damn got in a li'l scrimmage. No big thing, Benji."

"Yer wanna behave yerself, mate."

Looked down the bench, all eyes were on the game except for Coach. Damn mutha gave me a stare that paralysed my shit like a rattlesnake in my boxers. Damn knew this was the last time he'd allow my ass to suit up for the Warriors, but shit didn't bug me. Damn, all I needed was a chance to get in and handle the rock.

The half-time buzzer sounded. We were losin' badly, 48-30. Damn got off the bench for the first time since I sat down and followed the rest of the team into the tunnel. Everyone was havin' a go at everyone else—sounded like a damn fish market. Homie walked into the locker room and straight into Calvin's bullshit.

"Look, brotha man, I don't think you have any right being here."

"Damn yer mutha, homie got as much right as you."

"Brotha, you messed up once too often."

"Shit man, I apologise for being late, homiez." Damn went around everyone individually and slapped their hands, sayin' sorry to each one. Come to Calvin, he stared me out.

"Brotha, that's not good enough."

Then bang! Marcus punched his hand through the wooden bench.

"Whether de bloodclaat man come or not, we a play like a bunch of pussies out deh tonight, and me nah lose dis game. No way. So unnu bettah leave dis stupidness 'til after de game and work 'pon how we a go get back inna dis t'ing."

There was all-round applause for Marcus. Even Coach got up off his butt, took off his flat cap and rubbed his shining bald dome.

"Whassup, Coach, when I'm gonna git some burn?" I said as we came outta the locker rooms and head back for the court.

He stopped dead in his tracks, waited for me to catch up with him, then held me by my right arm. Damn nearly screamed as he put pressure on it.

"Me don't wanna hear no excuse, yuh gon too far dis time."

"Look, Coach, jus' git me in da ball game."

"Yuh wha', yuh mad? Man, yuh come four hours late an' yuh wan' play? Look, don't mek me swear, y'hear. Look 'ow yuh mash

258

up, an' yuh wan' me play yuh."

"Man, dis is my big opportunity. There's a scout from da States out there watchin' my ass."

"Well, y' should've t'ink 'bout dat before yuh get up late dis mornin'."

Shit, when we got back on court the others were warmin' up again. I tried to bounce the pill but my left hand was causin' too much stress and I couldn't set up to shoot 'cause my right hand just wouldn't go up.

Third quarter was in full swing but the only time my butt left the bench was when Coach called a time-out. This shit was eatin' away at my dome. Damn, the one time I had to be on the blacktop and this punk Coach was clampin' my ass like a bite from a bulldog.

Scout must think I'm a damn joker. Come three thousand miles to check my shit out and all homie's averagin' is splinters in my butt. The only time shit was free from membrane is when the silly ass MC shouted Marcus Codrington and that was regular. Marcus was dopin' out. Doin' some coast-to-coast, DIY shit. Man had heart, givin' it some. Brotha grabbed a re above Cheshire's six-foot-eight American, went the length of the court then BAM! Man went over two stupid-ass white dudes to slam it. Damn fools must have known with a man that size that he was goin' to step into their house no matter what shit they had behind the door. Marcus then gave the dudes a standin' eight count as they looked up at him, feet first from the depth of the hardwood. Damn got the crowd goin'. Man was imposin' on my shit. Should be out there takin' these dudes to school. But as I flexed my left hand the shit was still stiff as wood. Kept workin' it, tryin' to warm it up in case the fool decided to throw me in the game, and he better do that soon cause my shit's wearin' thin.

Minute to go in the third and Cheshire coach called a time-out as Andre registered another three after Calvin got him open. Damn didn't even bother to get off my butt to go to the huddle. If homiez didn't need me, then shit didn't need them. Felt like takin' a hike to the locker room, puttin' on my civilians and headin' back to my hood. When the time-out was over, walked straight up to Coach.

"When yer puttin' my ass in?" I demanded.

"Macca, jus' siddung y'hear, sa," he said like he tryin' to get me outta his face quickly to view the game.

"Man, yer can't diss me like dis."

Levi came between us and eased me back to my seat on the bench. Could see Calvin givin' me the stare from the court. Damn showed him the one finger and told him to play the game.

Into the last five ticks of the game and homie got the feelin' I wasn't goin' to get any burn. Coach wanted to school me in a vicious way. Man even used third-string guard Benji when he wanted to give Andre or Adam a rest. Damn, every time he did that the Cheshire score rocketed. But Marcus' forty points kept us in the game. Adam went up for a fade away jumper but came down hard on his ankle. Homie was in pain and was helped to the locker room. Coach looked down the bench, stared Benji out. Then looked at me and nodded his head. With the score at 80-73 the mutha couldn't afford another run on our asses—that would kill the game. Damn couldn't strip off my track top quicker.

"So is wha'ppen to yuh hand, Macca?"

Damn almost forgot that it was strapped tightly. "It's nothin' Coach."

"Wha yuh mean, nut'n. You sure yuh can play?"

"Man, I'm ready."

Damn I was in the ball game by default. But shit had to show the scout that I was still on top of my game. Homie could fake him. Say I had an injury. Damn don't have to know my ass was benched. Damn, as I ran onto the court the pain from Cheryl's beatin' was wreckin' me. As I jogged slowly past Andre the look on his face said it all. But I had to push my body through it...America depended on it.

There were three ticks to go when Marcus stole the rock from their American forward and raced in for a slam to make it 80-75. Coach bellowed: "Full cart press, full cart press."

Damn, my body was well and truly fucked up. My hand throbbin' as the ball tried to circulate and after my first attempt at pumpin' my arm to aid my sprint, homie could feel the thread in my arm tearin' with every tightenin' of my bicep.

Cheshire tried to play safe ball and run the clock down. I picked up Price deep in his house. Damn sucked up the pain cause I wanted this sucka.

"Man, yer ain't got shit," I shouted in his face.

"Damn bench is cold without your butt to warm it up," the punk-ass replied, as if he earned any right to trash-talk with me.

"C'mon, mutha. Show me wha' yer got," I replied as he tried to dribble the ball into my house.

Like a good press system, Andre blocked off the only avenue I was leavin' open for the sucka. When he reversed to get away I got my hand in and stole it like a pickpocket. I touched the rock loose. Andre grabbed the pill and sent it down court to Levi—replacing the rested Calvin—who went up for an unmolested two points.

It was a one-point ball game with a minute to go. Price tried to pull the same stunt, holding onto the ball as long as possible, then the sucka quickly looked up and sent a powerful right-handed pass that cut like a knife through our defence. Their other American had a simple lay-up.

Damn, some stupid-ass had missed their assignment but it wasn't the time to have an inquest.

There were forty seconds to go. I handled the rock for the first time. Shit, leather felt like a house brick rubbing against the palm of my hand. My right arm was wack and lying straight down by my side like it was paralysed, forcing me to play like a one-arm bandit. The crowd were bustin' eardrums as I brought the ball past centre court as quickly as possible and settled.

Price was again crouched in front of me as he had been since I came on the court.

"C'mon, bum," he said. "Show me what yer got."

"Man, yer ought to show some respeck to yer master."

I backed him in. Punk was playin' so close I could feel his sweat on the back of my shoulder. I tried to feint to the left and move to the right but he was playin' tough D. I sent the rock out to Marcus. He took the check just outside the paint, crashed it on the hard wood once before elevatin' for a jumper. I heard a bitch slap as for once Marcus' shot cannoned off the rim. But the ref called a defensive foul on him.

He went to the free throw line. Homie couldn't bear to look. Marcus was normally safe money from this range, but this was down the stretch, the pressure was on. Damn heard boi-i-ing and the crowd sighs overwhelmed the cheers, and I knew the homie had missed the first one. There was a roar on his second attempt and we were two down with just over half a minute to play.

The ginger-haired punk who was tryin' to restart the game for Cheshire after Marcus' free throw had a prob finding an open player, the crowd began to get on his back and the rock slipped from his sweaty paws right at Marcus' feet.

The big nigga reacted before his marker, he picked it up under the basket and jammed it through the hoop. Crowd went wild. Man was stealin' my limelight. Forty-three points. Scout must be thinkin' Tiffany got the names wrong. All the other players ran and hugged

Marcus but I stayed in our half.

There was still almost thirty seconds to go. Coach called for zone defence, hopin' to block every lane to the bucket. Cheshire got the ball in with the scores level. Price brought the ball up more quickly this time. Now it was my turn to slow him down by quickly closing off all the exits. Pain was reachin' unbearable levels. Damn was wishing Hector would appear from the crowd and inject my ass with some of that cortisone.

Price passed it out to the flank and made a quick move to the basket. Mutha checked abruptly and doubled back. Gave him enough distance from me to receive a pass and sink a jumper over me. Damn had no chance to issue a rejection slip on his shot as my nearest right arm was now so numb and stiff I could hardly move it from my side.

Coach immediately called a time-out.

"Gimme da shot, coach. I can take it in," I shouted as we huddled around each other.

"Ssshh, Macca. Look me wan' scheme A. Marcus is down to you. Yuh de man who goin' left open. Go fe de safe two and tek it into overtime. Dis shot fe de premier."

Damn man just dissed my request. This was my time and the man wanted me to give up the pill to a man who already had more digits than my mobile number. Goddamn, I didn't even have a bucket to my name. I had to do something to impress. Shit scout must see me put up something original. I bit my lip and sucked up the pain again. Blood was showin' through the strappin' but shit, this was make or break.

Joni took the rock from under the rim and threw it out to me. Damn brought it under control with my left hand, which was four times its normal size. I turned to face Price, dummied and moved easily past him. I could see Calvin and Joni making off-ball pick and roll moves. It left Marcus open for the money shot, but I decided not to play along with Coach's game plan.

Damn wanted to finish the game in style with a three. Everyone will remember that, even if I hadn't scored all game. Shit decided it was now or never. I sent a fade away in-yer-face jumper. Rock must have been in the air a lifetime as two shot blockers converged on me. Damn watched the ball as I fell back on to the hard wood. The rock ringed the rim once and fell out into the hands of a Cheshire player. Marcus rough-housed the rebounder to the deck as my dome hit the floor with the thud of a Semtex bomb exploding.

I closed my eyes. Couldn't believe the shit. I raised my head and all the Warriors were on their hands and knees. Looked over to the bench...man, the faces looked blank as a sheet of paper. Damn Coach was starin' at me. Didn't have to say a word. I knew I had messed up big time.

I got up and headed straight for the locker room. Damn didn't want to wait around to collect no loser's medal. Had to get over to a West End hotel to collect my tickets and get the hell outta this nation.

Half way through dressin', a white dude came in the locker room and handed me a note with number twenty-three written on it. Damn nearly fell down. Damn muthafuckin' scout said they won't be requiring my services this season. Just like that.

Cancelled the meetin', every damn thing, without givin' a homie a chance to explain why he had a wack game. Damn can't do this to me, it's my life—everything I've worked for. Shit, I got dressed, grabbed my rucksack and hurried to my wheels.

On the way out I could hear them callin' out the Warriors individual players for their medals.

Damn just about busted the heart of a homie.

16

Brothas Gonna Work it Out

Calvin pushed his clapped out BMW from fourth to fifth gear and cruised at sixty miles an hour along the A38 towards Birmingham city centre. His face was taut with frustration and his head still confused from trying to work out why Winston put up that shot when Marcus was clearly open.

He was even more disgusted that Winston didn't stay around to apologise or hang with the team in defeat; but he'd always known Winston was selfish and arrogant. He made himself a promise that if he was to take charge of the team next season, Winston would not be part of it.

As far as Calvin was concerned, this was the big one for Coach. His last game in charge, and to reach the Premier Division would've been a just reward for all his hard work over the years.

But Macca had other ideas.

Glory-hunting. Individualism over the team. Calvin believed from the off Winston was going to cost them a major game—and this afternoon his prediction had come true.

The disappointment on Coach Bailey's face at the end of the game was etched permanently on his memory. The tears, the heartache and the if-onlys...

He knew Coach was a tough nut. If he could survive a heart attack, he could soldier on for years to come. But Calvin was hurting for him. He knew how badly Coach had wanted it....and he had badly wanted to give it to him.

With his parents now back in Barbados, Calvin saw Coach Bailey and his wife as surrogate parents. Over the past month he had visited them at least twice a week. He poured out his troubles and fears about the youth conference, and they responded with encouragement and advice.

He even told Coach about the one-night stand he had with Heather, something his conscience wouldn't allow him to forget. He had to tell someone before it ate away his soul, and Coach offered him the sympathetic shoulder and words of wisdom.

He told him to keep it to himself.

No point disrupting a friendship that has lasted over twenty years, was the old man's advice. Calvin knew Coach was right but still he couldn't look Andre in the eye. And he couldn't sleep easy next to Lorna knowing he had knocked off one of her closest friends. But he had to let his head rule his heart and keep his mouth closed. Too many were going to be hurt if it came out in the open. As for Heather, he had neither seen nor spoken to her since that day.

Lorna found it peculiar that she hadn't phoned, but Calvin was always able to pass it off as Heather and Andre spending more time together trying to work ~~their~~ out their differences.

Calvin was a lonely, isolated figure driving into a city centre that mirrored his emotional state. It was a typical damp, dreary evening. He slipped through the empty city on his way to Mr Lindsey's home in Solihull to meet up with the Americans for the last time before tomorrow's main event at the X Centre.

He tried not to think about the death threats he'd received. But the images kept appearing, particularly the one Lorna had opened by accident. She almost fainted on the doormat. Calvin knew it was the dealers, and he couldn't be fazed by these phony gangsters trying to muscle him and the conference workers out of doing the right thing. He knew he had to stand up and be counted, and tomorrow he would be number one on the hit list.

After the success of the Black Pound Day a message was painted in bright red on the doors of the X Centre, threatening to burn the place down if the conference went ahead—so Calvin and Abdullah had called a meeting of all members to relay the full story of the dealers' plans to disrupt the conference. A vote was taken and the members voted unanimously, bar Kwesi, to stride forward with the project.

As far as Calvin was concerned no-one was going to put a stop to it. Not the dealers, not the councillors, not even the Home Office, who had heard about the plans at the last minute and wanted to ban it. But it was too late. Calvin knew he had defeated all opposition up until now—but he also knew the dealers still represented a small but powerful lobby, and a petrol bomb thrown on the day would be enough to get the media on his back and defeat the whole idea behind the conference.

It took Calvin about another thirty-five minutes to get down to Solihull. He pulled up outside Lindsey's house, which was large enough to disprove all that Lindsey had ever said about not having money. It had large steel gates guarding a front lawn that seemed as big as Handsworth Park.

Calvin got out, but the gates were locked. He pressed the intercom and Mrs Lindsey answered. Within seconds the gates swung open.

It took him a full minute to drive up the garden path to the front door. When he got out, he could hear dogs barking like they were hungry and could see their dinner on the doorstep.

He rang the bell and a taped message came on telling people to visit The Star Club for a night of superb entertainment. Lindsey never missed an opportunity to plug the club. The smile was still fresh on Calvin's face when Mrs Lindsey answered the door with a warm smile. She was the opposite of Lindsey. She was taller than him and her Caribbean Indian blood made her look real elegant. She tended to stay in the background while her husband hogged the limelight.

"Calvin, how are you?"

"Fine, Mrs Lindsey. You?" Calvin replied, stepping in.

"I'm well. But please call me Felicia," she said with an accent that had a hint of creole.

"I heard the team had a bad day in London."

"Yes, sista, missed a great opportunity."

"Well, I hope the owner isn't too disappointed, 'cause I know what he's like when things don't go his way."

"When I left he was down but not out," Calvin replied with a half-hearted smile.

"The other guys are in the living room," she said, pointing the way.

Calvin walked through to the living room. Distinct ghetto American accents hit him immediately, but because the expensively furnished room was L-shaped, he had to walk a full ten yards before he could put faces to the voices. When he turned the corner, Jamaal saw him first.

"Hey, whassup homie?" he said, looking like O.J. Simpson with devilish eyes in a Raiders baseball hat and a black tee-shirt that read 'Real Men Wear Black'. He stood up with the rest of them and they greeted Calvin by touching forearms.

"Hey, bro, we heard yer got yer butts kicked," Jamaal said. "Shit was close though."

"Yeah, man, we trailed it on whatcha 'call it? Pirate radio, y'know, that Black Man Radio," said Hakeem, who for some strange reason was wearing a thick 49ers Starter jacket, even though the room must have been touching seventy degrees.

"Yeah, brothas, we lost," Calvin replied.

"Some punk missed da muny shot, right?" Hakeem added.

"Brotha wasn't even suppose to take the thing. Believe me, I still can't take it in..."

"Homiez wanna teach da mutha a lesson. Damn punk messin' up a big-time victory!"

Hakeem said it like he was the Warriors' coach.

"Y'all should've invited us down, man," Jamaal said.

"Yeah, draft us on da rostah 'n' shit," Hakeem added. "Brotha man, yer'd see moves, man."

"Homie would've seen moves, but not yours 'Keem," said the baby-faced member of the four, Little Chris, who got his nickname because he was just over five feet tall.

"Whatcha' on 'bout, l'il man? Could handle da damn rock since homie came outta da cradle," Hakeem insisted.

"Brotha man, y' can't handle shit. Brotha's trippin', man," Chris replied, as if he had seen Hakeem perform on the Watts blacktop.

"Man, yer wanna tek me one-on-one?"

"Man, cut da shit out, we're 'pose to be here on bizness," Jamaal said, bringing the argument to a halt.

"Yeah, brothas. If I had arranged it in time I would have driven you down but I thought you'd need some rest to get over the jet-lag," Calvin replied, pulling up a seat between Little Chris and the group's adviser, Clayton Hoover.

"Man, yer didn't have to worry 'bout jet-lag. We was ready to hang large on da streets of London from da time dat big ass jet touched down on da tarmac," said Jamaal.

Terrell, the final member of the group added—in a slow, deep Barry White voice: "Yeah, man, homiez wuz ready to pay respecks to yer Queen. Y'know, bow and all dat shit dat y' English folks do."

"Man, shit. Homie don't know how yer black cats can bow down to some white hoochie. Hey cuz, dat schitt's deep," Terrell continued.

Calvin smiled, not just at what Terrell said but the way he said it. He was the spitting image of Mike Tyson. Calvin had joked with him when they first met that Mike Tyson's runaway dad had somehow found his way into his mother's affections. He even had the gold tooth and the lisp to go with it. Brotha had spent time inside for taking part in a drive-by shooting that killed an innocent six-year-old girl as she walked to school.

Both he and Jamaal, who was the most articulate of the group, belonged to the Crips, though to rival factions. Hakeem and Little Chris came from the same Bloods gang. Hakeem and Jamaal had explained to Calvin that they had been sworn enemies a year earlier.

267

Then the only way you were going to get them in the same building, let alone the same room, was if they were there to smoke each other.

"So, brothas, what you up to?" Calvin asked.

"Man, we're jus' chillin', goin' through some of da words for tomorrow. Wanna get it right, y'knowha'msayin'?"

Jamaal displayed a look that showed a real heart behind the tough macho exterior he always fronted.

"Y'know, we're gonna tell all yer English brothas da same message we talked down at yer project in Hockley. Dat is to stay away from all da gangbangin' shit 'cause it can only lead to one dead-end avenue, and da stories me and my homiez gon' tell is only a few years away from yer own 'hood."

Calvin nodded.

Hakeem, who was thinner than Jamaal and less fierce looking, added in a more sombre, deliberate tone:

"Yeah, brotha, we're gonna give yer da bottom line. Yer homiez either change now or die later 'cuz it's as simple as a damn heartbeat. Cats like us had no guidelines or anyone to imitate. Homiez were da prototype, if y'will. Now da brothas and sistas over here have a yard-stick y'all can measure yourselves by, and that's us, y'knowwhasayin'?"

"At the end of the day the brothas over here have the opportunity to take a new path," Clayton butted in with his intellectual, east coast accent.

"The guys in urban America didn't. It was a kinda experiment. Now these gangs stand as a reminder of what will happen if you don't nip the problems of inner-city deprivation and institutionalised racism in the bud."

The message was crystal clear to Calvin, and he only hoped they would talk with the same freeness and honesty on the stage tomorrow. They sat and talked for another couple of hours about life on the streets of South Central LA and in Handsworth, Birmingham.

Jamaal talked about the time he and one of his spars came out of a drug store near the corner of Florence and Normandie Boulevard; Calvin remembered it from the television coverage as the junction where the riots began in LA.

"Homie jus' came out man, knockin' back Night Train," Jamaal said.

Calvin looked confused.

"Night Train?"

"Homiez don't have dat shit ova here?" Terrell asked, with that unmistakable growl.

"Brotha, shit's ninety percent wine and meks a punk outta yer in ticks. Whole niggahood is full of it."

Calvin got the gist.

"Yeah, homie," Jamaal continued. "When me and my road dog come out we heard *boom! boom!* Mutha sounded like da cannons in Custer's las' stan'."

"Desert Eagle, homie," Little Chris jumped in on the story.

"Yeah, li'l man. Desert Eagle. We hit da deck but da shit tore outta me homie's face, man. Brotha was a corpse. *Damn!* Ain't never seen shit like it."

"Yeah, brotha, da ghetto Eagle muthafuckin' powerful. Shit rip a homie's head off from fifty feet. Bang! Everythin' gon'," Hakeem added.

Jamaal said he was lucky to be alive because the mega-force bullet grazed him before demolishing the contents of the drug store behind. He said he was in Martin Luther King hospital—the place where men of war are taken to recuperate—for almost six months. When he finally got out all he could think of was revenge.

"Same day homie got out. Got strapped to da neck. Man had ta git revenge. Saw da punks outside McDee's. Brothas rolled in our wheels then gave 'em every muthafuckin' cap we had. Brotha, AK-47's flyin' like birds in da sky, looked like Chi-Town in Capone days."

If Jamaal felt any remorse, Calvin thought, his features didn't let on.

He was so angry he didn't direct the bullets at any single person or persons and tried a catch-all policy, so only five people, all gang members, were killed. But seven innocent bystanders were badly injured. The incident earned Jamaal his OG status, the highest stripes bestowed on war-weary gangbangers.

After that, the Bloods made him public enemy number one and a contract was out on his head. But the authorities picked him up for another offence before members of the Bloods could.

"We wanted his muthafuckin' ass so badly we started tearin' up the shit," Hakeem added. "Sendin' dead bodies, any bodies, to the graveyard jus' to smoke this cat. We would've smoked man, woman or child to get ta him. Dat was da law we operated under at da time."

Calvin now knew that was how Jamaal ended up in the notorious youth detention centre, Kilpatrick, as a fourteen-year-old. Jamaal was able to meet the families of the innocent people he murdered. After seeing the pain he had caused he immediately changed his stance on

269

the need for gang violence.

His story moved Calvin, and he supposed it would touch the hearts of the most evil in the world. To see these guys come back from committing the most horrendous crimes to lead exemplary lives filled him with hope. If the young African brothas of today see there is an alternative, then there can only be hope for the future.

By the time Jamaal had finished his story it was time for Calvin to leave. He said his goodbyes as the five of them went off to bed.

As Calvin was about to get into his car, Mr Lindsey's big red Merc came up the path. He pulled up beside Calvin and let down the window.

"Calvin, man, me tell yuh me waste t-t-t-twelve t'ousand pound 'pon dat wotless piece a crap dem call Macca. W-w-why de hell 'im go fe-fe-fe dat shot, eh? Why? Me a go contac' 'im agent in de mornin' and ask fe me money back, but if I ketch 'im first, I goin' string 'im up, y'hear me. An' don't bother try stop me neither'!"

"Brotha, I wouldn't waste my time—but I did warn you," Calvin replied.

"D-d-dat's all yuh can say, yuh warn me? Dat's it?"

"The man was never for the Warriors, y'know that, brotha."

"Imagine, 'im never even wait fe collec' im medal. Jus' t'row up de shot and run 'im lickle ass out de place. Bwoy, im mek us lose all dat sponsorship fe nex' season. All me plans gone on one blasted lick-le good-fe-nut'n eediot bwoy. Me see it wid me two y'eye dem but me 'till cyan' believe it."

"Brotha, we gotta see what happens next season," Calvin said.

"So yuh wan' tek ova as head coach?" Mr Lindsey asked, a look of anticipation on his face.

"Brotha, I haven't decided yet," Calvin replied, yawning. The day's events were catching up with him.

"Wha yuh mean?"

"I mean, I might be lookin' at a complete break."

"C-C-Calvin man, me a look fe continuity. Wid Bailey gone you's de next man in line."

"Brotha, I appreciate your confidence, but I have to see nearer the time."

"Me 'ope you nah try and hol' out fe more money, 'cause after wha'ppen today me nah spend a penny more 'pon dis club 'til dem win somet'ing."

"We'll talk again another time, brotha. Right now I have to go, and you have house guests to see to."

Lindsey quickly looked in the direction of his house, as if he expected it to be on fire or something. Calvin climbed wearily into his car and began the drive back to Handsworth.

Chedda was sitting alone on a wall with his back to Calvin as he approached his block.

"What you doing out here so late, little brotha?"

Chedda turned around.

"Just come back from ravin'," he said simply, and turned back to face the drab night.

Times were changing so fast Calvin could barely keep pace. He remembered when he was fourteen—he'd never have been allowed out on the streets in the early hours of the morning. His dad never let him go to the toilet without knowing what time he'd be back.

"So why don't you just go up to your flat?" Calvin asked.

"I need some fresh air before I go in," Chedda replied.

"Is your mum in, bro?"

"Nah, still at work."

"Does she know you're out this late?"

"Man, it's not late, it's only one. Most days I'm not in my bed 'til three, even when she is here."

Calvin spent a short time explaining to Chedda the importance of going to bed early. Chedda's expression said he understood what Calvin was saying, but his answers said the allure of living on the edge and doing what his peers expected still outweighed any ideas he had of getting himself free of his current lifestyle. Seemed to Calvin it was just the shock talking.

Before he left he asked Chedda if he and his friends were coming to the youth conference.

"I don't know about the others, but I'll be there. I want to hear those American gangsters again. They were serious when they talked to us right on Saturday."

His eyes sparkled, but Calvin knew it was for the wrong reasons. Chedda seemed more interested in revelling in the violent stories the Americans had to tell. But that was okay, if that's what it took to get him to the conference. Tomorrow he would hear a different side of things; the maiming and killings.

"What about Maxwell, is he coming?" Calvin asked.

"Ganja Kid? I don't know. I don't see much of him these days. He's home for Easter from dat hospital, y'know, the one for cripples."

Calvin nodded his head.

"Even when he's here he hardly comes out, 'cause of the wheelchair. Doesn't like the gang seein' him," Chedda said in a saddened tone.

Calvin thought about Ganja Kid, confined to a wheelchair at the age of fourteen. The bullet severed some nerve in his spine. Lost the use of his bottom half. The young brotha who fired the shot, Boxer, had been detained at Her Majesty's pleasure at some borstal just outside the city borders. Calvin was happy that they had also charged Boxer's no-good father with possession of a firearm without a licence.

That case had yet to be heard. But the sooner they lock him up the better. The low-down no-hoper had been walking around boasting about how his son was locked up for shooting a brotha in the back, like it was some Jack City movie. He'd even tried to sell his story to the press for thirty thousand pounds; but since such shootings are now everyday happenings in inner-city Britain his offer met with little interest. In fact, one of the tabloids exposed his shortcomings as a father in a piece on the problems of British inner-city society.

Calvin told Chedda the Americans would have better things to say later this morning, and that he should bring as many kids as possible up to the conference. Then he left him and went up to his flat.

When he got in, everything was quiet. He walked along the narrow corridor and into the living room. Only the light from the half moon saved the room from pitch darkness. He walked over to his desk, looked out over Birmingham and rubbed his forehead.

For that split second all thoughts escaped him as he gazed into the darkness. He headed for the kitchen, but first put his head around the bedroom door. Lorna was out like a light. He stood for a while just looking at her neat little face partially hidden by the sky blue duvet and thought about the wrong he had committed against her. Calvin turned and continued onto the kitchen where he made himself a cup of coffee before heading back to the living room to sit in his favourite chair.

It must have been about three-thirty when he eventually got into bed beside Lorna. Her body was warm against his. She opened her eyes as Calvin put his arms around her.

"How did it go, darlin'?"

"We missed out, sis."

She pulled herself closer to him and kissed him.

"Never mind. Maybe next time," she said, before going back to sleep.

"One-two, one-two," Calvin spoke hesitantly into the silver mikes.

They were working fine and everything was in place, and everyone was ready—except Kwesi, no-one had seen or heard from him. Calvin was just glad he was not integral to the smooth running of the event.

Security was tight. Calvin had thirty brothas patrolling the nearby streets and the X Centre grounds. Another fifteen kept a close eye on things in the hall. Not even a kamikaze pilot could have got through the cordon today. Front Line Security had things that tight. Even cigarette lighters were confiscated at the door.

As Calvin walked onto the stage for one last look, he felt proud. His baby had been fathered through the rites of passage and was becoming a man today. He looked out; the hall was packed, the event could have been sold twice over. The four hundred seats were quickly taken as early as half-ten that morning, and there were at least a hundred more squeezed into the back of the hall.

The majority were black kids with their parents, but a few school teachers had brought along small delegations of pupils of all races. Some local councillors sat near the front, alongside two TV crews and a reporter from the local radio station.

The X Centre banner hung from the ceiling at the back of the hall, amid various posters promoting the centre. Mr Lindsey also wasted no corner of the hall bigging up the Star Club. He must have given everyone within the vicinity a copy of the same leaflet he had stapled to every free space on the wall.

Bang on time at eleven o'clock, Calvin called for silence on the microphone. He welcomed everyone, thanking them for coming and congratulated the X Centre and Mr Lindsey for making this day happen. The first hour of the conference was taken up by young British inner city brothas and sistas telling the audience what it was like growing up in Birmingham through personal or fictional stories, poems and songs.

One cute little brotha about ten years old came up on stage and said how the Birmingham decision-makers had neglected his family by allowing them to live in a rat-infested house, which they couldn't even decorate because there was so much damp that the wallpaper would fall off within a week of going up. He concluded by saying that he wanted to be a local councillor when he grew up, and would make sure no-one had to live the way he and his family did.

Everyone in the hall stood up and applauded him as he walked down the steps to be hugged by his mum.

At five past twelve it was time to introduce the guest speakers. As Calvin called their names, they entered from the back of the hall and walked down the gangway flanked by four shaven-headed Front Line Security guards dressed in black suits, white shirts and dark shades.

Public Enemy's *'Brothers Gonna Work It Out'* blasted through the speakers as the four Americans marched military-style towards the stage, their faces expressionless. They had come to deliver a message and this was their way of setting the mood. The track—his favourite from *'Fear of a Black Planet'*—might have been out since the turn of the decade, but Calvin believed it still had a resonance for today's black youth. He whispered the words softly to himself as the four approached the stage: *"As you raise your fist to the music. United we stand, yes divided we fall. Together we can stand tall. One day brothas gonna work it out."*

The four soldiers, dressed in black sweatshirts bearing the words *'Apart we can't do it, but together we can'* in red lettering, stepped up onto the stage. There were no handshakes with the committee members—who were all sitting at the large table on stage—just one approving nod, and a half-smile from Terrell in Calvin's direction.

Jamaal and Hakeem both wore dark shades and baseball caps, while Little Chris sported a Chicago Bulls ski hat and Terrell a kente dachiqui. The audience were going wild, tapping their knees and nodding their heads to the beat.

It was a good few minutes after the guests had taken their seats before Calvin could calm the audience down.

He quickly introduced the four and then let them run the floor. Each of them in turn told how they got into the gang and drugs scene. They talked about the peer pressure and racist practices, and each gave a personal account of his life as a member of an LA gang.

Calvin could see concern, horror, disbelief— a whole gamut of emotions—etched on the faces of the kids, parents, teachers and councillors alike as Little Chris gave an account of a drive-by shooting that he was part of. He also told of how he felt when he heard that a rival gang had caught his older brother and shot him through the head five times in cold blood, then amputated his legs and left him to die. Then they turned up at his funeral and shot his corpse again. He told how his time in Kilpatrick gave him the strength to turn his back on the gang violence.

Hakeem spoke about the streets of South Central as a war zone where:

"You either do or die. It no diff'rent from goin' to da Gulf except we took no prisoners. Our prisoner of war camps was da graveyard, y'knowyumsayin'?"

After each of them had been through his story, Jamaal again took the floor to describe what he'd seen on the streets of Birmingham. He warned that if it was not checked now, horror stories like those the audience were hearing from the States would be a British reality in less than five years.

He urged the black youth to start creating a community movement based at grass root level to help foster urban economic development, and lambasted the politicians for sitting back and doing nothing in the false belief that they could contain the violence within the ghetto areas.

"Let me tell yer, man, we four sittin' here didn't come from no ghetto. We're regular cats who got caught up in a way of life dat dissed all da values you people laid down," Jamaal said, pointing at the councillors.

"We set our own rules 'cause we had da ultimate power to say who lives or dies in our 'hood. That's what drove a lot of gangbangers, havin' da power to recreate reality in their own image."

The bulk of his speech was targeted at the African community.

"The power resides with you—the African people—to stop the killin' and wipe da drugs off da street," he said pointing at the audience.

"Da myth is dat we need someone high up in power. If they come correct da power structure can facilitate change, but ultimately it's up to you—da African people of Birmingham—to reject da black-on-black violence and boot da drug dealers out. It's time to say enough is enough. Nobody else can do that for you," he concluded.

As he sat down the whole audience and the panel sitting with him got to their feet and applauded. Even some of the local councillors and police were on their feet.

To round off the conference there were questions from the audience. The bald, white Tory councillor who had objected to the Americans being allowed into the country raised his hand and stood up, almost insisting that he should be the first to speak. Jamaal gave him the go-ahead.

"As all of you have said, you have murdered countless people. But yet you are free. Society cannot function if murderers are given soft sentences."

The audience groaned their disapproval at the statement before Jamaal rose to answer.

"How many cats did Ollie North smoke? How many did Stormin' Norman send to their graves? Yet the West acclaims these people as heroes. Look, we was takin' part in a war not in defence of country but in defence of our territory, our family, our gangs. Put it this way— if you seriously wanna stop what's goin' on, we are the only people who can do it. Da equivalent of a Tory councillor in LA has no jurisdiction over South Central. We're not proud of what we done in the past but we've been given the opportunity to make amends and that's why we're here. We're doin' more good now than we ever could behind bars."

The audience applauded and the red-faced councillor wanted to follow up his statement, but Jamaal moved on to other questioners.

A young black kid, no older than fourteen, stood up.

"How can I cope with the pressure of not being in a gang when all my friends are?" the little guy said, amidst the hum of the audience.

"Dat's mine," said Little Chris, standing up.

"Man, it's the same kinda pressure I was under, and grown-ups have got to realise dat dis peer pressure is a heavy thing. Real deep, man, 'cause if your not down wit' da gang you're an outsider, you can't be protected and you're fair meat for da gangbangers.

"I wasn't strong enough to fight da pressure and I got beat down. But for those of you who want to fight those pressures, you can come to a place like dis," Chris said, holding his arms out.

"Da homiez here will put yer on da right road. Always have in your mind dat what you doin' is da right thing. It's the gang members who got it wrong."

There was more loud applause and questions from the floor before the conference closed on time at two-thirty. An hour later the hall was still packed with people, all wanting personal words with the guests from America. Calvin gave a couple of quick interviews to the newspapers before going to the back of the hall to take a look at what the hard work of the committee had achieved.

As he turned to leave the hall, he almost tripped over a guy in a wheelchair. It was Ganja Kid. His face was drawn and sad, and his legs were covered by a tartan blanket. He held his right fist out and Calvin touched it with his. No words passed their lips, but they both knew the significance of what they'd heard.

His mum, standing behind his wheelchair, took Calvin's hands and said:

"Thank you. I just wish somet'ing wasn't done earlier."

It was five o'clock before the people started to disperse. The Americans were then free to come up and congratulate Calvin and the X Centre members for inviting them. They suggested that members of the X Centre and a party of youths should make a return journey to the States the following year, then all left for lunch at the Star Club together in two limousines driven by Front Line Security's guards.

"So how do you feel?" Lorna asked, as Calvin lay half-naked across the bed.

"About what?"

She playfully pinched him on his back before sitting down beside him on the bed.

"Sista, ask me in a month's time when it's worn off the young brothas. If we see a decrease in violence and less of them getting hooked or transporting drugs—then I'll feel great. If we don't, well—" he chuckled, "—I'll still feel great 'cause it opened the eyes of the young brothas and sistas to the possibility that things don't always have to be the way they are now."

"I'm proud of you," Lorna said, kissing him on his forehead.

"Don't forget the work you and all the X Centre members put in," Calvin said, sharing accolades.

"Don't worry, we'll claim our dues," she laughed.

"But if you hadn't come up the idea, the conference would never have taken place."

Calvin nodded and turned over onto his back, switching his thoughts to what to do next. He wanted to keep the message of the Americans ringing in the ears of the young brothas. He wanted to get more of them down to places like the X Centre on a regular basis. He didn't want to lose their attention while the conference was still fresh in their minds.

"Calvin, we'd better get ready," Lorna said.

"As hosts we should really be there before the other guests arrive."

Calvin was still stiff from playing yesterday. He dragged his aching body off the bed and had a long warm shower, then got dressed for the last event of the kickass Easter weekend, the Star Club party.

The bouncers on the door greeted him with a handshake instead of the normal nod of the head. He supposed they had heard about the conference. The Americans were there already, talking to Mr Lindsey. Calvin caught the end of their conversation and found that— as he expected—Lindsey was discussing some kind of business in America.

He left the table to circulate.

"Hey man, the brotha wants to invest in a movie round Li'l Chris' life," Jamaal said, as Calvin and Lorna sat down with them.

"Don't listen to Mr Lindsey, brotha. He says a lot of things but ask him to part with his money and that's different..." Calvin replied.

"Like dat is it, homie?" Hakeem chuckled.

"Better believe it, bro," Calvin replied.

The group had already got through two bottles of champagne when the hall started to fill up after ten-thirty. Lorna nudged Calvin and he followed her gaze to see Andre and Heather arriving.

They saw Lorna waving and came straight over. Calvin stood up when they got to the table. Andre bent to kiss Lorna and Calvin felt obliged to kiss Heather. He could see she was as nervous as he was. He grasped her by the elbows and kissed her on the right cheek.

He then introduced them to the Americans before they headed for the bar. Lorna and Calvin eventually left the Americans' table because so many people wanted to chat or dance with them.

The place was rammed; you couldn't move unless you stepped on someone's toes. Calvin and Lorna had to fight to get to the bar. When they got there Calvin saw Marcus, standing a few feet away. Calvin left Lorna to order their drinks and edged his way through the crowd towards Marcus.

"Brotha, what's goin' down!" Calvin shouted, tapping him on the shoulder.

"Calvin, man. Me 'ear say yuh had a wicked conference," Marcus shouted back.

"Yeah, brotha, went like a dream."

"Sorry me couldn't mek it but me had ta go a Wolver'ampton fe check me daughter. Yvette tell me say it did well nice!"

"Thanks, brotha. So, you over the game?"

"Cha, me nah even wan' t'ink bout it."

"What's happenin' with you and the case, brotha?"

"Bwoy, if yuh sight me tomorrow y'know it go good, if not, den yuh haffe come check me inside."

"Naa, brotha man you're not going down."

Marcus just shrugged his massive shoulders.

Calvin left him to make his way back to Lorna. As he did so Heather was coming in the opposite direction. The two met between dancers gyrating and bogling on the dance floor.

Heather took his arm to speak in his ear.

"I've just spoken to Lorna," she said.

Calvin's heart leapt.

"What about?" he asked, hesitantly.

"Don't worry, not about us," Heather replied.

"That was a mistake."

Calvin was relieved.

"I agree totally, sista."

"Andre doesn't know, and he's not going to," Heather told him.

"That's fine, sista. It's the same with Lorna."

"So when are you two getting married?"

"I haven't really thought about it."

"You better hurry before someone else asks her. You'll make a nice couple," she smiled,then released her grip on his arm and fought her way through the crowd. When Calvin eventually got back to Lorna, they had a couple more drinks and rubbed down several times to some lovers'.

Calvin didn't need to put the keys in the lock of the X Centre door. Someone had already done that. It was one in the morning and Calvin immediately became suspicious. He thought fleetingly that Abdullah had forgotten to lock up, but Calvin knew that after the threats and the break-in Abdullah would never be that careless. The X Centre was his life.

He slowly turned the handle, crept in and gently closed the door behind him. He tiptoed down the hallway, stopping suddenly when he heard the cracking of wood coming from the office the committee had used as their headquarters.

He began to sweat and thought, maybe he should have called the police? Then he decided that he had to deal with whoever was in the centre himself. The door was slightly ajar and one of the desk lights was on; he could see a shadow on the wall, and hear something that sounded like liquid being poured around the room.

Calvin burst in to find Kwesi with a lighter in one hand and a petrol can in the other. Both were almost paralysed with shock.

When Calvin was able to speak, all he could say was:

"Why, brotha?"

Kwesi dropped the canister and flung himself into a nearby chair.

"I'm sorry, bro," he said, lowering his chin to his chest.

"Sorry? You were going to torch the place. Why, brotha? Why?"

Calvin rushed over to him, grabbed him by the lapels of his jacket and pulled him out of the chair so they were face to face.

"Why, Kwesi?" he asked again.

The tears were flowing down Kwesi's black face.

"They got to me, brotha. They got to me. They threatened to cripple me if I didn't put a stop to the marches and the conference. I had to. I'm sorry brotha."

Calvin didn't need names. He knew who it was.

"But we had the meeting, brotha. We said we were going to stand firm against those ruff necks."

"I tried to...I tried to...but they kept comin' back again and again. They burgled my house, threatened my girl. Brotha, I had to man. I had to."

"You didn't have to do damn all," Calvin said angrily, pushing Kwesi back down into his seat.

"Why don't you finish the job, you damn yellow-belly coward."

He picked up the petrol can and thrust it onto Kwesi.

"Go on, finish it."

"I can't..."

Kwesi knocked the can to the floor.

"Why not? They're still going to be after you if you don't, brotha. What did they promise—to decapitate you, lynch you, burn you? 'Cause Kwesi, I'm going to do worse to you. Y'know what? We're going to sit here until Abdullah and the committee get here in the morning and you can explain all this. You hear brotha."

Kwesi looked around like he was looking for help.

"So what's it to be brotha? The choice is yours," Calvin said.

"You have no right to do this. Just let me go and I'll never come back, never," Kwesi pleaded.

Calvin thought how pathetic and scared he looked. He should have known that if there was going to be a weak link it would be him.

"You think you're so clever, don't you?" Kwesi said, his boldness coming from nowhere to surprise Calvin.

"You come in here five years after all the rest, start playing mister big shot. Start running things. Even steal my woman."

Calvin looked at Kwesi hard. His expression was one of aggression, as if he wanted to shift the blame for his weakness onto Calvin.

"Stole your woman?"

Calvin looked at him suspiciously.

"Yeah, that's right brotha," Kwesi replied, standing up.

"Come with all your fancy talk and she fell for it."

"Brotha, you and Lorna were dead and buried by the time I came on the scene."

"We had problems, but who doesn't? We could have worked them out. But you had to come along and kick a brotha's plans into touch."

"Why leave it until now, eh, brotha?"

"Just biding my time," Kwesi sneered. "Just biding my time."

"So, there was no gang threats, you just wanted to get me for stealing your dream girl. That's it, brotha? All the death-threats, the paint on the door, the petrol bombing...that was all you?"

Calvin didn't give him time to answer, just shot him a box across his face.

Kwesi flew over the desk and emerged seconds later with a busted lip.

"Brotha, get the fuck outta here before I call the police," Calvin shouted.

Kwesi ran like the wind through the door.

"I still won't forgive you for walking out of the party last night and not coming back," Lorna said.

"I understand, sis," Calvin replied, sprawling himself across the bed. He had told her that he went for a long walk just to relax. Luckily when he got back she had been fast asleep, so he could lie about the actual time he returned home.

He didn't tell her about Kwesi, because he didn't want to spoil what had been a successful conference. He had spent the whole night clearing up the X Centre, hoping no one would smell the petrol Kwesi had doused in the room. He didn't inform the police either. He believed there was no point getting the confused brotha locked up, since he knew Kwesi would never show his face at the centre again.

"Yeah, you missed this trampish-lookin' guy who came in asking the Americans to set up some kind of transatlantic drugs cartel," Lorna laughed. "I don't know how he got past security in that dirty old mac, it was supposed to be a high class affair."

"Yeah, what happened?"

"After Jamaal started cussing, security came and turfed him out." She chuckled.

"By the time they got him to the door the poor guy had a bleeding nose and mouth. But that'll teach him for making assumptions."

Calvin's head was spinning. He always hated the mornings after the nights he drank. The phone rang. It was Andre phoning from work—sounding ecstatic.

"What the hell's up, brotha?"

"Marcus was acquitted. Cleared on all charges!" Andre shouted with joy.

"For real, brotha?" Calvin whooped, just able to contain his relief.

"Got it from the horse's mouth. Simon, one of the legal execs, just gave me the news. One of the cops caved in and admitted they'd tampered with the original police statements. I knew it would be okay. Serve that bastard Theo right."

"What do you mean, brotha?" Calvin asked, curious that he should curse the man that had just got Marcus free.

"Never mind, legal talk. Let's just say there is such a thing as justice after all."

"That's legal talk, brotha?"

Andre laughed.

"Calvin, it's time for a real celebration."

"Brotha, you're right there. Come round for six, and bring Heather."

"You're on. Listen, my boss wants to see me. I'll speak to you later."

"Go in peace, brotha."

Lorna could see from his expression it was good news. Calvin punched the air and shouted:

"Yes!"

He lifted Lorna off off her feet and swung her round before locking her in a bear hug. Then he kissed her long and hard, and gazed into her eyes until he could hold back no longer.

"Marry me, sista," he said boldly, producing the ring he'd collected from the centre the night before.

Lorna's face softened and her eyes misted over as she looked at him and beamed.

"I thought you'd never ask."

She laughed and they stumbled and ended up on the floor. Calvin was still holding her around her thin waist.

"What kind of answer is that, sista?" he asked, as they lay side by side on by the sofa.

She looked deeply into his eyes.

"Yes, I'll marry you, Calvin. Yes, yes, yes, yes, yes, yes!"

Books with ATTITUDE

THE RAGGA & THE ROYAL by Monica Grant Streetwise Leroy Massop and The Princess of Wales get it together in this light-hearted romp. £5.99

JAMAICA INC. by Tony Sewell Jamaican Prime Minister, David Cooper, is shot down as he addresses the crowd at a reggae 'peace' concert. But who pulled the trigger and why? £5.99

LICK SHOT by Peter Kalu When neo-nazis plan to attack Manchester's black community they didn't reckon on one thing...A black cop who doesn't give a fuck about the rules! £5.99

SINGLE BLACK FEMALE by Yvette Richards Three career women end up sharing a house together and discover they all share the same problem-MEN! £5.99

MOSS SIDE MASSIVE by Karline Smith When the brother of a local gangster is shot dead on a busy Manchester street, the city is turned into a war zone as the drugs gangs battle it out. £5.99

OPP by Naomi King How deep does friendship go when you fancy your best friend's man? Find out in this hot bestseller! £5.99

COP KILLER by Donald Gorgon When his mother is shot dead by the police, taxi driver Lloyd Baker becomes a one man cop-killing machine. Hugely controversial but compulsive reading. £4.99

BABY FATHER/ BABY FATHER 2 by Patrick Augustus Four men come to terms with parenthood but it's a rough journey they travel before discovering the joys in this smash hit and its sequel. £5.99

WICKED IN BED by Sheri Campbell Michael Hughes believes in 'loving and leaving 'em' when it comes to women. But if you play with fire you're gonna get burnt! £5.99

FETISH by Victor Headley The acclaimed author of 'Yardie', 'Excess', and 'Yush!' serves another gripping thriller where appearances can be very deceiving! £5.99

PROFESSOR X by Peter Kalu When a black American radical visits the UK to expose a major corruption scandal, only a black cop can save him from the assasin's bullet. £5.99

UPTOWN HEADS by R.K. Byers Hanging with the homeboys in uptown New York where all that the brothers want is a little respect! A superb, vibrant humourous modern novel about the black American male. £5.99

THE CONJURE MAN DIES by Rudolph Fisher

Originally published in 1932, *The Conjure Man Dies* is the first known mystery novel written by an African-American. Rudolph Fisher, one of the principal writers of the Harlem Renaissance, weaves an intricate story of a native African king, who after receiving a degree from Harvard settles into Harlem of the 1930's. He becomes a fortune teller or 'Conjure Man' and quickly becomes a much talked about local figure. When the old man is found dead the rumours start spreading. Things are made even more confusing when he turns up very much alive!

THE AUTOBIOGRAPHY OF AN EX-COLORED MAN
by James Weldon Johnson

Until his school teacher points out to him in no uncertain terms that he's a "nigger", the anonymous narrator of *The Autobiography of an Ex-Colored Man*, believed that his fair skin granted him the privileges of his white class mates.

The realisation of what life holds for him is at first devastating, but as he grows into adulthood, he discovers a pride in his blackness and the noble race from which he is descended. However a disturbing family secret is soon to shake up his world.

THE HOUSE BEHIND THE CEDARS
by Charles W. Chesnutt

A few years after the American Civil War, two siblings, Rena and John Walden, 'pass' for white in the Deep South as their only means of obtaining a share of the American dream.

With a change of name and a fictitious biography, John starts a new life. But for Rena, the deception poses a bigger dilemma when she meets and falls in love with a wealthy young white man.

Can love transcend racial barriers, or will the dashing George Tryon reject her the moment he discovers her black roots?

Also Available *Black Classics*

Three more forgotten greats of black writing will be available from Jan 1996. Check out: *A LOVE SUPREME* by Pauline Hopkins, *THE WALLS OF JERICHO* by Rudolph Fisher and *THE PRESIDENT'S DAUGHTER* by William Wells Brown. Ask for details in any good bookshop. Only from **The X Press.**